Kentucky

Susan Reigler

Photography by Adam Jones

COMPASS AMERICAN GUIDES
An Imprint of Fodor's Travel Publications

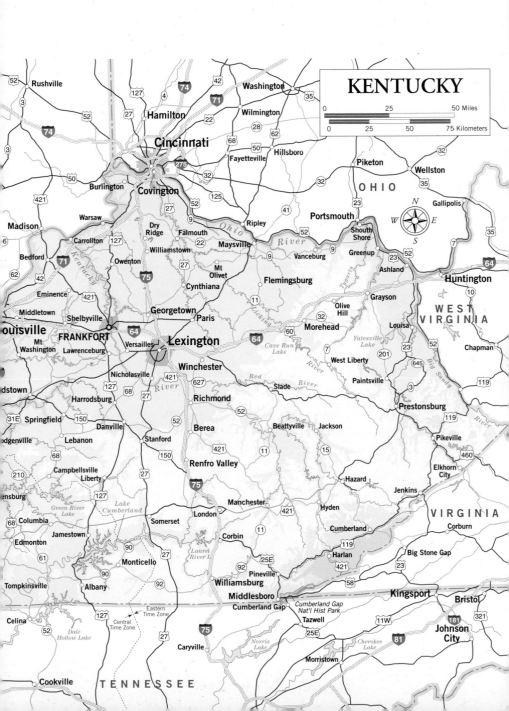

KENTUCKY

Compass American Guides: Kentucky

Editor: Jennifer Paull
Designer: Siobhan O'Hare
Compass Editorial Director: Paul Eisenberg
Compass Creative Director: Fabrizio La Rocca
Editorial Production: Jodie Gaudet
Photo Editor and Archival Researcher: Melanie Marin
Map Design: Mark Stroud, Moon Street Cartography
Cover Photo: Adam Jones

Second Edition

ISBN: 1–4000–1661–4
ISBN-13: 978–1–4000–1661–7

The details in this book are based on information supplied to us at press time, but changes occur all the time, and the publisher cannot accept responsibility for facts that become outdated or for inadvertent errors or omissions.

Compass American Guides, 1745 Broadway, New York, NY 10019
PRINTED IN CHINA

10 9 8 7 6 5 4 3 2 1

*To Marmalade and Puffers, who each provided invaluable assistance
in his and her own special way.*

■ AUTHOR'S ACKNOWLEDGMENTS

Many people helped with the seemingly endless details that a book like this requires. First I must thank Emilie Strong Smith who, with her late husband the Hon. Macauley Letchworth Smith, invited me to live and work in a piece of Kentucky history, the 1790 stone cottage on the farmstead now known as Blackacre. Gwynne Potts and Sam Thomas of the Blackacre Foundation helped me with questions about Kentucky's colorful past. William Bauer of the Ars Femina Ensemble provided tidbits about mountain folk music. Bob Stewart and Ann Coffey, Commissioner and Deputy Commissioner respectively, of the Kentucky Department of Travel, provided suggestions about regional highlights.

Guided travels around the state happened in the company of several people. Thanks are due to Ellen Ewing and Pat Owen for inviting me on those unforgettable houseboat trips on Dale Hollow. Also to my brother, Hunter Reigler, for the resident's tour of Owensboro. And, most of all to my parents, Harriett and the late Joe Reigler for dragging my brother and me all over the state on summer weekends when we were kids "so we could learn about our heritage." (The sacrifice of Saturday morning cartoons paid off.)

I also need to thank my writing colleague Martha Barnette for her constant encouragement and moral support when I switched careers from school marm to full time writer. "Technical assistance" was provided by Polly Blakemore, who let me use her Macintosh Powerbook until the advance from this book allowed me to buy my own, and by Joanna Goldstein, who gave me writing space in her study when the stone cottage was being remodeled.

I had lots of help from my wonderful colleagues at the *Courier-Journal.* Thanks go to my editors in the Features Department (Greg Johnson, Arlene Jacobson, Jena Monahan, and the late Maureen McNerney) for their flexibility while I was engaged in this project. And the ever-patient and skillful sleuths in the newspaper library (Sharon Bidwill, Patty Hauck, Amy Inskeep, and Mark Taflinger) who helped me find recent Kentucky statistical information. Thanks too to Pam Spaulding of the photography department who retrieved my author photo from the labyrinthine archives of the newspaper.

Finally big thank yous are in order to editor Kit Duane at Compass American Guides for her always-appreciated pushes in the right directions and Compass creative director Chris Burt for designing such a handsome volume.

C O N T E N T S

Literary Excerpts

Maps

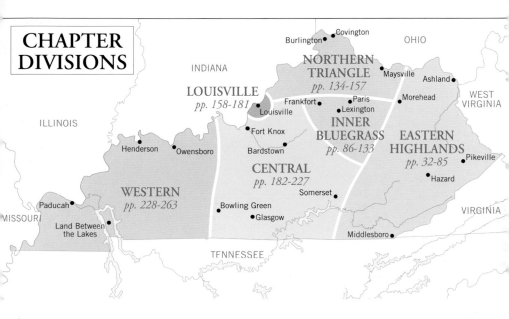

CHAPTER DIVISIONS

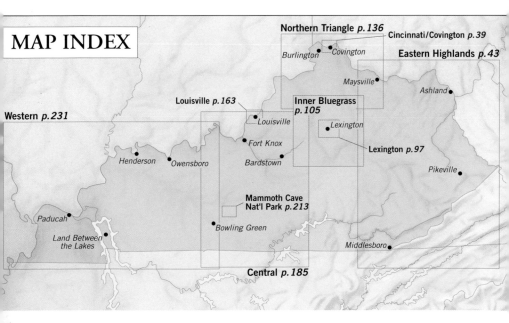

MAP INDEX

O V E R V I E W

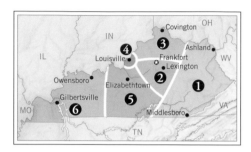

■1 EASTERN HIGHLANDS   *pages 32–85*

The mountainous region of eastern Kentucky is defined by the spine of the Appalachian Mountains, stretching from the northeast tip of the state to the Cumberland Gap in the southeast corner. This is a region of old-time mountain culture, coal mines, a boom-and-bust economy, and beautiful vistas of tree-covered, mist-shrouded slopes.

■2 INNER BLUEGRASS AND LEXINGTON
pages 86–133

This rolling green countryside, dotted with manicured horse farms and antebellum mansions, is the image most outsiders conjure when they think of Kentucky. About half of the state's renowned bourbon distilleries are here, too.

The city of Lexington, home of the University of Kentucky, is the commercial center. The state capitol, Frankfort, is located nearby.

3 NORTHERN TRIANGLE

pages 134–157

The Ohio River forms the northern boundary of Kentucky, and was long an important route for settlement and industry. River towns large and small remain, among them Maysville, Covington, and Newport. In the hilly country south of the river, farms, especially tobacco, dot the valleys.

4 LOUISVILLE *pages 158–179*

The state's largest city is famous for Churchill Downs racetrack and the Kentucky Derby. It's also the hometown of boxing legend Muhammad Ali. It was founded in 1778 when George Rogers Clark, leading settlers and soldiers in the area, decided to stop at the Falls of the Ohio, a rock outcropping into a river containing the world's largest exposed Devonian fossil beds.

5 CENTRAL KENTUCKY
pages 182–227

This is the part of Kentucky where Abraham Lincoln was born. Largely agricultural, there are vast fields of corn, used in the making of bourbon. (The rest of the distilleries are here.) The world's largest cave, Mammoth Cave, is here, preserved as a national park.

6 WESTERN KENTUCKY
pages 228–263

Among the destinations for nature lovers here are the Land Between the Lakes in the southwestern portion of the region and John James Audubon State Park, which also houses a museum with exhibits of the artist/naturalist's paintings. Cities overlooking the Ohio River in the northern part of the region are Owensboro and Henderson.

Located at the westernmost tip of the state, the Jackson Purchase has a strikingly different landscape from the rest of the state. There are wetlands and swamps rich in wildlife in a region bounded by three rivers: the Ohio, the Tennessee, and the Mississippi. The largest city is Paducah, located where the Tennessee flows into the Ohio.

(opposite) Autumn reflection on Mill Creek Lake in the Daniel Boone National Forest.

HISTORY & CULTURE

KENTUCKY CONJURES UP ROMANTIC VISIONS of Bluegrass horse farms and bourbon distilleries, of mountain "hollers" and moonshine stills, and the most famous American horse race of all, the Kentucky Derby.

"Colonels," of course, live in mansions on those horse farms—Southern gentlemen dressed in white who puff cigars and drink mint juleps as they gaze out at their sleek Thoroughbreds. In Kentucky's mountains? The Sunday funny paper's "Li'l Abner" lives there—that sweet-tempered hillbilly whose cantankerous Mammy smokes a corncob pipe. "Coal miner's daughter" country singer Loretta Lynn hails from eastern Kentucky, and Kentuckian Merle Travis's song "Sixteen Tons" evokes the harsh truth of a miner's life.

Like most archetypes, those above are part of the story. Southern gentlemen do live here, of course, as do coal miners' daughters who become country music stars, and horse trainers who count on the Derby to make their reputations. Alongside them live the rest of us, and we aren't too different from the Midwesterners who live along our northern border. Most of us live in cities, work in industry or in offices, and wouldn't mind moving to the suburbs. Despite the scars mining and industry have left on our land, we enjoy the beauty that abounds in the rhododendron-covered Appalachian mountains, the lush meadows of the Bluegrass, and hundreds of lakes and streams.

We're proud that Daniel Boone was our founding father and that Abraham Lincoln was born here. We like our chicken fried Southern and our ham salt-cured and smoked, but we're of two minds when it comes to our great American whiskey, bourbon. We're proud we invented it, but we've made liquor illegal in half the state.

■ TOPOGRAPHY

The 40,411-square-mile state, 37th in size among the 50 states, is shaped like a rough-edged right triangle. The Appalachian Mountains in the east form the short side of the triangle, separating Kentucky from neighbors West Virginia and Virginia. The straight border with Tennessee to the south runs west along the triangle's base. At the right angle is the Cumberland Gap, through which many of the first settlers arrived in the 18th century. The Ohio River, the other gateway into the state, is Kentucky's hypotenuse, marking a clear boundary with Ohio, Indiana,

Cumberland River at dawn, Daniel Boone National Forest.

and Illinois to the north. At the western tip, where the Ohio meets the Mississippi River, Missouri is the state across the water.

Variation in topography is considerable, starting with the eastern mountains and ending with swampy bottomlands at the westernmost tip of the state. In between are picturesque foothills of the Appalachians that gradually give way to the rolling pasturelands of the Bluegrass region and the level farmlands of the central and western portions of the state. Here fields are pockmarked with sinkholes, clues to the vast system of caves that lies beneath the surface. The land flattens out even more in the far western tip of the state, which contains extensive wetlands, including cypress swamps.

■ NATIVE PEOPLE

Kentucky was named by indigenous people who hunted and fished in its forests and streams. By some accounts *Kentucky* was a Wyandot word meaning "land of tomorrow." It also may have come from Iroquois for "land of meadows." For generations, Kentucky schoolchildren were taught that the name meant "dark and bloody ground"—which of course appealed to the bloodthirsty nature of some kids. This idea probably came from a warning given to Daniel Boone by Cherokee chief Oconostota after whites coerced the sale of his people's land rights: "There is a dark cloud over that country." Before the historic tribes of Wyandot, Iroquois, and Cherokee roamed the Bluegrass region, cultures of nomadic Paleo-Indians made their homes here. Flint tools have been found in Kentucky that date from the end of the last ice age, 8,000 to 12,000 years ago, when glaciers reached the northern banks of the Ohio River.

During the Archaic Period (which ended about 3,000 years ago) people survived by harvesting foods from wild plants and trees, especially walnuts, hickory nuts, and chestnuts, and they may have cultivated squash and domesticated dogs. Bits of copper, which would have come from the Great Lakes region, and shells

from the Gulf of Mexico have been found in sites from this period, demonstrating that Kentucky's early people were connected to a vast trading network.

(opposite) Arrows, beads, and spears from ancient cultures give mute testimony to lives lived long ago in Kentucky. (above) An artist envisions life in the Mississippian culture, a few remnants of which can be seen at Wickliffe Mounds on Kentucky's western border.

The Woodland Period people (1000 B.C.E. to A.D. 1000) constructed burial mounds. Beans and corn were first cultivated by Indians a thousand years ago, and the bow and arrow came into use for hunting deer and bison. What is now known as the Mississippian culture, extended to western Kentucky, developed about a thousand years ago among people who lived in villages constructed around temple mounds. Tribes belonging to this culture still lived in western Kentucky and in what is now the southern United States when Europeans arrived.

■ LAND SPECULATORS AND LONG HUNTERS

French explorers traveling south along the Mississippi River visited western Kentucky briefly at the end of the 1600s, but the first sustained venture into the interior by people of European descent was made by Virginians coming through the Cumberland Gap. In the 1740s, the colony of Virginia decided to encourage settlement west of the Appalachians in order to secure British claims over the territory. The catch was that Virginia could only grant settlers the right to claim land not already occupied by someone else, and Kentucky was occupied—by Indian nations.

Emissaries from development companies hoping to purchase land from the Indians began arriving in Kentucky in the mid-1700s, the first being Dr. Thomas Walker of Virginia, an agent of the Loyal Land Company, who led an expedition through the Cumberland Gap and explored the Cumberland River basin. His party built a small cabin near present-day Barbourville, but the group failed to find open, tillable land. Disappointed, and under constant threat of Indian attack, they turned back. (Walker later returned to Kentucky and made the first survey of a boundary with Tennessee, known, not very originally, as Walker's Line.)

Those who followed in the wake of Walker were the "long hunters" of the 1760s. Parties of one to two dozen men would pass through the Cumberland Gap into Kentucky and fan out along the Cumberland River Valley in small groups of two to four. They would stay for weeks, shooting and trapping. They got their name not from the long rifles they carried, but because they left home for months at a time. Theirs was a risky business. Consider the luck of Abraham Bledsoe, a member of a 1769 hunting expedition. His cache of pelts was destroyed by Indian

Kentucky pioneers sometimes stayed away from home for months hunting for beaver pelts. They came to be known as long hunters, not for the long rifles they carried, but for their long absences.

FRONTIER KENTUCKY

By 1775, settlers following Daniel Boone's expedition had established a number of permanent communities in Kentucky. In 1792 the territory became a state. French botanist François Andre Michaux spent the summer of 1802 in the region and described the land, people, and customs in a book published in Paris. It gives an idea of what Kentucky was like 10 years after statehood.

*T*he inhabitants of Kentucky, as we have before stated, are nearly all natives of Virginia, and particularly the remotest parts of that state; and exclusive of the gentlemen of the law, physicians, and a small number of citizens who have received an education suitable to their professions in the Atlantic states, they have preserved the manners of the Virginians. With them the passion for gaming and spirituous liquors is carried to excess, which frequently terminates in quarrels degrading to human nature. The public houses are always crowded, more especially during the sittings of the court of justice. Horses and lawsuits comprise the usual topic of their conversation.

If a traveler happens to pass by, his horse is appreciated; if he stops, he is presented with a glass of whiskey, and then asked a thousand questions, such as: Where do you come from? Where are you going? What is your name? Where do you live? What profession? Were there any fevers in the different parts of the country you came through?…

The inhabitants of Kentucky eagerly recommend to strangers the country they inhabit as the best part of the United States, as that where the soil is most fertile, the climate most salubrious, and where all the inhabitants were brought through the love of liberty and independence!

—François Andre Michaux, *Travels to the West of the Alleghenies,* 1804

raids and animal predation. Bledsoe carved his lament on a poplar tree: "2,300 deer skins lost. Ruination by God."

The most famous of the long hunters was Daniel Boone, who first came through the Cumberland Gap in pursuit of pelts, but returned in 1773 with his family and a group of settlers. Their attempt to establish a first settlement failed, however, and after Boone's son was tortured and killed by Indians, the family returned to North Carolina. Boone's party was followed in 1774 by a group led by James Harrod that made the first permanent white settlement in Kentucky, establishing a log fort at Harrodstown (now Harrodsburg).

HISTORY &
CULTURE

In 1775, Boone returned. He had been hired by Richard Henderson of the Transylvania Company to extend the trail from the Cumberland Gap, known as the Wilderness Road, into the Bluegrass. The new route, called Boone's Trace, extended to the Kentucky River, where Fort Boonesborough was built. Henderson negotiated a treaty with the Cherokee (the occasion of Oconostota's aforementioned ominous remark).

Henderson claimed to have purchased 17 million acres. The Virginia legislature begged to differ, later reducing his holdings to a mere 200,000 acres. When Henderson tried to make Kentucky an independent colony, the legislature at Williamsburg declared his Transylvania Company to be illegal and claimed Kentucky as Jefferson County, Virginia.

Daniel Boone Escorting Settlers Through the Cumberland Gap *was painted by George Caleb Bingham in the early 1850s, almost a hundred years after the event. (Courtesy Washington University Gallery of Art, St. Louis; gift of Nathaniel Phillips)*

■ REVOLUTIONARY WAR AND STATEHOOD

After the Revolutionary War broke out in 1775, Virginia was no longer interested in protecting British interests in Kentucky. The British, for their part, no longer wished to encourage "disloyal" Virginians to settle Kentucky. Thinking strategically, the British encouraged Indians to attack settlers. To protect their kinsmen, the Virginia militia sent a detachment into Kentucky under the leadership of George Rogers Clark, a young lieutenant colonel. Clark traveled into Kentucky by navigating the Ohio River (which forms the state's northern boundary), and took some settlers with him. They established a fort at the Falls of the Ohio near the site of what would become Louisville.

An artist's rendering of Fort Boonesborough. It was attacked by Shawnee, allies of the British in 1778.

In 1778, Shawnee in the employ of the British Crown attacked Boonesborough (by now a camp) but were defeated. In 1780 the British launched attacks into Kentucky down the Licking River from the Ohio. In 1782 they overwhelmed colonists at the bloody battle of Blue Lick, but the Indians with them retreated north.

❖

When the new United States of America was formed after the end of the war, thousands of settlers moved into Kentucky over the Wilderness Road and down the Ohio River. A growing movement for statehood arose among this thriving population, which was effectively separated from Virginia by the Appalachians, and in 1792 Kentucky became the 15th state, and the first west of the Appalachians. Isaac Shelby, a Revolutionary War hero, was elected governor, and the state capital was established at Frankfort.

■ ANTEBELLUM KENTUCKY

Kentucky's horse-racing industry has its roots in colonial days, as the fertile pastures and plentiful water supply of the Bluegrass region attracted horse breeders almost as soon as they saw the area. One of the first laws passed at Boonesborough established rules for breeding quality horses. Thoroughbreds were introduced in 1793 by John Breckenridge, who had started Cabell's Dale Farm outside of Lexington. As early as 1797, horses were being raced in Lexington. In fact, the Kentucky Jockey Club was founded that year.

By the 1830s, horses from the Bluegrass were in demand all over the United States. One contemporary account declared, "Horses are raised in great numbers and are of the noblest kinds.... Great numbers are carried over the mountains to the Atlantic states; and the principal supply of saddle and carriage horses in the lower country is drawn from Kentucky...."

Corn and tobacco grew well in the fertile Bluegrass, as did hemp, a crop valued for oil and rope fiber up through World War II. (Recent attempts to revive industrial hemp production have met with opposition, since the plant is closely related to marijuana.)

Corn was as valuable on the frontier as money, but even more valuable was corn distilled as whiskey. Mice wouldn't touch it, and whiskey barrels were easy to transport and exchange. Many a combination gristmill and distillery cropped up around the state, so Kentuckians could have their corn bread and wash it down with bourbon, too.

Much of the labor for Kentucky agriculture was supplied by black slaves, a practice introduced by settlers from Virginia. By 1830, nearly a quarter of the people living in the state were slaves, so it's a wonder that Kentucky didn't actually secede from the Union when the Civil War broke out. This was due in great part to the efforts of statesman Henry Clay—Speaker of the House of Representatives from 1811 to 1825 and U.S. Senator from Kentucky from 1831 to 1842.

A slaveholder himself, Clay nonetheless advocated gradual emancipation and promoted the idea of recolonization of blacks to Africa. He defended the right of Congressional committees to consider abolitionist petitions (these had a way of being tabled before they could even get to legislators), and he opposed a bill that would have made it illegal for abolitionists to use the U.S. mail to distribute their literature. A fierce defender of the Constitution, Clay is famous for uttering the words "I'd rather be right than be President." This was just as well, since he ran unsuccessfully for the office three times.

CHILD OF STARRWOOD PLANTATION

*M*y father's name was Aaron Pendleton Starr. His father, Rodney Pendleton Starr, had come to Kentucky in the 1790's, bringing with him the marks of his rank and privilege, the silver and china, the linen and damask, the portraits in peeling gold frames. I do not wish to make these items of household plunder sound too grand. The silver teapot was dented, the linen was thriftily mended, and since not every ancestral likeness had been limned by the brush of a maestro, dignity, despite scarlet coat, and foamy lace at stalwart throat, sometimes seemed merely bovine, and beauty, despite the sheen of silk and the glitter of diamond, sometimes seemed merely a simper. I have seen far grander things since, in Louisiana, where ostentation indulged a pitch that old Virginia people like my father, might have considered vulgar—as people are accustomed to regard anything as vulgar that overreaches their own attempts at self-justification. But when I was a child, it all seemed grand enough to my limited perspective.

The house which old Rodney Starr had built in the country south of Lexington, near Danville, was of brick, two stories, a chimney at each end of the main bulk, with an L. running back, and there was a portico with pillars, not very high or imposing. There were, however, some fine trees about the place, for trees grow well in that part of Kentucky, and these had been left from the time before the white men came over the mountains. I sometimes see in my mind's eye those towering masses of green that characterized *Starrwood*—beech and white oak and maple and tulip trees rising in sun-guilded steep and terraces of boughs and shade-dark grottos giving into the inwardness of the tree. The upper leaves move in some cool visitation of air, not enough to be named a breeze but enough to refresh your cheek, and the shade lies blue-dark on the cropped grass under the trees. Then coming back to the reality of things, I remember that the house may have been burned long since, burned by carelessness, violence of soldiery, or stroke of lightning, and the trees may be fire-blasted or have bowed to axe or age.

From the happy time before I was nine and left *Starrwood*, I remember things only in starts and patches, for from childhood you remember things only in portentous disconnection, each in a kind of mystic isolation.

From a novel by Kentucky native Robert Penn Warren (see page 243). The novel tells of a young woman raised on a Kentucky plantation who discovers after her father's death that her mother was in fact a slave, and that she will be sold into slavery.

—Robert Penn Warren, *Band of Angels*, 1955

■ CIVIL WAR: THE BORDER STATE

It's one of history's ironies that the chief protagonists of the Civil War—Abraham Lincoln, President of the United States, and Jefferson Davis, President of the Confederate States of America—were both born in Kentucky, a few miles apart and within a year of each other (Davis was nine months the elder.) Kentucky was the only state to have native sons in cabinets of both governments. The attorney general of the United States during the war was Louisvillian James Speed. The Confederate secretary of war was John Cabell Breckenridge of Lexington (who had

been defeated for election as U.S. President in 1860 by, of course, Lincoln).

While no major battles of the war took place in Kentucky, its location on the border between two warring countries, and the fact that its people were divided in their loyalties, resulted in years of civic upheaval. Kentucky remained in the Union, yet it was a slave state. Brothers fought brothers; cousins fought cousins. One hundred thousand (about one-fifth of whom were black) fought for the North. The number of Kentuckians who joined the Confederate army was smaller, but at 40,000, certainly significant.

One of the most colorful figures of the war was Confederate General John Hunt Morgan, a cavalry officer whose Morgan's Raiders executed a series of daring attacks on Union strongholds in Kentucky and neighboring states. In one three-week campaign in 1862, the Raiders took 17 towns, captured 1,200 Union soldiers, and burned significant caches of Union supplies. When a sympathetic telegraph operator sent misleading reports of Morgan's rapid movements to Union commanders, Lincoln responded by wiring one of his generals, "They are having a stampede in Kentucky. Please look into it."

Thomas Crittenden (above) and his brother George (below) were the sons of Sen. John J. Crittenden, whose attempts at compromise in Kentucky failed. Thomas became a Union general, while George enlisted with the Confederate Army.

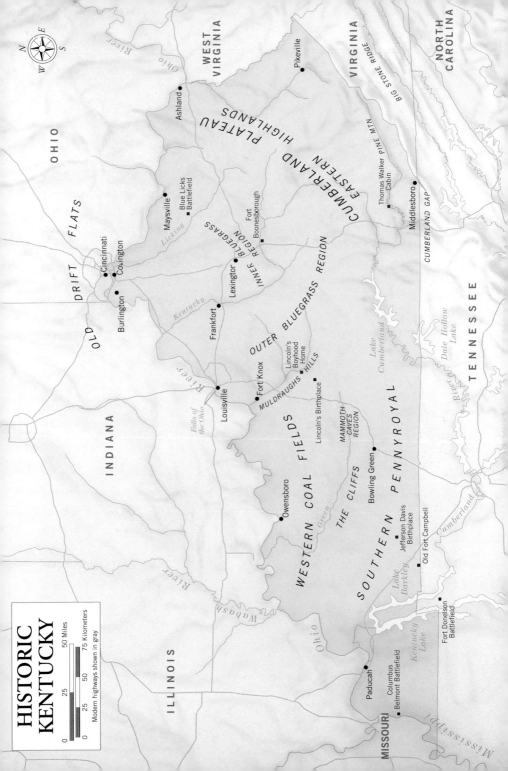

HISTORIC KENTUCKY

0   25   50 Miles

0   25   50   75 Kilometers

Modern highways shown in gray

N
W   E
S

OHIO

WEST VIRGINIA

VIRGINIA

NORTH CAROLINA

TENNESSEE

INDIANA

ILLINOIS

MISSOURI

Ohio River

Pikeville

Ashland

EASTERN CUMBERLAND PLATEAU HIGHLANDS

BIG STONE RIDGE

Thomas Walker PINE MTN
Cabin

Middlesboro

CUMBERLAND GAP

Blue Licks
Battlefield

Maysville

Licking

BLUEGRASS REGION

Fort
Boonesborough

INNER BLUEGRASS REGION

Cincinnati
Covington

OLD DRIFT FLATS

Burlington

Lexington

Kentucky

Frankfort

OUTER BLUEGRASS REGION

Lincoln's Boyhood
Home

MULDRAUGHS HILLS

Fort Knox

Louisville

Falls of
the Ohio

River

Lincoln's Birthplace

MAMMOTH CAVES REGION

THE CLIFFS

Lake Cumberland

Cumberland River

Dale Hollow
Lake

WESTERN COAL FIELDS

Owensboro

Green

Bowling Green

SOUTHERN PENNYROYAL

Jefferson Davis
Birthplace

Old Fort Campbell

Cumberland

Wabash River

Ohio River

Lake
Barkley

Fort Donelson
Battlefield

Kentucky Lake

Paducah

Columbus
Belmont Battlefield

Mississippi River

■ INDUSTRIAL REVOLUTION AND THE EARLY 20TH CENTURY

Kentucky was not as hard hit economically as the rest of the South after the war. Its infrastructure was not badly damaged, and as it had remained in the Union it was not under occupation. The goods produced here were much in demand: whiskey and tobacco. Its central location as a trading crossroads, with borders on the Ohio and Mississippi Rivers, meant that merchants and traders prospered.

Large coal deposits were discovered in eastern Kentucky mountains in the late 19th century and were soon providing energy for America's industrial revolution. Kentucky's waterways were harnessed to provide hydroelectric power, and timber was abundant. All of these factors drew industry into the state, and in the early 20th century, manufacturers producing aluminum and appliances became major employers. Inhumane working conditions in the coal mines led to the Harlan County "Coal Wars" of the 1930s, which in turn led in the Wagner Act of 1935, allowing miners to unionize.

Coal mining in the early 1900s.

THE ORIGINAL PICKANINNY BAND, ORGANIZED BY PROF. J.H. BRISTER ESPECIALLY FOR "IN OLD KENTUCKY" AND DIRECTED BY MASTER WALTER BRISTER. THE YOUNGEST BANDMASTER IN THE WORLD.

A promotional lithograph ca. 1894.

■ "OLD KENTUCKY HOME" TODAY

Today Kentucky is the 23rd most populous state in the country, with nearly four million residents. Most of us live in the Bluegrass region, since the largest urban areas—Louisville, Lexington, Covington/Greater Cincinnati—are there. Most of us are white, just over 92 percent. Only seven percent of us are of African descent, and the last one percent covers the few Hispanics, Asians, and Native Americans.

Our Southern identity is manifested in a love of bluegrass and country music, homemade biscuits with cream or red-eye gravy, and serious churchgoing (51 percent of Kentuckians identify themselves as Southern Baptists).

In its urban areas, the state has a lively restaurant scene; performing arts organizations such as orchestras, operas, and ballets funded by citizen contributions, and high-tech medical research centers affiliated with universities in Louisville and Lexington.

Nearly three-fifths of us live in cities and work in manufacturing (automobiles, electronics, appliances), service-sector jobs (restaurant industry, health care, tourism), or government (state and local). Although Kentucky traditionally has been an agricultural state, only six percent of its population are farmers now. Tobacco is grown in 118 of the 120 counties. Farmers also grow corn, wheat, rye, and barley, some of which is malted, mashed, and distilled into bourbon.

The state's most famous export after Thoroughbred horses is bourbon whiskey. Yet nearly half of the 120 Kentucky counties are dry (meaning that you can't buy alcohol of any description). Kentucky has the highest high-school dropout rate in the country. No wonder then that "Welcome to Kentucky, Where Education Pays" has been replaced by "Kentucky: Unbridled Spirit" on the highway signs that greet visitors.

The bison of Daniel Boone's era are gone, as are most of the bears, but the horse population of the central Bluegrass region is thriving. In fact, there are more than 460 horse farms located on the rolling green pasturelands surrounding Lexington, representing the largest concentration of such facilities in the world. They are presided over by owners who range from fifth-generation Kentuckians (who are

Renowned photographer Lewis W. Hine captured this Nicolas County farm in 1916.

A massive flowering catalpa tree stands along Route 7 at Bennett's Mill covered bridge, near the town of Greenup.

usually sporting windbreakers, not white suits, and sipping coffee, not juleps) to Arab potentates (usually represented by proxies).

The mountains of eastern Kentucky are populated by independent-minded individuals whose Southern accents have a notable twang. Many of these folks earn their livings in the coal mines or the timber industry, but that is changing. The beautiful but rugged mountain landscape has historically isolated the region from the rest of the state. New economic development has been very slow, but tourism and recreation have provided jobs for many people.

Outdoor sports thrive. Kentucky provides endless opportunities for outdoor recreation with its millions of acres of federal land, such as the Daniel Boone National Forest and Land Between the Lakes, as well as its 53 state parks.

If you enjoy the juxtaposition of old and new, Kentucky is a good place to travel. Louisville and Lexington, with their glass-and-steel skyscrapers, share the state with towns boasting century-old Main Streets. Log cabins and covered bridges still dot the landscape along country roads. Few states boast as many beautifully restored 19th-century homes, all filled with antiques and history. You can visit a replica of the log cabin near Hodgenville where Abraham Lincoln was born, as well as the elegant Lexington mansion in which his wife grew up.

The state where Louisville Slugger baseball bats are made has no major league sports franchise. But it does have a tradition of fiercely loyal college basketball fans who sweat blood for the University of Kentucky Wildcats, and, to a lesser extent, the University of Louisville Cardinals. (Louisville is sometimes considered a separate "country" by other Kentuckians.) Finally, of course, there's that Most Famous Two Minutes in Sports, the Kentucky Derby, run at Churchill Downs in Louisville the first Saturday in May. When the first horse sets hoof on the track to lead the rest of the field to the starting gate, the crowd raises its collective voice to sing the best-known state song, which begins, "The sun shines bright on my old Kentucky home." The pride of Kentuckians is such that even if it's pouring rain at Churchill Downs at that moment, they believe every word they're singing.

As seen from Clarksville, Indiana, the Ohio River reflects Louisville's colorful skyline.

EASTERN HIGHLANDS

■ HIGHLIGHTS *page*

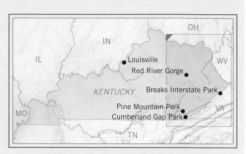

Food & Lodging *page 264*
Also see map page 43, towns in yellow.

■ TRAVEL BASICS

Area Overview: Mountainous eastern Kentucky offers dramatic scenery, camping and hiking, unique folk art (quilts, furniture, and musical instruments), and significant historic sites. Much of the area is heavily forested, peaceful, and beautiful, but the traveler will encounter some strip-mined and deforested mountainsides, as well as a good deal of poverty.

Travel: Four-lane interstates and parkways—I-64 and I-75—will get you into the area quickly and easily. The region's two-lane highways spiral around and between the steep, wooded mountainsides, which are so close together that simple, up-and-down roads would be absurd. Allow plenty of travel time between points that look close on a map, and stay alert, as fully loaded coal and logging trucks also use these narrow mountain roads.

If you're driving into Kentucky from the east, you might begin a tour of the Highlands at the Cumberland Gap and head northeast towards Ashland, then head back south through Daniel Boone National Forest to the Cumberland Falls region.

Weather: The elevation in the mountain region somewhat moderates the humid summer weather, when temperatures max at 90 degrees. Winter seems to hit eastern Kentucky hard. So while it's a beautiful area to tour when the trees are turning in the fall, avoid traveling when ice and snow are likely. Such conditions make roads very dangerous, if not downright impassible.

Food and Drink: Fast-food chain restaurants are the most reliable places to stop. At independent roadside cafes, apron-wearing waitresses may call you "hon," but those they work for aren't big on quality control. Servings of lumpy, sticky grits and occasionally authentic red-eye gravy are accompanied by fried foods. Don't even think about asking for a beer in most places, as most of the Appalachian Kentucky counties are "dry"—a circumstance that, given human habits of alcohol consumption, has led to a thriving trade in mountain moonshine.

Lodging: Many of the state parks in the mountains have log cabins fitted with all the modern conveniences, nestled in the woods where visitors can sleep in comfort. The area also has its share of chain accommodations. Refer to the **Food & Lodging map,** page 265; toll-free numbers for chains on page 266. Towns are listed in alphabetical order beginning on page 267. For charts relating towns to chapters see page 311.

■ ABOUT THE HIGHLANDS

Approximately one quarter of Kentucky's population lives in the 10,500 square miles of the Eastern Highlands—also known as the Eastern Coal Fields region—which stretches across all or part of 35 counties, from Bell County in the south to Greenup County in the north.

Technically the mountains here are the remains of an eroded plain, part of the folded and faulted Appalachian Plateau. Wind and water have worn down the peaks over millions of years, so there are no snowcaps in the eastern mountains, none of which rise above 7,000 feet. To the west and northwest the mountains gradually lower and merge with the uplands of the Bluegrass and Pennyroyal regions *(see map page 25).*

The primeval forest, heavily logged, has regrown and includes yellow poplar, black cherry, black walnut, oak, and hickory. Underground, rich coal deposits are the remains of the vast Carboniferous-era forests of hundred-foot-tall horsetails and club mosses. Their growth was so thick that the fossilized remains of the plants resulted in vast seams of carbon, compressed over the course of 300 million years. These coal and natural gas deposits were elevated by a period of mountain building that started 290 million years ago and lasted for 50 million years.

(following pages) Fog rests in a valley below hills bright with fall color in Pine Mountain State Resort Park.

A dogwood tree blooms in The Breaks Interstate Park.

■ STUDY IN CONTRASTS

This mountainous region of the state provides a study in contrasts between tremendous natural beauty and man-made ugliness, caused by mining, lumbering, and casual garbage dumps.

Mist rising off of the Appalachian ridges in the springtime clears after sunrise to reveal mountain laurels, dogwoods, and redbud trees in bloom. In the autumn, forests of oak, hickory, and maple turn the mountainsides into spectacular patchworks of red, orange, and gold. Some mountainsides, once densely forested, are scarred from the effects of coal mining and logging, the twin boom-and-bust industries of the region. Recently the state has stepped in to replant forests and contain toxic waste. A local group, PRIDE (Personal Responsibility in a Desirable Environment), has identified almost 2,000 creek-bed garbage dumps and is working to clean them up. According to an article published in the *New York Times*, when Breathitt County announced a five-dollar reward for each appliance reclaimed from a dump or creek, within three days mountain folk brought in 5,000 rusted appliances. The county had to float a loan to keep up the program.

Public education came late to this region. In the first half of the 20th century, churches set up settlement schools, meant to bring literacy, farming expertise, and basic health information. Public schools followed. Yet today in the southeastern counties, school dropout rates approach 50 percent. In the year 2000, 30 percent of the region's adult population was considered functionally illiterate—unable to do the simplest math, to read a map or a recipe.

This population is among the poorest in the United States. Appalachian historian and attorney Harry Caudill's *Night Comes to the Cumberlands*, published in 1963, was a moving account of how "this rich and beautiful land was changed into an ugly, poverty-ridden place of desolation." The book is credited with having brought the attention of the federal government to this economically blighted area. The result was the formation, in 1964, of the Appalachian Regional Commission, an agency charged with aiding people in Kentucky and in a dozen other mountainous states. But the social programs of the 1960s, which provided food and shelter for the destitute, didn't improve the situation. By the end of the 20th century, much of the area's population was dependent on welfare.

It was thought that the intractable social problems of the area would be improved once roads were built across the mountains, but jobs didn't follow. Yearly per capita income today averages about $12,000.

Strip mining scars the hills near Middlesboro.

Tourism is proving to be a more reliable industry than coal and is bringing a measure of prosperity—there aren't as many battered mobile homes crouching in narrow hollows between the mountains as there once were. The dozen state resort parks in the region are oases of natural beauty, as is vast Daniel Boone National Forest, The Breaks Interstate Park, and the Cumberland Gap National Historic Park—all of which protect hardwood forest, rushing streams, and wildlife.

■ MOUNTAIN CULTURE

♦ MUSIC

Traditional mountain folk music is the direct descendant of the rural music of the British Isles. Settlers living isolated lives sang ballads that scarcely changed as they were passed down through generations, including "Queen Jane," from the time of Henry VIII; the 15th-century "Cherry Tree Carol;" and the more familiar "Barbara Allen" and "Sweet William." (The melody of the popular fiddle tune "The Lamp-lighter" derives from a violin sonata by Italian composer Arcangelo Corelli (1653–1713; Opus 5, No. 3.)

Singing schools and songbooks were popular in old-time Kentucky. In 1816 singing teacher Ananias Davisson compiled *Kentucky Harmony,* a book of songs common to the rural South, all written in four-part harmony. Samuel Metcalf's *Kentucky Harmonist* followed in 1817, and *Southern Harmony* by "Singing Bill" Walker in 1854. Clapping and foot-tapping were part of singing games at parties. Old-time dance tunes played by string or "hillbilly" bands became known to the rest of the country with the advent of the radio. The repertoire of these folk songs has been preserved by Berea College *(see page 118)* and at settlement schools.

Modern bluegrass and country evolved from this traditional music. Many of America's most famous country music singers are native to this part of Kentucky, including sisters Loretta Lynn and Crystal Gayle, Dwight Yoakam, Patty Loveless, and Tom T. Hall *(see pages 76–77).*

Many towns and state parks host folk music and crafts festivals. Exact dates vary from year to year, but you can get a complete list of events from the **Kentucky Department of Tourism** in Frankfort; *502-564-4930.* These include:

March: Kentucky Hills Weekend, Cumberland Falls State Resort Park
April: Mountain Folk Festival, Berea
May: Mountain Laurel Festival, Pineville
September: Kentucky Highland Folk Festival, Prestonsburg

This dulcimer, crafted by Warren A. May, is housed in a collection of musical instruments at Berea College.

◆ CRAFTS

Eastern Kentucky crafts match grace and beauty to utility. A hand-stitched patch-work quilt, antique or modern, will brighten a bed as well as keep its occupants warm. The silky-smooth wood of white oak is used to make baskets and furniture as well as dulcimers and fiddles. Clay dug from the mountainsides is turned into simple, graceful pottery, which is usually glazed with plant dye in hues of dark blue and pink.

Some crafts shops are stocked with decorative objects, such as bark-covered birdhouses and Rube Goldberg-ish contraptions called whirligigs. These hand-carved and painted whimsical lawn ornaments have pinwheel-like mechanisms which, when the wind blows, set the whole thing in action: for instance, a whirligig mule might kick when the bladed wheel attached to it turns with the breeze. Near Pineville you'll find the following shops that sell traditional crafts:

Eastern Kentucky is known for its utilitarian crafts, such as homemade baskets.

Kentuckian folk artist Willie Massie, who built this birdhouse of wood, paint, foil, and tape, is widely known for exquisite adaptations of the Appalachian craft vernacular.

Henderson Settlement

On KY-190 southwest of Pineville; 606-337-3613.

Settlement crafts shop sells quilts, baskets, and furniture made by locals.

Log House Craft Shop

On KY-190 off Hwy-25 out of Pineville; 606-337-5823.

Sells weavings, locally made crafts. Also, a place to stay or attend work camp; call 606-337-3613.

Red Bird Mission

On Hwy-66 north of Pineville in Beverly; 606-598-2709.

United Methodist mission complex. Hickory bark furniture, willow baskets, hand-woven rugs.

◆ WRITERS

Many native authors have captured the spirit and reality of life in the mountains. John Fox, Jr.'s novels, such as *The Knight of the Cumberlands* and *The Trail of the Lonesome Pine,* have mountain settings. His most beloved work, *The Little Shepherd of Kingdom Come* (1903), is a story of the impact of the Civil War on the region and the state. Jesse Stuart (1907–1984) wrote novels and poetry, but the work that best describes life in his native Greenup County is his autobiographical *The Thread That Runs So True,* about his experiences as a teacher in a one-room schoolhouse.

Possibly the best of all eastern Kentucky novels is Harriette Simpson Arnow's masterpiece, the 1954 novel called *The Dollmaker.* Winner of the National Book Award, the book tells the poignant story of a mountain family that moves from eastern Kentucky to Detroit to find work in the factories.

■ CUMBERLAND GAP NATIONAL HISTORIC PARK *map page 43, B-6*

A good way to begin a tour of the Eastern Highlands of Kentucky is to start at the same place the early settlers did, the Cumberland Gap. Ridges and valleys in this area generally run north-south, so westward travel was rough going—up and down, up and down, up and down. The Gap was the one east-west opening in a hundred miles. Today it divides Kentucky from Virginia and Tennessee and is flanked by mountains thickly covered with rhododendron and laurel.

Coming from Virginia or Tennessee in the southeast, you'll enter Kentucky through the Cumberland Gap Tunnel. This twin-bore tunnel is nearly a mile long, and its computer-controlled lighting system mimics natural daylight. On the Kentucky side of the tunnel, the road exits at the entrance of the Cumberland Gap National Historic Park. (The next left turn, KY-74, leads into Middlesboro.) Covering some 20,000 acres, this is the second-largest national historic park in the United States. Within it are 70 miles of hiking trails.

A view of the Cumberland Gap.

◆ PINNACLE POINT

Unless you plan to hike the four-mile ascent, you'll probably want to drive from the highway-level visitors center parking lot up the wooded mountainside to the head of the paved footpath leading to Pinnacle Point. About 20 minutes slow progress up the steep, winding road will bring you to another parking lot and the beginning of a path. Follow it into the woods and past great outcroppings of limestone. It leads to the literal high spot of the park, Pinnacle Point.

As you look eastward, the mountains below stretch left to right, forming the spine of the Cumberland range. You can appreciate the difficulty of crossing into Kentucky, because the Cumberland Gap is the only break as far as you can see in either direction. Middlesboro sits below in a bowl-shaped depression. The tunnel entrances look like twin mouse holes in the mountainside.

The mountains here are close together and densely wooded. They almost seem to be the keepers of ancient secrets. This feeling of mystery can be strong on a late summer morning when mist shrouds the hillsides. Tiny patches of gold appear among the green on the trees, and it's a pleasant shock to feel cool air on your face after the heat and humidity of the Kentucky summer at low elevations. Early in the day you are not likely to encounter other visitors along the path, and the stillness and magic of the place invite contemplation of the lives and struggles that went on in the forests and valleys below.

◆ REFLECTIONS ON HISTORY

Long ago the Cherokee, Wyandot, Delaware, and Shawnee followed game into this area and warred with each other for control of the bountiful hunting grounds.

When Dr. Thomas Walker and his party came through the Gap in search of new farmland for settlers, they hiked westward through dense forests for weeks, finally stopping and turning around a few days' walk short of exactly what they were looking for—the fertile land of the Kentucky Bluegrass.

Excerpts from Walker's 1750 journal help paint a picture of those early ventures into the wilderness. When Walker's expedition returned to the men they had left to guard their base camp, Walker recounts that they had built "an house 8 x 12, cleared and broke up some ground and planted corn and peach stones. They had also killed several bears and cured the meat." This cabin was the basis of a land claim, but eventually the party returned to Walker's Virginia plantation. (One can subsist on bear meat for just so long.)

A sunrise as seen from the overview at Pinnacle Point.

Frontiersman Daniel Boone first traveled through the Gap in 1767, returning with hunting companions a few years later. Then in 1773 Boone brought his own family and several others into Kentucky hoping to settle, but they were challenged by Cherokee, who tortured and murdered Boone's son, James. In 1775 Boone and 28 others were hired by Richard Henderson's Transylvania Company to blaze a trail into Kentucky. Their success became the most important immigrant trail into the west, the Wilderness Road. Between 1776 and 1783 an estimated 12,000 white settlers came into Kentucky along this route.

During the Civil War, both the Confederacy and the Union understood the strategic value of the Gap. Lookouts from both armies must have hiked to the overview here at Pinnacle Point, surveyed the landscape, and reported back to their superiors how soldiers and ordnance might be directed through this area.

Some 10,000 Union troops commanded by Major General George Morgan occupied the Gap in the spring and summer of 1862. But in August, Confederate General Kirby Smith used 25,000 troops to surround the area and cut off supplies to the Federal soldiers. The Union troops, who had managed to live on wild food and meat from butchered Army mules, finally abandoned the Gap after a two-month siege. The following spring, the Confederates, now under the command of General John W. Frazier, built a fort overlooking the Gap.

Soon more Union troops arrived, led by hired Irish nobleman, Col. John Fitzroy De Courcy. De Courcy could tell that the fort wouldn't yield to a direct attack, so he ordered his troops to march over the ridge near the fort and down the mountainside into the forest, as though they were assembling for an attack. Once out of sight of the fort, the men circled back and repeated the procedure, but in different formation and with different battle flags.

De Courcy had them do this twice more, creating the impression of a massive troop movement. He then sent a message to Frazier suggesting that he surrender in order to save unnecessary Southern bloodshed in light of the superior Union strength. Frazier, knowing De Courcy's nationality and assuming he must have some good Irish whisk-y on hand, requested a sample as a goodwill gesture. De Courcy complied with quite a bit more than a sample. Apparently after considering the situation over numerous sips of Irish, Frazier surrendered. Not a single shot had been exchanged. When De Courcy arrived at Frazier's tent to accept the surrender, he discovered the general in a state he tactfully described as "off poise." The Cumberland Gap remained in Union hands through the rest of the war.

PROMISED LAND

Moses Austin traveled through Kentucky in the 1790s. On the way, he encountered men and women who had made their homes in the wilderness. He recounts their trials in his account of the journey, commenting, "should [my son] live to my age, not doubting but by that time the country I have passed in a state of nature will be overspread with towns and villages; for it is not possible a country which has within itself everything to make its settlers rich and happy can remain unnoticed by the American people."

*I*cannot omit noticing the many distressed families I passed…traveling a wilderness through ice and snow; passing large rivers and creeks without shoe or stocking and barely as many rags as covers their nakedness; without money or provisions, except what the wilderness affords—the situation of such can better be imagined than described. To say they are poor is but faintly expressing their situation— Life, what is it, or what can it give, to make compensation for such accumulated misery? Ask these pilgrims what they expect when they get to Kentucky. The answer is land. "Have you any?" "No, but I expect I can git it." "Have you anything to pay for land?" "No." "Did you ever see the country?" "No, but everybody says it's good land."

Can anything be more absurd than the conduct of man? Here are hundreds, traveling hundreds of miles—they know not for what nor wither, except it's to Kentucky—passing land almost as good and easy obtained, the proprietors of which would gladly give on any terms. But it will not do. It's not Kentucky. It's not the Promised Land. It's not the goodly inheritance, the Land of Milk and Honey. And when arrived at this Heaven in Idea, what do they find? A goodly land, I will allow, but to them forbidden land. Exhausted and worn down with distress and disappointment, they are at last obliged to become hewers of wood and drawers of water....

—Moses Austin, 1797

A replica of the first home in Kentucky in Thomas Walker State Park.

◆ **WILDERNESS ROAD**   *map page 43, B-6*

In the 20th century, the original Wilderness Road—the trail blazed by Daniel Boone in 1775—became a paved highway leading to Pineville. The new US-25E has replaced the old route, but recently a portion of the old road has been restored to its 18th-century state. In this section, during the summertime, overhanging and interlacing branches of oaks and maples form a green tunnel over the 15-foot wide dirt road. As you walk along in the gold-green gloom you may begin to fantasize that unfriendly Indians or large bears are watching you, or that at any moment you'll hear the crack of a pioneer's rifle.

In springtime the forest seems less intimidating—redbuds and dogwoods of the understory bloom and sunlight penetrates the still bare branches, reaching to the ground. The ruts of wagon wheels cut into the road during the Civil War era are still visible in the road.

◆ **HENSLEY SETTLEMENT**   *map page 43, B-6*

Remote Hensley Settlement, a 500-acre site located on top of Brush Mountain within the boundaries of the park, is a restored mountain community that is now

The zigzag pattern of a split-rail fence at Hensley Settlement.

an outdoor museum. The reason for the remoteness of the site is found in the reclusive eccentricity of the family that settled here.

The cluster of log houses and barns surrounded by a split-rail fence looks like it dates from Daniel Boone's era. Oddly, it's almost entirely a 20th-century community. In 1903, 21-year-old Sherman Hensley and his 17-year-old wife, Nicey Ann, moved to the mountaintop so that, in his words, they "could make a living and there was plenty of outlet for stock." The young couple and their two-year-old son lived in a one-room log cabin that had been built by an earlier settler, who had grazed his cattle on the plateau pasture. Hensley brought his own livestock, including a horse, two cows, and 18 hogs.

A straw broom in a Hensley Settlement cabin.

Other members of the Hensley family moved onto the mountain, and by 1925, the population numbered some 100 inhabitants. The Hensleys had their own church, one-room schoolhouse, and (illegal) whiskey still. There were no paved roads, electricity, or indoor plumbing.

During the Depression and World War II, younger residents left the settlement. In 1951, founder Sherman Hensley, the last remaining occupant, left too, and the property became part of the park.

Today, the homestead is populated (in the summer) by guides wearing homespun clothing while they attempt to recreate life on a primitive farmstead (no, this is not reality television). Other than that, the peace and quiet of the farmstead is broken only by the steady hum of insects and the calls of birds, which are very appealing—as are the tidy log buildings that seem to fit naturally into the landscape. But the farm feels almost desperately isolated, and it's easy to see why the younger members of the settlement got out when they could.

Getting to Hensley: The easiest (term used loosely here) way to get to the settlement is to take the shuttle from the park visitors center. The van lurches along narrow roads up and down the steep mountainsides. June through October, there's a four-hour, round-trip shuttle tour to Hensley which leaves from the Cumberland Gap National Historic Park Visitors Center; or you can hike the Ridge Trail up to the settlement. *Reservations for the shuttle are required seven days in advance; call 606-248-2817.*

◆ CUMBERLAND GAP HIKING

There are about 50 miles of hiking trails in the park, ranging from easy nature walks to steep, strenuous climbs, to overnight treks (get a permit from the visitors center if you plan to backpack). The walk along the trail to **Skylight Cave Trail** makes for a moderately difficult hike that can be done in an hour and a half. This

1.2-mile (round-trip) hike is a steep, steady climb to a wild cave you can explore with a flashlight.

The trailhead is in the Wilderness Road Picnic Area, off US-58 in Virginia. Start from the campground entrance on the Lewis Hollow Trail, heading through a hardwood forest. At mile .24 turn right at the **T**, onto the Skylight Cave Trail. Passing through hickory and oak woods, the trail steepens, and you'll pass several false trails (the main trail is broad,

Early pioneer utensils on display at Cumberland Gap National Historic Park.

A black bear cub.

well-maintained, and very obvious). Continue past limestone cliffs to a set of stairs leading to Skylight Cave. The mouth of the cave is low, but it opens into a high-ceilinged chamber. **Warning:** *Don't enter the tunnel below the skylight without a flashlight, and don't explore it alone.*

After exploring the cave you can turn back the way you came or, for a more strenuous hike, continue to the Ridge Trail and up to the Pinnacle (2.8 miles).

Cumberland Gap Visitors Center: Displays in the visitors center detail the history of the area, including Native American culture (Cherokee, Wyandot, Delaware, and Shawnee hunted here) and the adventures of the early white explorers. *Located on KY-25E, south of Middlesboro at the last light.*

Park information: No entrance fee, open year round; campsites available; check at the visitors center for parking information along the Wilderness Road. *606-248-2817.* For a guided tour of the area, contact **Wilderness Road Tours,** *224 Greenwood Rd., Middlesboro; 606-248-2626.*

The historic Alexander Alan Arthur Home.

■ MIDDLESBORO

map page 43, B-6

Since the early settlers just kept going once they made it through the Cumberland Gap, Middlesboro (pop. 13,000) is a relatively new town. The surrounding terrain is rugged, but Middlesboro (originally spelled Middlesborough) is built into a deep, circular depression in the mountains some geologists think may be a meteor crater.

Though a few intrepid souls mined coal from the banks of nearby Yellow Creek as early as 1850, the city of Middlesboro wasn't incorporated until 1890. A Scots mining engineer named Alexander Alan Arthur, who must have fancied himself to be the next Andrew Carnegie, had bought up 100,000 acres in the area with the funds of the American Association Limited, a company he had formed with other European backers. Arthur thought that local iron deposits could be turned into steel with fuel from the rich store of coal in the region. The iron deposits turned out to be less than extensive, and the American Association went bust in 1893.

Before the down-turn, company executives built grand, English-style houses on the hills overlooking the town, in a neighborhood called Arthur Heights. Many of these beautiful homes still stand. One is an inn called the **Ridge Runner,** which commands striking views of the surrounding mountains from its verandah and bedroom windows.

The main street of Middlesboro, Cumberland Avenue (KY-74 as it passes through town), is lined with brick and frame buildings dating from the late 19th century. Some light manufacturing occurs in the town, notably clothing and tanning, but Middlesboro's main industry is tourism. Roads into town are lined with chain lodgings and restaurants.

Tourism Bureau

Regional tourist information.
800-988-1075. www.mountaingateway.com

Cumberland Mountain Fall Festival

This festival's most exciting event is the Official Kentucky State Banjo Playing Championship. Held in late September or October. *606-248-1075 or 800-988-1075.*

Coal Museum and House

Mining equipment is on display here and includes a mine locomotive (part train, part trolley), a coal cutting machine, and hand tools used by miners, dating from the late 1800s through the 1960s.

Next door to the museum is the rather weird Coal House, now used as the headquarters for the Bell County Chamber of Commerce and Tourism Commission. It was built in 1926 with 42 tons of coal mined in the area and is one of only two buildings in the United States made from blocks of the fossil fuel. *Located in downtown Middlesboro, near the public parking lot at 238 North 20th St., one block off Cumberland Ave.; 606-248-1075.*

Bell County Historical Society Museum

Housed in a building originally built as a Carnegie library, this museum displays Indian relics, furniture dating from the pioneer period, Civil War memorabilia, coal mining artifacts, and materials from Middlesboro's days as the South's "Little Las Vegas." The town earned that nickname during the 1930s through the '50s, when coal money funded growth of gambling parlors, brothels, and bars. (In 1955, the townspeople formed a "Mop and Broom Party," voted Bell County dry, and the "goings on" ceased.) *242 North 20th St.; three doors from Coal House; 606-242-0005.*

Saint Mary's Episcopal Church

One block behind the museum is Saint Mary's Episcopal Church, built in 1890 by the English families who had come to the region with would-be industrialist Alexander Arthur. The woodwork is of hand-carved oak; one window is Tiffany stained glass. *131 Edgewood Rd.; 606-248-6450.*

The porch of the Ridge Runner B&B in Middlesboro.

Centennial Park

Behind the church, on the other side of the city parking lot, is Centennial Park, with fountains, plantings, and war memorials to the fallen from the Cumberland Gap region. City Hall overlooks the park. A footpath along a restored canal originally built by the American Association city planners leads from the park to the Alexander Arthur Museum, where visitors can learn about the history of the town. *21st St. and Lothbury Ave.*

Golf Course

Another legacy of the Scots-English vision for Middlesboro, the Middlesboro Country Club's nine-hole golf course, the oldest continuously played in the United States, is open to the public. There's a stunning view of the Cumberland Gap from the Number Five tee. *Off of North 25th St. at the end of Cirencester Ave.; 606-248-3831.*

Lost Squadron Museum

This new museum in Middlesboro houses a reconstructed P-38 World War II "Lightning" plane. It was recovered from the site in Greenland where it and other planes were lost when their transport mission failed. *1400 Dorchester Ave.; Middlesboro–Bell County Airport, west along Cumberland Ave. to North 30th St.; 606-248-1149.*

The Lost Squadron Museum in Middlesboro has exhibits relating to the recovery of a World War II P-38, found in Greenland.

A view of Pineville from Chained Rock in Pine Mountain State Resort Park.

■ PINE MOUNTAIN STATE RESORT PARK   *map page 43, B-6*

Within Pine Mountain Park stand magnificent groves of old-growth timber, some of which have been maturing for close to three centuries. These include towering beech poplar and hemlock (take the Hemlock Garden Trail to appreciate them). A few pockets of old-growth oaks and maples, protected from logging, flourish with newer growth in a seemingly endless vista of rolling, forest-covered mountains. Given the size and density of these trees, a lone hiker will be again struck at the incredible determination it must have taken for the long hunters and early settlers to venture into this landscape. There are numerous hiking trails, naturalist-led programs throughout the spring, summer, and fall, and recreation such as golf and swimming. Pine Mountain is known for its flowering bushes: rhododendron and a native Cumberland azalea; as well as for its wildflowers: pink lady's slipper, rare pale corydalis, and even rarer blue and horse gentian.

A ruby-throated hummingbird feeds on the nectar of a trumpet creeper flower.

Late spring is my favorite time to visit, since the nights are crisp and the fog burning off the mountainsides in the mid-morning reveals floral clouds of white mountain laurel suspended in their background of leathery green leaves. On the other hand, there are few better simple pleasures than standing with a hot mug of coffee on the porch of one of the park's log cabins on a cold October morning. The scent of the wood burning in the stone fireplace mingles with the papery-peppery smell of the autumn woods. The view is of a deep valley of hardwoods blazing red and gold. And that rustle in the undergrowth could be a white tailed deer or a lumbering box turtle.

Basics: Kentucky's oldest state park, created in 1924, Pine Mountain Resort State Park has a 30-room lodge that almost seems to be part of the landscape, with its stone pathways, stairs, and columns. Each room has a covered balcony overlooking dense woods that begin just a few feet away across a grassy border. There are also nine one-bedroom log cabins, some of which have fireplaces.

The park is located 15 miles north of Middlesboro off US-25 in Pineville. Open year-round; campground open April through October. (kystateparks.com/ agencies/ parks/pinemtn.2.htm) Information: 606-337-3066; reservations: 800-325-1712.

A trio of Kentucky lady slippers.

(opposite) Flowering shrubs in full bloom at Herndon J. Evans Lodge in Pine Mountain State Resort Park, Pineville.

■ SETTLEMENT SCHOOLS

Because travel was arduous in the roadless, narrow valleys of eastern Kentucky until well into the 20th century, many small communities remained completely isolated—their inhabitants living in primitive conditions without health care or schooling. (Of course, coal from these mountains helped fuel the nation's booming industries, but a miner's pay was minimal, and the wealth coal brought flowed out to absentee mine owners.)

To help these impoverished areas, social activists, usually church affiliated, came to eastern Kentucky to start settlement schools and health clinics. One of the most fascinating was the Frontier Nursing Service, founded in 1925 by Mary Breckenridge, an American nurse-midwife.

Breckenridge trained other nurses, who became famous for riding through the difficult terrain on horseback in order to attend women in labor. The Nursing Service acquired a Jeep in the 1940s, and the organization has now evolved into a modern health care service. The Mary Breckenridge Hospital in Hyden is its most visible presence today.

TAKING THE GED*

*T*aking the GED was the first time I'd ever been stubborn over the doing of something, instead of the not doing. Right there's where Dad and me were different. He was hardheaded over things he never had a say in.

In the morning I left the hill and walked halfway to town before getting a ride that dropped me off at the test place. The lady was surprised to see me. She wrote my name on a form, and asked for fifteen dollars to take the test. I didn't say anything.

"Do you have the fee?" she asked.

"No."

"Do you have a job?"

"No."

"Do you live with family?"

"Mom."

"Does she have a job?"

"No."

"Do you receive welfare assistance?"

"No, Ma'am."

"Then how do you and your mother get along?"

"We don't talk much."

She tightened her mouth and shook her head. Her voice came slow and loud, like I was deaf.

"What do you and your mother do for money?"

"Never had much need for it."

"What about food?"

"We grow it."

The lady set her pencil down and leaned away from the desk. On the wall behind her hung a picture of the governor wearing a tie. I looked through the window at the hardware store across the street. Dad died owing it half on a new chain saw. We got a bill after the funeral and Mom sold a quilt her great-aunt made, to pay the debt.

(continues page 61)

*The GED is the high school equivalency exam.

(opposite) Marion Post Wolcott took this photograph in 1940 of an arithmetic lesson at a one-room school in eastern Kentucky. *(Farm Security Administration)*

> I was thinking hard and not getting far. There wasn't anything I had to sell. Warren would give me the money but I could never ask him for it. I turned to leave.
> "Junior," said the lady. "You can take the test anyway."
> "I don't need the help."
> "It's free when you're living in poverty."
> "I'll owe you," I said. "Pay you before the first snow."
> She led me through a door to a small room with no windows. I squeezed into a school desk and she gave me four yellow pencils and the test. When I finished, she said to come back in a month and see if I passed. She told me in a soft voice that I could take the test as many times as necessary. I nodded and headed out of town toward home. I couldn't think or feel. I was doing good to walk.
>
> —Chris Offutt, "Sawdust," in *Kentucky Straight*, 1992

Today, the settlement schools serve as community centers and educational institutions, most often for the purpose of introducing people from outside the region to Appalachian traditions such as woodworking, pottery making, storytelling, and folk music.

◆ **PINE MOUNTAIN SETTLEMENT SCHOOL**   *map page 43, B-6*

Founded in 1913 by pioneer settler William Creech for the children of the area, this rustic 632-acre campus was home to the first school here at a time when there was no public school in the area. Now the campus serves as an educational center for elementary school students from as far away as Louisville who come here to learn to identify plants and study the lives of Native Americans and pioneer settlers. Classes include weaving on hand looms, learning folk dances, and identifying plants traditionally used as folk remedies. (Yes, there really is such a beverage as sassafras tea, made from the bark of the sassafras tree.) The log buildings are nestled in a flat hollow surrounded by forested, rhododendron-covered hills. Visitors are welcome. ***Directions:*** *drive east from Pineville on KY-66N for 1.5 miles and turn right onto KY-221E. This will take you 32 miles to KY-510. Bear to the right; immediately take another right and you will see the entrance to the school. 36 Highway 510; 606-558-3571.*

(opposite) A costumed interpreter at Cumberland Gap National Historic Park demonstrates how wool is carded by hand.

◆ HENDERSON SETTLEMENT *map page 43, B-6*

This 1,300 acre working farm, community center, and child care facility started in the 1920s as a Methodist mission school. Those who run it describe it as a social organization meant to help mountain people with housing and food. Located 22 miles from the nearest town, the settlement provides help and some employment in an area with few jobs and little transportation to nearby cities. It offers GED training, and teaches prospective mothers how to care for their children.

The settlement **crafts shop** sells traditional, homemade mountain crafts—quilts, baskets, and furniture—the sale of which provides many nearby residents their only earned income.

Although most visitors who come here have some connection to the Methodist church, all visitors are welcome and are usually given a history tour. *Southwest of Pineville on KY-190; 606-337-3613.*

From the Pine Mountain area you can either head northeast, deeper into the mountains and eventually up to Ashland *(see page 80),* or west to the Cumberland Falls area and northward into the Daniel Boone National Forest, eventually heading toward Lexington.

■ CUMBERLAND FALLS STATE RESORT PARK *map page 43, A-6*

This state park is located at the southern end of Daniel Boone National Forest. Here, the Cumberland River drops off a cliff to form a 60-foot-high waterfall with a 125-foot-wide curtain. East of the Rockies, only Niagara Falls in New York is larger.

In 1939, the falls were beautifully described in the WPA guide, *Kentucky, the Bluegrass State.* The following description is still correct.

*I*mmediately behind the falling sheet of water is a recess in the rock wall, which makes it possible to go almost across the river through the arch formed on one side by the rock and the other by the flashing waters. Below the falls are are many whirlpools and rapids in the river as it flows for seven miles through a boulder-strewn gorge, whose cliffs are 300 to 400 feet high. A winding trail leads from the falls half a mile down the river to Little Eagle Falls, small but picturesque, surrounded by heavily wooded hills. It is said that this spot was regarded as a sacred place by the

Indians who guarded it day and night and even fought a battle (the Indian Battle of Shiloh) in its defense. On the south side of the river is a Cliff Walk, a narrow ledge high above the water, which winds around the shoulders of the hill until it reaches a shelter house at the top.

A fine growth of yellow pine crowns the ridges, while on the steep slopes and ravines leading down to the river is a mixed forest growth of hemlock, tulip, magnolia, oak, sweet gum, dogwood, and holly, the latter especially abundant and of large size. Azalea, rhododendron, spicebush, Stewartia, blueberry, St.-John's-wort, and strawberry bush are among the many plants.

A multi-colored "moonbow" is visible in the rushing water of the falls on clear nights when the moon is full—as well as two nights before and two nights afterward. Cumberland Falls is one of only two known places in the world where this occurs predictably (the other is Victoria Falls on the Zambezi River in Zambia). You have the best chance of seeing the moonbow in the winter, since cold nights are often clearer. The trail to the falls is silvery in the winter moonlight, and the hooting of great horned owls carries in the woodlands on these crisp nights.

A rainbow at Cumberland Falls.

Numerous recreational facilities are available here, including guided white-water rafting trips on the Cumberland River from May through October. Displays at the **Bob Blair Museum** describe the area's plants, animals, and geology, as well as Native American artifacts.

Basics: Park lodging includes campgrounds, cottages, and Dupont Lodge—one of the most beautiful in the Kentucky State Parks system—its high ceilings supported by hemlock beams and golden knotty pine paneling. In the wintertime, the massive stone fireplaces in the lodge blaze with big, open wood fires. *Information: Cumberland Falls State Resort Park, 7351 Hwy-90, Corbin; 606-528-4121.*

■ NEAR CUMBERLAND FALLS PARK *map page 43, A-5/6*

From the state park take KY-90 to US-25W and head north to Corbin. From there, and off I-75, several sites are within easy distance. Note: If you are coming from Middlesboro, don't be fooled by a map into thinking that the shortest route is west along KY-74 and TN-90. What the map doesn't show is that these are winding two-lane roads through mountains.

Harland Sanders Cafe & Museum
map page 43, A-6
From I-75, take Exit 29 at Corbin and you'll find the Harland Sanders Cafe & Museum. This is the little restaurant where Colonel Sanders developed his famous chicken recipe. (Which, believe me, was much better before fast-food giant Tricon, also the parent company of Taco Bell and Pizza Hut, got its corporate oven mitts onto it.) Be warned that it's modern KFC that's served up at the cafe.

Thomas Walker State Historic Site
map page 43, A-6
This may be the smallest "by-the-way-this-is-a-historic-site" in the nation. Its 12 acres contain a replica of the cabin built by the first white explorer in the region, Dr. Thomas Walker (the hut looks a lot like it was made from giant Lincoln Logs). There's also a basketball court, a miniature golf course, picnic facilities, and a playground. It feels like "kinderhistory." That said, the manicured site is beautifully maintained. *Located on KY-459, six miles off US-25E in Barbourville.*

Levi Jackson Wilderness Road State Park
map page 43, A-5
There are eight and a half miles of hiking trails that incorporate portions of the original Wilderness Road as well as of two other significant trails, Boone's Trace and Warrior's Path. If you choose to hike along Boone's Trace, you are literally following

(opposite) Autumn leaves in a pool at Cumberland Falls State Resort Park.

Daniel Boone's footsteps, since it was part of the 100-mile track that Boone originally blazed through the Kentucky wilderness. The narrow dirt trail feels a little like a woodland equivalent of a cathedral aisle, since the oaks, beeches, and walnuts tower above the path like leafy columns.

Also on the park grounds is a working grist mill, McHargue's Mill, a recreation of an early 19th-century facility. It's surrounded by the largest collection of antique millstones in the country They face upward like sundials and are mounted in a bed of gravel. Inside the mill, you can watch the giant cogged wheels turn to the rhythm of the water flowing in broad, shallow Little Laurel River. The scent of fresh flour mingles in the air with the mellow smell of the old log walls of the mill. *On US-25S. (It's easy to find from I-75, Exit 38.) For park information call 606-878-8000.*

Renfro Valley   *map page 3*

Renfro Valley, off Exit 26 of Interstate 75, is known as "Kentucky's Country Music Capital." The entertainment center hosts concerts nightly from Memorial Day to Labor Day and on weekends year round. Renfro Valley is about an hour's drive south of Lexington and just south of Berea, described on page 118.

■ HARLAN COUNTY

Head northeast from Pineville along US-119 to go deeper into the mountains of eastern Kentucky. Harlan County is famous as one of the major coal-producing regions of the state and the site of many confrontations between miners and management. It contains Kentucky's highest point, Black Mountain at 4,145 feet.

Families in the area have been here for generations, and although many young people leave in search of work, they don't seem to yearn to depart. People are conservative, the main institutions being church and family. In this close-knit community, most people don't lock their cars or houses. Go to a store or a gas station and people are helpful and friendly—although they might be a little less so if you tried to move in.

The Kingdom Come Festival, first weekend in October, offers a glimpse of their world. Demonstrations include molasses making, bowl making, chair making, lye soap making, hominy making, and apple cider making. Moonshine making, however, is not demonstrated—even though it's a highly developed art in these mountains. It's illegal to own a still here, but moonshine is still picked up from local dealers by customers carrying brown paper bags. At 100 to 108 proof, moonshine is either clear or "charred"—the latter being made in barrels burnt on the inside.

COPPER KETTLE SONG

This famous old folk ballad celebrates distilling moonshine whiskey.

Get you a copper kettle
Get you a copper coil
Cover with new-made corn mash
And never more you'll toil.

Refrain:
You'll just lay there by juniper
While the moon is bright
Watch them jugs a filling
In the pale moonlight.

My daddy he made whiskey
My granddaddy he did too,
We ain't paid no whiskey tax
Since 1792.

❧ *Refrain* ❧

Build you a fire with hickory
Hickory, ash, and oak,
Don't use no green or rotten wood
They'll get you by the smoke.

❧ *Refrain* ❧

Kentucky's other legendary whiskey: moonshine.

Serpent handlers at the Pentecostal Church of God in Lejunior, Harlan County, 1946. (National Archives)

Kingdom Come State Park *(map page 43, C-5)* is named after a sentimental Civil War novel, *The Little Shepherd of Kingdom Come,* written by John Fox, Jr. and set in Harlan County. Its land is unspoiled and trails along the ridge tops offer remarkable views of the surrounding mountains.

For information on the area, call the Tri-City Chamber of Commerce, 606-589-5812.

◆ CUMBERLAND   *map page 43, C-5*

In 1870, six families settled down to form the town of Cumberland. Their community was incorporated as Cumberland 41 years later with a population of 186.

Today it is the home of **Southeast Community College,** which maintains the **Appalachian Cultural and Fine Arts Center**. The center exhibits mountain arts and crafts, and it archives photographic and oral history. On the walls you'll find pictures of coal mining camps from the 1900s to the '40s as well as exhibits that include critters made from seashells, medicine vials, and various gourds (this ain't the Louvre). You'll also find a 2,200-item pocket knife collection and works by local artists and craftspeople. For information about the museum call the college: *606-589-2145, Ext. 2102.*

On Main Street in Cumberland, at a shop called Poor Folks Arts and Crafts, you can purchase goods made by contemporary artisans.

If you're curious about coal—or the life of singer Loretta Lynn—visit the **Kentucky Coal Mining Museum** at Benham, two miles southeast of Cumberland on KY-160. The community was founded by International Harvester in 1911 as a company coal town and the museum is housed in what was the commissary building. The center has exhibits of local mountain arts and crafts and archives of photographs and oral histories. Upstairs in ithe museum, **Loretta Lynn memorabilia** is on display and a 7,000-record collection of country music from the 1930s to '70s; *606-848-1530.*

Miners with a locomotive, ca. 1920.

■ LILLEY CORNETT WOODS   *map page 43, C-5*

If you've chosen to head further into the hills and go northeast from Pine Mountain, make time to visit Lilley Cornett Woods in Letcher County, just a few miles north of Kingdom Come State Park. Here is one of the last stands of virgin forest in the eastern United States. Along stream beds and climbing up hillsides some 900 feet grow trees that were saplings when the Pilgrims landed at Plymouth Rock. The massive branches of sycamores, sweet gums, and slippery elms hang over the rushing water of Line Fork Creek. Hackberry trees, identified by their distinctively bumpy bark, produce pea-sized, purplish-black fruits, attractive to birds. Ridges are populated by stands of sugar maple, tulip poplar, buckeye, hemlock, and beech. Even the virtually extinct American chestnut has made a last stand here. In the woodlands you can spot old trunks that still send up shoots, which reach sapling stage before they die back from chestnut blight.

This magical preserve makes it possible to imagine what Daniel Boone and

Bad Branch (creek) runs through a stand of new forest.

other settlers felt when they first encountered the Kentucky wilderness. Most of Kentucky's woodlands are second- or third-growth, with young trees too densely packed to allow an understory to flourish. But here that flora has been preserved: you can walk the trails beneath the soaring canopy and spot hundreds of native wildflower species. On my last walk here, in late August, tall Joe-Pye weed stalks were capped with clusters of tiny purple blossoms; jewelweed lay in brilliant orange carpets, and yellow and white asters in full bloom were attended by hovering butterflies.

A question mark butterfly (Polygonia interrogationis) with its fall coloration.

Two- and four-hour guided hikes are offered at the park; call for reservations; *Located at the end of KY-1103, off KY-160; 606-633-5828.*

■ THE BREAKS INTERSTATE PARK   *map page 43, D-4*

The Breaks of the Big Sandy River, on the border of Kentucky and Virginia, is an area of magnificent natural beauty. Over the course of millions of years, the Russell Fork of the Big Sandy managed to carve the largest canyon east of the Mississippi, some five miles long and 1,600 feet deep. It winds around a half-mile-long, one-third-mile-wide rock formation called The Towers. (There's a legend dating back to Boone's time that an English explorer named John Swift hid a fortune in silver near the Towers.) The view of this area has been described thusly:

A Gray's tree frog sings in the forest.

A thousand feet or more below, in the most striking water gap of the Big Sandy Valley, flows Russell Fork which begins as a thin mountain stream in Virginia and flows into the Big Sandy in Kentucky. The river has worn a deep gorge through an uplift dating from the Paleozoic era. In this great upheaval other streams that once crossed the land here in an east-west direction were thrown back upon themselves or else were diverted to form Elkhorn Creek and Pound River. In a succession of waterfalls and rapids—called "jumps" by the natives—the river plunges over and around boulders that fill the bed of the stream and descends about 350 feet in traversing the tortuous five miles of the Breaks. Rising on each side of the turbulent stream are palisades bedecked with rhododendron, evergreens, and hardwood. *(Kentucky, the Bluegrass State,* WPA, 1939.)

Today, if you take a raft trip along the river, the view up the steep slopes from below reveals rock faces and a forest of oaks and maples whose deep green leaves turn scarlet and gold in fall. The white-water rapids of the Russell Fork charge and bolt among boulders as big as boxcars, and the river twists and turns along its bed as it loops around the Tower. You'll want to be travelling with experienced rafters.

Basics for The Breaks Park: The 4,600-acre park has a lodge, camping facilities, cottages, and a swimming pool. Hiking, horseback riding, and whitewater rafting, and fishing in Laurel Lake are all available. Breaks Interstate Park; *Park entrance on Hwy-80; 800-982-5122.*

■ PIKEVILLE AND THE HATFIELDS AND MCCOYS   *map page 43, D-4*

At the center of a coal-producing region, Pikeville (pop. 6,300) is the county seat of Pike County, the state's easternmost county. The town is best known as the site of the trials and executions of participants in the infamous Hatfield–McCoy Feud.

Kentucky's McCoy clan lived in Pike County, the Hatfields across the border in West Virginia. Their patriarchs were Randolph (Ran'l) McCoy born in 1825 and father of 16 children, and his counterpart Devil Anse Hatfield, born in 1839 and father of 13 children. Members of both families were tall handsome people of Scottish descent who farmed, hunted, logged, and made moonshine. During the Civil War most supported the Confederacy, and their men returned from the war sore and ornery. One McCoy, however, joined the Union Army, and upon coming home, was shot at and killed. The McCoys blamed the Hatfields.

Relations reached a climax in 1878, when Ran'l McCoy accused Floyd Hatfield of holding a McCoy hog in his pen. A trial over the ownership of the animal ensued, and members of both families attended, most carrying guns. A jury of six Hatfields and six McCoys found Hatfield innocent of pig-napping.

Pretty soon it got out that one of the McCoy jury members had found for Hatfield. Not surprisingly, he was kicked out of his clan. Over the next decade, altercations continued with killings on both sides. A clandestine romance then came to light—between Johnse Hatfield and Rosenna McCoy. Ellison Mounts, convicted of killing Ran'l McCoy's daughter Alifair, was hung in Pikeville.

After that, things began to simmer down.

Historians in Pike County are working on a Hatfield–McCoy Trail in hopes that visitors will come to take a look. If you stop by Pikeville's Dils Cemetery, you'll see that many members of the McCoy family are buried there.

This family portrait of the Hatfields was taken during their feuding days.

EASTERN HIGHLANDS

■ US-23 COUNTRY MUSIC HIGHWAY   *map page 43, D-4 to C-1*

It's pretty easy to follow US-23, dubbed "The Country Music Highway." From the Virginia border near The Breaks, US-23 heads north to Ashland. Markers along the highway pinpoint the birthplaces of several country music and bluegrass stars including Patty Loveless (Pike County), Dwight Yoakam (Floyd County), Loretta Lynn (Johnson County), The Judds (Boyd County), and Billy Ray Cyrus (Greenup County). *(See page 76.)*

◆ PRESTONSBURG   *map page 43*

US-23 will take you from Pikeville through the mountain towns of Coal Run Village, Betsy Layne, and Water Gap before you reach Prestonsburg. The **Mountain Arts Center** on Hal Rogers Drive is a state-of-the-art concert facility with a 1,050-seat auditorium. Home to the Kentucky Opry, it features country and bluegrass music. For ticket information, call 1-888-MACARTS.

This is also a crafts center. The **Country at Heart** complex on South Front Street has items such as walking sticks, hand-made baskets, stained glass, and rustic furniture for sale, made by local craftspeople. If this isn't enough of a selection, you can take a detour six miles southwest of the town on KY-404 to a wide spot in the road called David, where **David Appalachian Crafts** dominates the crossroads. Look for quilts, baskets, and woodcrafts. *606-886-2377.*

◆ JENNY WILEY STATE RESORT PARK   *map page 43, C-3*

Jenny Wiley State Resort Park is located between Prestonsburg and Paintsville, off of US-23 on KY-3. The park commemorates pioneer woman Virginia "Jenny" Wiley, who was kidnapped from her log cabin by Indians in 1789. She endured many hardships among the Indians, including the death of the small son captured with her and of the baby born several months after she was abducted. But she managed to escape and return home where she and her husband Tom had five more children. Wiley lived to the age of 71 and is buried in Johnson County near Paintsville. An outdoor drama performed each summer in the park's amphitheater reenacts the story of her life.

The park has a trail that follows the route taken by Wiley and her captors; this trail also connects to other rugged hiking trails which eventually lead to the Ohio River. But even the shorter trails within the park offer scenic views of the surrounding mountains.

Court Street and South Front Street in Prestonsburg.

STARS OF THE COUNTRY MUSIC HIGHWAY

It's pretty easy to follow US-23, dubbed The Country Music Highway. From the Virginia border near The Breaks, US-23 heads north to Ashland. Markers along the highway pinpoint the birthplaces of several country music and Bluegrass stars.

PATTY LOVELESS
b. 1957
Pikeville, Pike County

One of eight children, she was singing and writing songs by the age of 13. She married Terry Lovelace after she graduated from high school, and later Emory Gordy, Jr., her producer. A fine songwriter, she has been inducted into the Grand Old Opry.

Songs: *Long Stretch of Lonesome, Trouble with Truth, When Fallen Angels Fly*

Patty Loveless
(photo by T. C. Farley)

DWIGHT YOAKAM
b. 1956, , Floyd County
Yoakam learned to play the guitar at the age of six and was a member of several bands in high school before he headed to Nashville in the late 1970s.
Has acted in various movies, including *Sling Blade.*

    Songs: *The Heart That You Own, It Only Hurts When I Cry, Ain't That Lonely Yet*

Dwight Yoakam

(All photos courtesy Michael Ochs Archives, Venice, CA)

LORETTA LYNN

b. 1935, Butcher Hollow, Johnson County
A coal miner's daughter (the second of eight children), Loretta Lynn was raised in a small shack. She married at 13, and had six children and a grandchild by 29. She recorded 16 number 1 and 60 hit singles; today she lives on a huge ranch 70 miles from Nashville.
Songs: *Success, Before I'm Over You, Blue Kentucky Girl, You Ain't Woman Enough, Fist City, Don't Come Home A-Drinking (With Lovin' On Your Mind), Pregnant Again.*

Loretta Lynn

THE JUDDS

Naomi b. 1946, Boyd County; Wynonna b. 1964
Blurring the line between popular and country singing, Wynonna Judd and her mother Naomi Judd have been the most popular mother-daughter singers in the nation. By 1985 they had two platinum albums, a gold album, and six number- one singles. Their final concert in 1991 grossed $21 million. Wynonna's younger sister Ashley, born in California, is a singer and actress.
Songs: *Mama He's Crazy, Why Not Me, Girls Night Out, Cry Myself to Sleep, Have Mercy*

The Judds: Naomi and Wynonna

BILLY RAY CYRUS

b. 1961, Flatwoods, Greenup County
As a child Cyrus sang with his father's gospel quartet and his mother's bluegrass group. By 19 he was playing guitar and performing with the band Sly Dog, named after his one-eyed bulldog. Made his Grand Ole Opry debut in 1996. Cyrus married wife Leticia in 1993. He lives with "Tish," his six children, and many dogs and horses on a farm in Tennessee.
Songs: *Achy Breaky Heart, Some Gave All, Shot Full of Love.*

Billy Ray Cyrus

Basics: The Jenny Wiley State Resort Park has a lodge and restaurant, cottages, a campground, golf, boating, fishing, and a sky lift to the top of Sugar Camp Mountain. The park is open year-round, but some facilities change days and hours seasonally. *Call 606-886-2711 for information.*

◆ PAINTSVILLE   *map page 43, C-3*

Paintsville is 15 miles north of Prestonsburg, on US-23. The town was named for Indian drawings that early settlers found on tree trunks on the banks of nearby (and similarly named) Paint Creek.

Another of the centers for coal commerce in eastern Kentucky, the growth of the town was influenced by John C. C. Mayo, a Pike County native who amassed a personal fortune by acquiring mineral rights in the region. (When he died in 1914 at the Waldorf-Astoria Hotel in New York City, he had become the richest Kentuckian.) Mayo was responsible for two buildings in town. The first is the United Methodist Church, a beautiful Gothic-style stone church; inside is an

organ donated by Andrew Carnegie (705 Court Street). The second is a 40-room mansion that now houses Our Lady of the Mountain School (405 Third Street).

If you are a country music fan and want a closer view of a landmark than the signs along US-23, stop by the Paintsville Visitor Center (housed in a red caboose) and get the directions to Butcher Hollow (say "Holler"). Here is the childhood cabin of Loretta Lynn and her singer sister Crystal Gayle—a ramshackle wooden

The John C. C. Mayo Mansion in Paintsville.

Loretta Lynn's childhood home off US-23 near Paintsville.

dwelling built against the mountainside, its front porch supported by stilts. Lynn left home at 13 to get married, and by 14 she was a mother. Once she started a career as a singer and songwriter, Lynn became, in the words of one critic, "the spokeswoman for every woman who has gotten married too early, pregnant too often, and felt trapped by the tedium and drudgery of life." *(Also see "Country Music Highway" on page 76.)*

The Mountain Home Place is a few miles west of Paintsville on US-460. This is a living history farm. "Residents," properly dressed for their era, do daily chores using farming techniques from around 1850. Oxen, rather than tractors, pull plows. Butter is churned by hand. *Call 606-297-1850 for information.*

You now have the option of going back to US-23 and driving 50 miles to Ashland, or taking a less direct route to Saylersville, where you can pick up the Mountain Parkway and have a straight shot to Slade, the town nearest the scenic Red River Gorge district of the Daniel Boone National Forest.

■ ASHLAND AND THE GREENBO REGION   *map page 43, C-1*

Ashland, built on the banks of the Ohio River, was first settled in 1786 by members of the Poage family of Shenandoah Valley, Virginia, who had come to Kentucky through the Cumberland Gap. Known as Poage's Landing, the town turned out to be located in a region rich in the materials—coal, timber, and limestone, that could be used to process pig iron. Its location on the river meant that manufactured goods could be easily transported.

The early iron furnaces used charcoal, but in the 19th century, as coal was starting to be mined, the furnaces switched to the hotter-burning fossil fuel.

In 1854, a group of Ohio industrialists and Poage family descendants formed a development company, called the Kentucky Iron, Coal, and Manufacturing Company and hired an engineer to lay out a plan for the town, which was renamed Ashland in honor of the U.S. senator from Kentucky, Henry Clay, whose Lexington home was called Ashland.

Central Ashland has several opulent homes built by the men who made fortunes from the industry of the city. These are concentrated on Lexington and Bath Avenues.

At the town center is the ample and aptly named Central Park, the site of an annual brass band festival in June and the Poage Landing Days Festival in September. Five prehistoric Indian burial mounds on the park grounds date from the Adena Period (800 B.C.E to A.D. 800).

The most important business presence in modern times has been Ashland Oil, Inc. The refinery company, one of the 100 largest industrial companies in the United States, has contributed substantial amounts of its profits to secondary and higher education in Kentucky. It maintains its refining operations in Ashland, but recently moved its corporate office to Covington, Kentucky. *Ashland is about a one-and-a-half hour drive from Lexington.*

◆ GREENBO LAKE STATE RESORT PARK   *map page 43, C-1*

Fifteen miles north of I-64 (Exit 172) at Grayson is Greenbo Lake State Resort Park, at the center of which is Greenbo Lake, home to enormous largemouth bass, as well as catfish, trout, and bluegill. Also located on the grounds of the park are the ruins of the historic Buffalo Furnace, which was active in the region's iron production in the mid-1800s.

The park has 25 miles of hiking trails and a 36-room lodge. The lodge contains a library and reading room dedicated to the works of Jesse Stuart, novelist and poet, who lived nearby.

Someone in the park's past had the idea of hanging hummingbird feeders from the railings of the lodge porches. If you are visiting in the summer and can stand very still by these feeders, you'll be treated to the sight of dozens of jewel-like little hummers hovering at the tube-shaped feeders.

◆ JESSE STUART HOMEPLACE

KENTUCKY STATE NATURE PRESERVE   *map page 43, B/C-1*

Beloved in his home state, but little known outside Kentucky, author Jesse Stuart (1906-1984) lived most of his life in Greenup County where he taught school and wrote more than 2,000 poems, 460 short stories, and nine novels. His autobiographical novel, *The Thread That Runs So True,* was based on his experiences as a teacher. Stuart's family home (private) is located within 733 acres of woods and fields that have been designated a state nature preserve. To get to the Jesse Stuart Homeplace from Greenbo Park, *take KY-1 north about five miles and turn left on KY-2433, W. Hollow Rd.; 606-473-7324.*

◆ COVERED BRIDGES   *map page 43, B/C-1*

Of Kentucky's remaining covered bridges, two are in Greenup County. The **Old-town Bridge,** dating from 1880, is nine miles south of Greenbo Lake Park on KY-1. The 1855 **Bennett's Mill Bridge** is 12 miles north of the park, on KY-7.

◆ CARTER CAVES STATE RESORT PARK   *map page 43, B-1/2*

Heading west from Ashland towards Morehead on I-64, you'll pass through Olive Hill, the town closest to Carter Caves. This Kentucky state park has beautiful forested hills on its surface and more than 20 caves meandering below. Tours are offered of the caverns, including Cascade Cave, which has a 30-foot-high underground waterfall. The largest of the caves is **Bat Cave,** home in the winter to thousands of rare bats. Not surprisingly, tours for humans are given only in the summer. The park has lodging, a campground, and a swimming pool, stables and cave tours. *Information: 606-286-4411.*

Millcreek Lake in Natural Bridges State Resort Park.

◆ **MOREHEAD**   *map page 43, B-2*

On US-60 near I-64 is Morehead, the seat of Rowan County and a good place to pick up supplies if you are planning a trek in the Daniel Boone National Forest.

Morehead State University oversees the following attractions pertinent to the culture of the area. The **Cora Wilson Stewart Moonlight School** is a preserved one-room school located at the end of West First Street. The **Kentucky Folk Art Center** specializes in pieces made from found objects and is located at 102 West First Street.

The university library's **Appalachian Collection** contains documents, including genealogical materials, important to the area as well as collections of materials related to Kentucky authors James Still and Jesse Stuart.

(opposite) Yahoo Falls in the South Fork River and Recreation Area.

◼ DANIEL BOONE NATIONAL FOREST

The vast Daniel Boone National Forest stretches northeast to southwest across the width of the state, all the way to the Tennessee border. This is a hikers' and back-packers' paradise and there are plenty of scenic roads through the various sections of the forest, including the nine-mile Zilpo Road National Forest Scenic Byway. Visitors centers at Slade and Winchester have maps.

◆ MOREHEAD RANGER DISTRICT

At the north end of the forest, game fish such as bass, crappie, and muskie can be caught in **Cave Run Lake** (*map page 43, B-2/3*). If you have long-hunter fantasics that need fulfilling, there is a Pioneer Weapons Wildlife Management Area where, with flintlock rifles, muzzle-loading shotguns, and crossbows or long bows, you can stalk wild turkey and white-tailed deer in season. Be advised that you need a license to hunt or fish in Kentucky; local stores and Wal-Marts sell hunting and fishing licenses. *For queries try 606-784-6428.*

The aforementioned **Zilpo Scenic Byway** is in this part of the forest. It passes the **Tater Knob Fire Tower,** the last watchtower in the forest. It's no longer used to watch for fires, but it's open March through October to anyone who wants to climb the stairs to the tower cab and enjoy the panoramic views.

The Byway also goes past the Clear Creek Iron Furnace. Smelting was one of the early industries in the region.

◆ RED RIVER GORGE   *map page 43, A/B-3*

Protected as a National Geological Area, the 25-mile-long Red River Gorge contains more than 100 natural sandstone arches formed over 70 million years by erosion. There's evidence that prehistoric people lived in the gorge as early as 10,000 years ago, many in the cave-like openings in the cliffs. In more recent times, Daniel Boone is thought to have explored the area and may have spent the winter of 1769–70 here. Boone would feel at home if he were to show up today, although he might be surprised to find others canoeing in the Red River. (For canoeing information: *800-K-CANOE-1)*

Gladie Creek Cabin, a reconstructed log house, sits amid fields near the gorge on KY-715, beside a blacksmith shop and a moonshine still. A small resident herd of bison graze nearby. The cabin serves as a visitors center and provides trail maps and information on the National Forest.

The Red River Gorge became a protected area after a well-publicized campaign by environmentalists to save vast parts of it from being inundated by an Army Corps of Engineer dam project. In 1967 Supreme Court Justice William O. Douglas hiked in the gorge to attract support for its conservation.

The topography of the gorge is spectacular, with sandstone arches, chimney rocks, and multistory ledges that were popular camping places for prehistoric Indians. The trails are lined with a diversity of wildflowers unmatched for an area this size anywhere else in Kentucky. Resist the temptation to stray from the trails and explore the rhododendron-covered hillsides. A seemingly gentle slope can come to a sudden end at a cliff's edge with a shear drop of 300 feet.

◆ NATURAL BRIDGE STATE RESORT PARK   *map page 43, A-3*

Named for an impressive sandstone arch, the park is located within Daniel Boone National Forest. There are more than 150 natural stone arches, formed over millions of years, within five miles of the park. The park's namesake, a 65-foot-tall span is the most famous. (Kentuckians don't quibble over the difference between a bridge and an arch from a geological point of view.)

Natural Arch at Natural Bridge State Resort Park.

About half the park is preserved to protect the unique Cumberland Plateau landscape, and in the preserve section only hiking is allowed. There are over 18 miles of trails in the park. Trails pass moss-covered rocks and small waterfalls. In spring and summer, violets, trillium, and iris bloom, as do yellow lady's slipper, dogwood, and the pink and white buds of the mountain laurel. *For information call 606-663-2214.*

◆ **SHELTOWEE TRACE**

Sheltowee in Shawnee means "Big Turtle," which is the name the tribe gave to Daniel Boone. The trace is a 268-mile long National Recreation Trail that will certainly give your hiking boots a workout. In addition to Boone, conservationist John Muir, founder of the Sierra Club, walked portions of what is now the trace.

It begins 10 miles south of the Kentucky border in Tennessee, but the trace runs the entire length of the Daniel Boone National Forest, and you can pick it up at numerous points (the trail is marked with a white diamond or turtle-shaped blaze). It extends northwards past Morehead. If you haven't had enough of a hike, it joins the Jenny Wiley Trail. *Points further south in the Daniel Boone National Forest, such as Cumberland Falls State Resort Park, are described beginning on page 62.*

INNER BLUEGRASS

■ HIGHLIGHTS *page*

Food & Lodging *page 264*
Also see map page 105, towns in yellow.

■ TRAVEL BASICS

Area Overview: This is horse farm country, a region crisscrossed with scenic two-lane, tree-canopied roads lined with wooden fences. April is my favorite time to travel in the Bluegrass, because the meadows are so vividly green and there are hundreds of adorable little foals frolicking in the fields next to their mothers. Flowering trees such as dogwoods and redbuds add extra texture to the landscape. In late summer, the green is interspersed with large, yellowing soybean fields.

Travel: To experience the flavor of this region, drive the back roads that wend their way though small, tidy towns and past mile after mile of horse farms. These roads often circle around a town square sporting a 19th-century courthouse that is as likely to be faced by the local Dollar General Store as by antiques shops.

Weather: The Bluegrass is graced by a temperate climate, so unless there's a drought, pastures and lawns here remain green year-round. Rain falls throughout the year, most of it in the spring. It can get very cold in winter, hovering in the 20s and 30s in January, although it's possible to experience an odd spring-like day in February with temperatures climbing into the 60s or even 70s. Summers are very hot—80s and 90s in July and August with 70 percent and higher humidity. Fall temperatures are typically in the 60s, creeping up to the 70s and 80s on warm days.

Food: In the Bluegrass, traditional inns serve fried chicken and corn pudding. In the past few years new restaurants have served ethnic dishes.

Lexington boasts a growing restaurant scene, and many restaurants have excellent wine lists as well as a fine selection of bourbons. Lexington is packed on winter days when the University of Kentucky Wildcats are playing basketball at Rupp Arena. You won't get into a restaurant after an afternoon game or before an evening contest. Friday and Saturday nights are also problematic for dining during the spring and fall meets at Keeneland Race Course, which are held in early April and early October.

Lodging: A wide choice is offered between well-known hotel and motel chains and historic inns and B&Bs. Refer to the **Food & Lodging map,** page 265; toll-free numbers for chains on page 266. Towns are listed in alphabetical order beginning on page 267. For charts relating towns to chapters see page 311.

■ OVERVIEW

When most people think of Kentucky, they picture the lush, green, meticulously manicured fields of horse farms where the valuable Thoroughbred residents are bred, trained, and pampered. Such fields, lined with white fences and punctuated with palatial horse barns and fine homes, do indeed exist in the heart of the Bluegrass region. In the counties surrounding Lexington—Fayette, Woodford, Jessamine, Scott, and Bourbon—there are more than 460 horse farms, the greatest concentration of such operations anywhere in the world. Racehorses account for one-third of the economic base of the Bluegrass. Until recently, burley tobacco and bourbon whiskey made up the other two thirds. Ironic, isn't it, that in a state where more than half of the residents identify themselves as Southern Baptists, so many traditional livelihoods are based on bourbon, tobacco, and horseracing?

Burley tobacco is the variety used for making cigarettes. More of it was grown in Kentucky than in any other state. Correspondingly, the state has the highest rate of adult smokers in the United States, at just about 50 percent. Not coincidentally, Kentucky also has the nation's highest rate of smoking-related illnesses. Federal tobacco buyout programs are encouraging most tobacco farmers to grow other crops.

Since corn grew prolifically in the rich soil of the Bluegrass region, it was the grain favored by the Scots-Irish settlers for distillation into whiskey. Corn was often used as barter in exchange for other goods, and turning it into whiskey not only preserved it, but made it easier to transport. All of Kentucky's remaining commercial distilleries are located in the Bluegrass region, and three are found near Lexington and Frankfort: Buffalo Trace, Woodford Reserve, and Wild Turkey.

Agriculture is still important in the Inner Bluegrass, but Lexington and its suburbs have experienced considerable manufacturing growth in the past two decades. The former IBM compound on the city's outskirts is now the headquarters of Lexmark International, a major manufacturer of computer printers and keyboards. Toyota Motors has a plant in Scott County that produces about 400,000 automobiles a year.

The University of Kentucky in Lexington, the state's land-grant university, provides over 10,000 jobs, making it the region's biggest employer. (In light of the near-religious fervor with which many natives follow the University of Kentucky Wildcat basketball team, one is tempted to designate the U of K as a church with an even larger membership than that of the Baptists'.)

Tobacco leaves dry in an open-sided tobacco barn.

A Thoroughbred colt grazes beside his mother in a meadow off Ironworks Pike near Lexington.

And, speaking of sports, state government is concentrated in the Inner Bluegrass. The Kentucky General Assembly meets every year in Frankfort. This august body passed the Kentucky Education Reform Act, which has served as a model for similar initiatives around the nation. Yet this same assembly has also decreed that it's fine for ministers to carry concealed deadly weapons in church, but *not* acceptable for Kentuckians to have wine shipped directly from its producers.

■ HISTORY

The elegant horse farms with their rolling pastures bounded by plank-and-stone fences seem such a natural feature of the landscape that it's easy to forget that this is human-sculpted terrain and that the bluegrass itself is not native to Kentucky. In his 1949 classic, *Sand County Almanac,* conservationist Aldo Leopold put the ecological history of central Kentucky in perspective:

> *I*t is time now to ponder the fact that the cane-lands [of Kentucky], when subjected to the particular mixture of forces represented by the cow, plow, fire, and axe of the pioneer, became bluegrass. What if the

INNER BLUEGRASS

With the sideways cast of morning sunlight, bluegrass really does appear bluish.

plant succession inherent in this dark and bloody ground had, under the impact of these forces, given us some worthless sedge, shrub, or weed? Would Boone and Kenton have held out? Would...there have been overflow into Ohio, Indiana, Illinois, and Missouri? Any Louisiana Purchase? Any transcontinental union of new states? Any Civil War?...[I]n the case of Kentucky, we do not even know where the bluegrass came from—whether it is a native species or a stowaway from Europe.

Actually, the famous bluegrass, *Poa pratensis,* is native to Eurasia. It was a popular pasture grass for centuries in Britain, where it was known as smooth-stalked meadow grass. English immigrants to North America may have brought seeds with them as early as 1625. Seeds had somehow established themselves as far west as Kentucky by the early 18th century. The opportunistic plant sprouted easily in the rich limestone soil.

(previous pages) Manchester Horse Farm on Van Meter Road in Lexington.

By the time Daniel Boone and Simon Kenton brought settlers into Kentucky, bluegrass was well-established in the region that now takes the plant's name. (No one quite knows why it's called "bluegrass." Some claim that in springtime when the grass blooms and grows tall, and wind sweeps the meadows, bluegrass really is blue, while others say that it's the seeds that are bluish. Still others assert that bluegrass looks blue in direct proportion to the amount of bourbon imbibed by the observer.)

Underlying central Kentucky is a vast shelf of Ordovician (450 million-year-old) limestone, progenitor of the fertile soil in which bluegrass thrives. The grass propagates by spreading a network of roots and so makes an excellent sod grass. Buffalo, and later cattle, grazing on the native cane (a coarse grass) that once grew in the region, soon depleted that plant. Bluegrass replaced cane because it tolerates close cropping.

The topsoil of the region also was, and remains, very fertile. In addition to containing calcium carbonate (the mineral in limestone), it is rich in nitrogen and phosphates. Central Kentucky's late 18th- and early 19th-century farmers noted that their animals grew more robust than they did elsewhere in the state or in neighboring Ohio and Tennessee. By the early 1800s, Kentucky horses were already renowned throughout the fledgling United States for their beauty and stamina.

Hemp, used in making rope and sailcloth, was an important crop in the antebellum Bluegrass, replaced by tobacco only after the Civil War. Hemp farming is a labor-intensive activity, and in the first half of the 19th century, those who did the work were slaves.

After emancipation, many blacks remained on the Bluegrass farms as paid laborers, some as highly skilled and valued employees of the horse farms. (Most jockeys in the 19th century and the early part of the 20th were African American.)

Harvesting hemp at the turn of the 20th century.

■ LEXINGTON   *maps page 97 and 105, B-2*

Kentucky's second largest city (population nearing a quarter million) lies in the heart of the Bluegrass region and is the center of Thoroughbred horse racing in America. In fact, it can reasonably claim to be the Horse Capital of the World. The countryside surrounding the city is home to nearly five hundred farms breeding Thoroughbred and standardbred horses. The city itself embraces several charming, historic neighborhoods; offers a variety of good restaurants; and enjoys the intellectual and cultural benefit of the state's largest university—all of which makes it an enjoyable place to visit.

◆ SETTLEMENT HISTORY

Pioneers in the early 1770s were drawn to the site they named Masterson's Station because of nearby lush pasturelands. In 1775 a group of frontiersmen from Pennsylvania renamed the settlement Lexington in honor of the Revolutionary War battle fought in Massachusetts. A fort was established at Lexington to help defend against the British and the Indians.

After the war, streets were laid out and Lexington grew into an attractive city of elegant homes and bustling commerce. In 1780, Transylvania Seminary, later called Transylvania University, was chartered as the first institution of higher learning west of the Appalachians. Artists, writers, craftsmen, and musicians were attracted to Lexington. It was the home of portrait painter Matthew Jouett and site of the American premiere, in 1817, of Beethoven's Symphony No. 7. By 1820, Lexingtonians were referring to their city as "The Athens of the West."

◆ LEXINGTON TODAY

Arts and education continue to thrive in this modern city, home of many historic sites, museums, a resident symphony orchestra, several art galleries, and the University of Kentucky. Culturally conservative, Lexington may be the blue blazer, khaki trouser, and shirtwaist dress capital of America. And this doesn't bother its citizens one bit. They are proud of their traditions.

The downtown, in decline in the 1960s, was revitalized in the following decade. Several highrise hotels were built, along with the new Civic Center and the Rupp Arena, the latter home of the Kentucky Wildcat basketball team (many-time NCAA

Posing around an equestrian statue in Lexington, ca. 1911.

champions). Victorian Square, a complex of restored redbrick 19th-century warehouses, contains retail stores and restaurants. The 1886 Opera House on the edge of the city center, near one of the historic districts, was restored as a concert hall.

In Lexington, downtown streets are mostly one-way. And don't make the mistake of getting on New Circle Road thinking you'll skirt around the city center. It's a strip-mall-lined nightmare with closely spaced stoplights that don't seem to be synchronized.

◆ VISITING HISTORIC LEXINGTON

A good way to get an idea of the character of the city is to tour some of Lexington's many historic houses. All are located in residential areas that have retained their period feel.

Ashland   *map page 97, C-3*

This 18-room mansion was home to one of Kentucky's most famous citizens, Senator Henry Clay (1777–1852), who lived here with his wife and their 11 children. The mansion, built between 1806 and 1808, sits on 20 acres planted with several species of fine old trees, including descendants of the ash trees after which the estate was named, and ginkgoes, a species Clay introduced to Kentucky.

Clay, a Virginian by birth, came to Lexington as a young man and became a well-known lawyer. In 1799 he married Lucretia Hart, the daughter of a wealthy Lexington businessman. Clay's farm, then 600 acres, was planted with hemp and corn and was worked by slaves—emancipated in his will.

Ashland is furnished with 19th-century antiques. *Open 10–4 Mon-Sat, and Sunday afternoon. Just a few minutes' drive from downtown, off Richmond Rd. at 120 Sycamore; 859-266-8581.*

A view down the spiral stairway in Hunt-Morgan House.

A parlor at Ashland, home of Henry Clay and his wife, Lexington native Lucretia

Hunt-Morgan House   *upper map page 97*

This house was built in the early 1800s by John Wesley Hunt, the first man to make a million dollars on the western side of the Appalachians. (Hunt, who had a general store in Lexington, made hemp yarn for cotton bales and his product was used in packaging cotton for shipment.)

Hunt's grandson, Capt. John Hunt Morgan, who also lived at one time in the house, was the notorious cavalry officer who led Confederate raids on Union strongholds during the Civil War. Morgan's nephew, Thomas Hunt Morgan, a childhood resident, was Kentucky's first native Nobel science laureate. T. H. Morgan was the first scientist to use fruit flies in genetics experiments, and he discovered the relationship between genes and chromosomes. *201 North Mill St. in the Gratz Park district; 859-233-3290.*

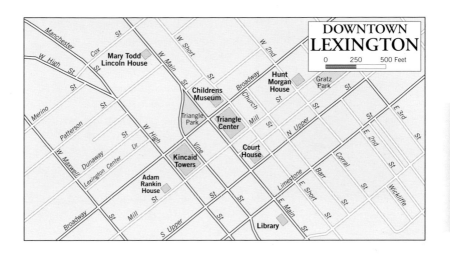

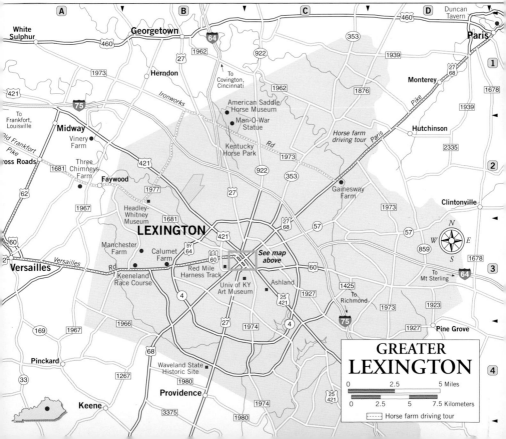

The porch at Mary Todd Lincoln House.

Mary Todd Lincoln House

upper map page 97

Between the ages of 13 and 21, Abraham Lincoln's wife, Mary Todd (1818–1882), lived in this 200-year-old Georgian house on Main Street. She was a witty, exciting young woman with a good education and an active social life. At five foot two, with blue eyes and light brown hair, she had the manners of a Southern belle.

She met Lincoln while visiting her sister in Springfield, Illinois. Mary and Abe Lincoln and their two sons stayed here for three weeks after Lincoln had been elected to Congress in 1847, and again in 1849.

The house is furnished with antiques and artifacts. *Mon–Sat, 10–4; 578 W. Main St.; 859-233-9999.*

Waveland State Historic Site

map page 97, B-4

The redbrick 1847 Greek Revival mansion with its columned portico is a fine example of antebellum architecture. Situated on 10 acres, the site is a model plantation with smokehouse, ice house, slave quarters, and formal gardens. Waveland was built by Daniel Boone Bryan, nephew of the famous frontiersman. *10 miles south of Main St. on US-27 (Nicholasville Rd.); 859-272-3611.*

Explorium of Lexington

upper map page 97

Interactive exhibits including a simulated moon walk and a walk through a cave. *Open Tues–Fri; Downtown at 440 W. Short St.; 859-258-3256.*

University of Kentucky Art Museum

map page 97, C-3

Fine collections of 19th-century regional paintings, 20th-century photography, and prints, many from the WPA years. *On campus in the Singletary Center for the Arts, Euclid Ave. and Rose St.; 859-257-5716.*

Headley-Whitney Museum

Headley-Whitney Museum *map page 97, B-2*
The Bluegrass equivalent of London's Victoria & Albert, it houses decorative arts: collections of furniture, textiles, metalwork, and porcelains. It also has a large collection of jewelry and jeweled sculpture by artist-designer George W. Headley. The museum hosts a notable chamber music series as well. *Just outside of the city, 4435 Old Frankfort Pike; 859-255-6653.*

Harness racing at the Red Mile Harness Park.

Kentucky Horse Park *map page 105, B-2*
This huge park is part museum, part theme park. An **International Museum of the Horse** has exhibits and videos about the evolution and breeding of every variety of horse on the planet, from miniature ponies to draft horses. A daily feature in the summer is a Parade of Breeds in which visitors get to meet the horses in the flesh, so to speak. **Tours of the grounds** are given in horse-drawn trolleys, and there are horseback and pony rides. The legendary **Man O' War** is buried in the park, his grave marked by a life-size bronze statue. A thousand people came to the horse's funeral in 1947, and he lay in state after his death. One of the most important international cross-country and steeplechase races, the **Rolex 3-Day Event,** is held here every April.

Also located on the grounds of the park is the **American Saddle Horse Museum.** The saddlebred horse was developed in Kentucky in the 19th century and soon became *the* riding horse of choice. *Six miles north of Lexington, 4089 Iron Works Pike; 859-233-4303.*

Horse Races *see map page 105*
There are a couple of places where you can go to bet on the races. Elegant, tree-dappled **Keeneland Race Course,** located next door to fabled Calumet Farm on US-60, has racing dates in April and October. A red-coated bugler walks onto the track to sound the call to the post before each race. If you didn't know you were in Kentucky, you might think you were at Ascot. But the Kentucky burgoo stew served at the concession counters (rather than England's strawberries and bubbly) gives away the location. *4201 Versailles Rd.; 859-254-3412.*

High-stepping standardbred horses race pulling two-wheeled sulkies at **Red Mile Harness Track**. Racing dates are April through June and in September and October. *1200 Red Mile Rd.; 859-255-0752.*

KEENELAND RACE COURSE

A day at intimate Keeneland Race Course can make you feel like a guest at an extended party of horse-racing insiders—even if you don't have box seats and don't know a soul in the Thoroughbred business.

The three-week meets in April and October attract all kinds, from blueblooded breeders in tailored suits to college students in khakis. You'll rarely see jeans, though: Keeneland's clubhouse dress code forbids denim in any color, as well as miniskirts, turtlenecks, and athletic shoes.

The track's surroundings are a big part of its appeal. The ivy-covered limestone complex on Versailles Road is near some of the world's finest Thoroughbred farms, including legendary Calumet, the birthplace of nine Kentucky Derby winners. Keeneland's grounds are so pretty that people often choose to arrive early to tailgate under a blossoming dogwood or crabapple in the spring, or a blazing maple in fall.

To people in Lexington, where so many make their living from horses, it's considered almost a civic duty to attend the races at Keeneland at least once a season. It's a place to be seen and catch up with old friends while sipping bourbon or iced tea and eating burgoo, a thick local stew of meat and vegetables. But the fine-boned horses are the true stars here. Keeneland's purses—the prizes paid to the first three finishers in a race—are the highest in North America, averaging more than $600,000 a day.

Racing has deep roots in Lexington. The city's first organized horse race was recorded in 1787, five years before Kentucky became a state. During the 1800s, races took place in various open spaces around town. Racing fell on hard times during the Great Depression, prompting a group of central Kentucky breeders to pool their money in 1934 and build Keeneland on a portion of a stud farm owned by breeder Jack Keene. Back then, as now, betting was encouraged but by no means mandatory. As one founder, Hal Price Headley, said in 1937: "We don't care whether people come out here to bet or not....We want them to come out here to enjoy God's sunshine, the fresh air and to watch horses race."

Keeneland offers a rare chance to fully experience the sights, smells, and sounds of a racetrack. It is believed to be the only track in the country that allows visitors to wander freely through its bustling backstage—the barn area—where horses prepare for a race and are hosed down and rubbed afterwards. Just don't try to pet or get too close to these powerful, high-strung animals. They might bite your hand or knock you down with a swift kick of a hind leg.

Early morning is my favorite time at Keeneland., I love pulling on a sweater and heading out to the track to watch the sun come up and a dozen or so fillies and colts make their laps. The countryside is quiet and you can hear the horses' hooves hit the soft dirt and see steam blowing out their nostrils. A few other hardy horse-lovers will be there, leaning up against the fence or peering through binoculars. Afterward, I like to walk over to the utilitarian track kitchen tucked back among the barns, where muddy exercise riders pull off their helmets, wipe their brows and dig into a breakfast of ham, eggs, and biscuits and gravy. By then, it's usually 9 A.M. and the rest of the world is just starting its day.

For information on Keeneland races, call 859-254-3412. Location is 4201 Versailles Road. See map page 105, B-2.

—Kirsten Haukebo

Thoroughbred horse racing at Keeneland Race Course.

■ ABOUT BLUEGRASS HORSE FARMS

A map of France's Bordeaux wine country will be dotted with little icons of wine bottles or grape bunches marking the region's vineyards and palatial winery-chateaux. On maps of Kentucky's Bluegrass, the icons are of horse heads or up-turned horseshoes, and they mark the homes of equine aristocracy. These famous Thoroughbreds live in climate-controlled barns (many featuring gables, cupolas, stained glass, and even bell towers), and their owners live nearby in antebellum manor houses.

The world's largest population of pedigreed racehorses lives in the Bluegrass, grazing on acre after acre of rolling green meadow inside plank-and-stone fences. In the spring, when graceful dogwoods are blooming white and pink along the fence rows, gangly foals trot out beside their mothers on these pastures. In the heat of the summer, horses rid themselves of flies by rolling on the grass, hooves in the air. By the time the fall colors start to paint the old oaks and maples that form canopies over the lanes, these graceful animals are growing their winter coats (no matter that they have heated stalls).

Retired Thoroughbred race horses run at the Kentucky Horse Park in Lexington.

THE THOROUGHBRED

The Thoroughbred is the fastest, most beautiful, and most valuable, breed of horse in the world, combining great speed with endurance. Standing between 16 and 16.2 hands high, Thoroughbreds have long, sloping shoulders which support a graceful neck, and powerful hindquarters supporting the long legs responsible for their impressive stride.

Though the Thoroughbred is a fixture of Kentucky horse farms, it traces its roots to England. In the 17th and 18th centuries, wealthy English horsemen—Captain Robert Byerly, Thomas Darley, and Lord Godolphin—imported three Arabian stallions which have come to be known as the Byerly Turk, Darley Arabian, and Godolphin Arabian. Bred to English horses developed for running, the matches resulted in three renowned Thoroughbred stallions: Matchem (foaled in 1748), Herod (1758), and Eclipse (1764).

By a strange coincidence, the breeder of Herod and Eclipse (the horse to which some 90 percent of all of the Thoroughbreds in the world today trace their direct ancestry) was the Duke of Cumberland, the very same English nobleman after whom Kentucky's first white explorer, Dr. Thomas Walker, had named Kentucky's Cumberland Gap, Cumberland Mountains, and Cumberland River.

Horses were obviously important on the frontier for travel and for agricultural work. And they served another valued service as well—high-spirited pioneers liked to match horses against each other in order to gamble and to settle disputes. Racing was taking place in Harrodsburg and Lexington in the 1780s. There was a "Lexington Course" in the 1790s, and in 1797 the Kentucky Jockey Club was formed. That was the same year that the first English "blooded" horse, the stallion Blaze, arrived in Kentucky. Kentucky's bluegrass grows on limestone soil, which like England's is rich in calcium and phosphorous.

One horseman who recognized the potential for breeding top horses in Kentucky was Dr. Elisha Warfield of Lexington. In 1806 he advertised the stud serves of Tup, a stallion whose pedigree was vouched for in England's *General Stud Book and Racing Calendar.* Warfield helped organize similar record-keeping for American race horses, though the first compilation of horse breeding records in this country, the *American Stud Book,* was not put together until 1868. Warfield also bred Lexington (1850-1875), the most successful Thoroughbred sire in history. He led the international sire list for 16 years, producing 238 winning offspring, 84 of which were of the quality that would now be classified as stakes racers.

Sunrise on a horse farm between Frankfort and Versailles.

Thoroughbred foals are born of pairings as closely planned and recorded as the historic family alliances of the princes and princesses of Europe. But instead of the Houses of Hapsburg, Bourbon, or Windsor, the blue-blooded names that echo through the Bluegrass include Man O' War, Whirlaway, Citation, and Secretariat. And it's money, not political power, that's at stake.

The combined stud fees for stallions at the Bluegrass region's 460 Thoroughbred farms tops $250 million, and the progeny of those unions bring at least three times that much at the spring and fall sales at Keeneland Race Course. Yes, altogether, we're talking about one billion dollars or so a year in revenue for Kentucky's horse industry. That ain't hay. No wonder the farms, especially so many of the older, more established ones, have the air of a royal estate.

Seeing the horse farms. Basically you have two choices. Follow the self-guided driving tour of the countryside (that follows) or sign up for a guided tour with a tour company. A driving tour will allow you to see the farms from a distance and see foals and champions grazing behind white fences.

Individuals cannot visit these private farms except by guided tour. Tour companies that offer this opportunity are listed on page 109.

◆ SELF-GUIDED DRIVING TOUR OF HORSE FARM COUNTRY

Hundreds of picturesque horse farms—some historic, some modern—can be glimpsed on a drive through Bluegrass horse country. Take three hours or so for a leisurely tour. You might want to have breakfast at Keeneland Race Course before setting out, then stop for lunch in the town of Paris before heading back.

Route: A route that will take you past many famous farms and beautiful scenery goes west on Versailles Road (US-60) from downtown Lexington to US-62, then north along 62 to Frankfort Pike (turn right) and east to Yarnallton Road. Go north on Yarnallton and take a right onto Ironworks Pike (KY-1973), which will take you east to Paris Pike. When you turn right onto Paris Pike, continue north

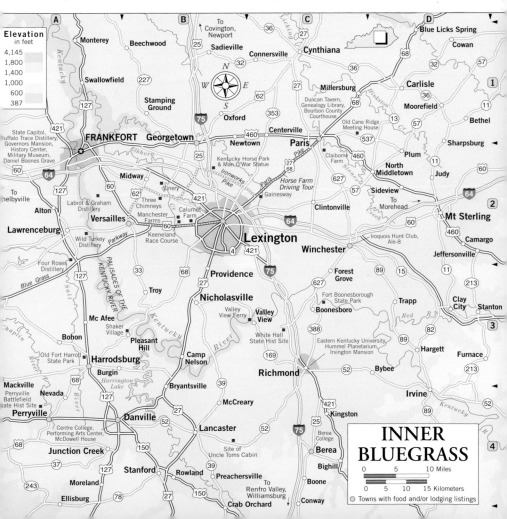

about 15 minutes and you'll pass Claiborne Farm. Finish your tour by traveling back down the Pike to Lexington. Keep in mind that the roads are narrow and traveled by horse vans and farm equipment.

Horse farms are not open to the public except via official horse farm tours listed on page 109. Take this driving tour to see the countryside and the farms from the road.

INNER BLUEGRASS

Calumet Farm *map page 97, B-3*
About five miles southwest out Versailles Road (US-60) from midtown Lexington, you'll see on your right the white plank fences of Calumet Farm. (If leaves are off the trees, you can also get a glimpse of the red and white painted barns with pointed cupolas and dormer windows.)

Calumet was named for founder Warren Wright's business, Calumet Baking Powder of Chicago, which, like the horse farm, comes in a red and white package. Calumet has produced a record eight Kentucky Derby winners, including Triple Crown champions Whirlaway and Citation. Calumet's current owner is Henryk de Kwiatkowski. *3301 Versailles Rd. (US-60).*

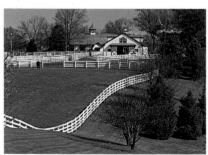

Calumet Farm

Keeneland Race Course *map page 97, B-3*
The grounds of Keeneland Race Course are directly across the road from Bluegrass

Airport, just past Calumet Far. Turn right at the first Keeneland entrance onto the beautifully landscaped grounds, which seem more like those of an antebellum plantation than of a racetrack. You're welcome to get out of your car and walk the grounds. Get there just after sunrise, and you might catch the horses' morning track workouts. After, you can breakfast in the Track Kitchen and rub elbows with trainers, owners, and track staffers. *See page 100.*

Manchester Farm

Manchester Farm *map page 97, B-3*
Behind Keeneland is the 275-acre Manchester Farm, which has miles of white plank fence and striking blue and white barns with dormers and cupolas. It's named for Manchester Spring, located on the property, which was a popular rendezvous point for early settlers. On the farm is an antebellum mansion that's a dead ringer for

(and some say the inspiration for) "Tara" in the movie version of *Gone With the Wind.* *2500 Rice Rd.*

Three Chimneys Farm   *map page 97, A-2*
The most famous stallions to stand at stud at this picturesque farm were 1977 Triple Crown winner **Seattle Slew** and two of his sons: Slew o' Gold and Capote. The farm is open to the public by appointment only, and no tours are offered in December or January. *Old Frankfort Pike.*

Vinery

Vinery   *map page 97, A-2*
More than 30 stallions stand at stud here, including 1991 Derby winner Strike the Gold, and Dare and Go, who broke Cigar's 16-win streak in 1996. Call in advance and you may be able to visit the horses up close. *Weisenberger Mill Rd., Midway.*

Continuing Toward Paris Pike
map page 97 & 105
Return to Old Frankfort Pike (Hwy-1681) and head east to Yarnallton Road. Go north on Yarnallton and take a right onto Ironworks Pike (KY-1973), which will take you east to Paris Pike. The Paris/Lexington

Pike (US-27/68), a National Scenic Byway, is lined with historic stone fences surrounding horse farms and their antebellum mansions. Century-old oak trees line many stretches of the road, and create green tunnels in the summer. Spring may be the most charming time of year, when the air smells of new bluegrass and the horses trot, rather than walk, over their pastures.

Gainesway   *map page 97, C-2*
The barns here are **A**-frames grouped along pathways and set under trees. If you take a guided farm tour from one of the companies listed following this section, you can walk through this equine village. From the entrance to the breeding barn the view is of a fountain flowing into a 170-foot channel that serves as a watering trough. On either side, the channel is lined with flat headstones marking the graves of famous Thoroughbreds, among them the winner of the 100th Derby, Cannonade.

Gainesway's most famous current resident is Winning Colors, the filly who led right out of the gate in the 1988 Derby to beat all of her male rivals. *3750 Paris Pike.*

Gainesway

Claiborne Farm   *map page 97, D-1*
Claiborne, which produced such champions as Gallant Fox, Nashua, and Bold Ruler, is situated on 3,500 manicured acres. It has 97 miles of fences, 27 miles of roads, and a village worth of buildings—including three owners' homes, 30 employees houses, and 40 barns. All of these are painted a distinctive buttery hue called Wheatland Yellow, the copyrighted color of Claiborne Farm.

"Barn" is not a generic term in horse country. There are breeding barns; foaling barns; separate barns for stallions, brood mares, and yearlings; and barns used in training. Most of the farms have their own tracks where the yearlings learn to break from a starting gate and are tutored in the interaction between horse and jockey.

The Claiborne staff is typical of that of the larger farms. Farriers keep the horses' hooves in trim. Veterinarians look after the horses' physical well-being. Trainers prepare the colts and fillies for racing. There are grooms, exercise riders, and hot walkers "to warm down a horse after a run."

Among the stallions in residence at Claiborne today are two Kentucky Derby winners, Unbridled (1990) and Go for Gin (1994). The horse that many think may have been the greatest ever—Secretariat, whose 1973 Triple Crown records have yet to be bested—is buried at Claiborne. (Usually, just the head, heart, and hooves of the champions are buried. Secretariat, in honor of his extraordinary achievement, was interred intact.)

The Hancock family has presided over Claiborne since the early 20th century, when Nancy Clay Hancock, wife of A. B. Hancock, Sr., inherited the farm. Their grandson Seth Hancock, who runs Claiborne today, was in the foaling barn on a spring morning in 1997 when a colt was born that he had a "special feeling about." Three years later, at Churchill Downs on the first Saturday in May, that colt, the three-year-old Fusaichi Pegasus, won the Kentucky Derby by one and a half lengths, flying past 14 rivals to finish first. *703 Winchester Rd.*

◆ GUIDED TOURS OF HORSE FARMS

Most Bluegrass horse farms do not admit individual visitors. Several tour companies based in Lexington have access to the farms for group tours.

Lexington Visitors Center

Here you'll find information on daily van tours, private tour guides, a driving tour map, and a list of horse farms that are open to the public. *301 E. Vine; 800-845-3959. www.visitlex.com*

Bluegrass Tours

Lexington's oldest tour company offers two tours daily, March through October, and by appointment the rest of the year. Each tour includes a stop at a working horse farm, a driving tour of other horse farms, a stop at Keeneland and/or the Red Mile, and a tour of Lexington's historic downtown. *1116 Manchester St.; 859-252-5744.*

Historic & Horse Farm Tours Inc.

This is the company to use if you want to visit Calumet (the farm famous for breeding Derby winners). Three-hour tours are offered seven days a week, with a changing itinerary. The standard tour passes by Calumet and visits Keeneland. To visit Calumet, take the Monday morning, Thursday afternoon, or Saturday morning tour. There are two tours a day, but note that there is often a two- to three-week wait for tours of Calumet. *3429 Montavesta Dr.; 859-268-2906.*

The Lexington Connection

Customized tours are by appointment only and are led by "step-on" guides in your own vehicle. A standard tour hits Keeneland in time to watch early morning training (and might include breakfast in the track kitchen), visits a working horse farm, and tours a bourbon distillery and/or a historic Lexington home. *859-269-4040.*

SIX GREAT KENTUCKY HORSES

Man O' War.

MAN O' WAR

1917–1947

Foaled at Nursery Stud
near Lexington
Sired by Fair Play, out of
Mahubah, by Rock Sand
Kentucky Derby: Never ran

America's first legendary racehorse decisively won 20 out of his 21 career races, losing only to the appropriately named Upset in a short, six-furlong race at Saratoga. Sired and then retired to stud in Kentucky, Man o' War never raced in the state, but he spent most of his life here, tended by his adoring groom, Will Harbut, who told visitors to Faraway Farm where the big chestnut stallion lived that he was "the mostest hoss that ever was." Hard to argue with that. His trainers insisted that Big Red, as he was nicknamed, was never allowed to run flat out, for fear that he would injure himself. His jockeys usually were trying to slow him down at the finish line. He won the 1920 Belmont Stakes by 20 lengths. Among his champion offspring are two Derby winners, Clyde Van Dusen (1929) and War Admiral (1937).

CITATION

1945–1970
Foaled at Calumet Farm,
Lexington
Sired by Bull Lea, out of
Hydroplane II, by Hyperion
Kentucky Derby: Won 1948

Citation was one of Calumet Farm's Triple Crown Champions in the 1940s, the other being Whirlaway (1941). The bay colt

*Citation winning the 1948 Kentucky Derby.
(Kinetic Corp./Churchill Downs)*

raced into Triple Crown history, winning the Preakness and Belmont Stakes, as well as the Derby, under the steady hand of legendary jockey Eddie Arcaro. Citation had the two most desirable traits in a great racehorse, terrific speed and excellent endurance. Other horses seemed to just give up when they tried to run with him. He won the Derby by 3¹/₂ lengths, the Preakness by 5¹/₂ lengths, and the Belmont by 8 lengths. When Citation retired from racing in 1951, he had become Thoroughbred racing's first millionaire, winning a total of $1,085,760 in purse money. It was to be a quarter of a century until another horse, Secretariat, won the Triple Crown.

SECRETARIAT

1970–1989

Foaled at Meadow Stud,
    Doswell, Virginia
Sired by Bold Ruler, out of Some-
    thing Royal, by Princequillo
Kentucky Derby: won 1973

Secretariat.
(Kinetic Corp./Churchill Downs)

Meadow Stud's owner, Penny Chenery Tweedy, won the chestnut foal in a coin toss. It didn't seem like much of a deal when Secretariat finished a mere fourth in his first race as a two-year-old. But he had been bumped into the rail at the start of the race at Aquaduct and moved from 10th place at the head of the stretch. It was the only time he finished out of the money. Secretariat went on to win seven of his other eight races as a two-year-old and then, in 1973, to become the first Triple Crown Winner since Citation. His record times for the Derby and the Belmont still stand. (He is the only horse to have run the Derby in under two minutes.) Anyone who saw, either live or on television, his astounding 31-length victory in the Belmont will never forget it; he seemed to be flying. Big Red (he had the same nickname as Man o' War) stood stud at Claiborne Farm near Paris, Kentucky for 15 years. He sired more than 300 offspring, including Risen Star, winner of the 1988 Preakness and Belmont Stakes. An autopsy upon his death revealed that his heart was nearly twice the size of an average Thoroughbred's, which may have had something to do with his extraordinary speed and stamina.

John Henry. (Photo by Barbara Livingston)

JOHN HENRY

1975–

Foaled at Golden Chance Farm, Kentucky

Sired by Ole Bob Bowers, out of Once Double, by Double Jay

Kentucky Derby: Never ran

The dark, testy yearling with faulty confirmation (he has a condition called "back knee" which makes his legs look bent the wrong way) sold at auction for the unbelievably modest $1,100. It was his almost uncontrollable temper (and the reason he was named after the mythological "steel driving man") that lead to his being gelded as a two-year-old. This did calm John Henry down and he went on to become one of the leading racehorses of all time. In an eight-year racing career he won 30 stakes races (a record 25 of them graded) and over $6.5 million. He was named Horse of the Decade for the 1980s by the Thoroughbred Racing Association. Since he can't have a breeding career, John Henry now lives in retirement at the Kentucky Horse Park in Lexington, where his stable mate is Cigar, who retired after having won nearly $10 million in the 1990s. Both horses are regularly brought out of their quarters to see visitors.

SEATTLE SLEW

1977–2002

Bred in Kentucky by Ben S. Castleman

Sired by Bold Reasoning, out of My Charmer, by Poker

Kentucky Derby: won 1977

A group of friends pooled their money to buy Seattle Slew at the Keeneland Yearling Sales for $17,000. He went on to earn over a million dollars in purse money, which has, in turn, been dwarfed by his multi-millions in stud fees. When he won the Triple Crown in 1977 he became the first undefeated horse to do so. He was the only living Triple Crown winner when he died in 2002. He is one of only 12 Derby winners having offspring that have won the race. His was Swale, in 1984. His other champion offspring include A. P. Indy; Slew O' Gold; and Capote, who, like his sire, is one of the stallions in residence at Three Chimneys Farm, near Lexington. His daughter, Solar Slew, was the dam of Cigar, making the all-time-richest horse (to date) Slew's grandson.

Seattle Slew winning the 1977 Kentucky Derby. (Kinetic Corp./Churchill Downs)

WINNING COLORS

1985–

Foaled at Echo Valley Horse Farm, Kentucky
Sired by Caro, out of All Rainbows, by Bold Hour
Kentucky Derby, won 1988

Only three fillies have won the Kentucky Derby. They are Regret (1915), Genuine Risk (1980), and Winning Colors (1988). The roan filly, Winning Colors, had another notable Derby accomplishment—she lead the race from the starting gate, setting a pace that her male rivals couldn't best. Hall of Fame jockey Gary Stevens won his first Derby aboard her, and she was trained by D. Wayne Lukas, whose horses have dominated the Triple Crown races in the 1990s. Winning Colors won eight out of her 19 races and earned over $1.5 million in purse money. She retired to a career as brood mare in 1989 and lives at Gainesway Farm.

Winning Colors winning the 1988 Derby. (Kinetic Corp./Churchill Downs)

■ PARIS   *map page 105, C-1/2*

If you drive to Paris from Lexington along the Pike (US-27/68), you'll find it's like driving through one long postcard of Kentucky horse country. After you drive past Claiborne Farm (described page 108), you'll find yourself in Paris proper. The town was founded in the 1780s as Hopewell, but the name was changed after the Revolutionary War to honor the help given to the new nation by the French. (Surrounding Bourbon County was named in honor of the French royal family.)

So what's the connection between Bourbon the place and bourbon the drink? That's a little complicated.

The region around Paris was one among many where settlers made whiskey. In the early 19th century, Paris entrepreneur Jacob Spears started shipping whiskey in oaken barrels to places as far away as New Orleans. To make sure his buyers knew where the beverage was from, he called it "bourbon." Ironically, there are no bourbon distilleries in Bourbon County today.

Paris is an enclave of historic architecture. At Fourth and High Streets, the 1788 **Duncan Tavern,** which was visited by Daniel Boone, has been a boarding house as well as a tavern. It now houses the **John Fox, Jr., Genealogy Library,** the second-largest genealogical library in the country, and is the headquarters for the Kentucky chapter of the Daughters of the American Revolution.

The tavern is just behind the majestic, century-old **Bourbon County Court House** at Third and Main Streets. Storefronts in the center of town offer a pleasing amalgam of styles: Federalist, antebellum, and Victorian.

Eight miles east of Paris on KY-537 is the **Old Cane Ridge Meeting House,** a log structure preserved inside a stone outer building. In the 1800s it was the site of revival meetings that attracted tens of thousands. The Protestant denomination called the Disciples of Christ began here.

■ WINCHESTER   *map page 105, C-2*

Winchester, county seat of Clark County, is home to a pair of Kentucky institutions, **The Iroquois Hunt Club** and **Ale-8-One** soda.

The former is a horse-and-hounds hunting club, headquartered in a restored gristmill just west of the town. Riders in formal "pink" coats pursue quarry cross-country, in the traditional British manner, from October to March. It's not uncommon on a crisp November day to see the spotted hounds and mounted riders dashing across the rolling countryside of Clark County, especially if you are driving along one of the winding state roads between Lexington and Winchester.

Crack your car window, since you'll probably
hear the baying of the dogs before you see the
horses. By the way, the hunters no longer
chase foxes (who are thriving despite the fact
that they can't steal chickens from modern
wired chicken houses). Coyotes, considered
a pest because they kill calves, are the object
of hunts today.

Ale-8-One is a ginger-flavored soft drink invented by manufacturer G. Lee Wainscott during the Depression and marketed only in central
Kentucky. (Quaff a bottle to cool off after hiking at
Boonesborough.) Its sea-green vending machines can be
found in stores and along sidewalks. (Don't make
the mistake of asking for a "Coke" in Winchester.
You'll be treated to a lecture/testimonial on the su-
periority of Ale-8-One, which really is pretty boda-
cious for a soft drink. Must be all that ginger.)

Henry Clay.
(North Wind Picture Archives)

Winchester is also renowned as the town where Henry Clay, the Civil War–era
U.S. senator from Kentucky (nicknamed "The Great Compromiser"), delivered
the first and last public speeches of his illustrious political career. These occurred
in the Clark County Courthouse, a stately white 1855 building topped with a
handsome cupola.

The courthouse is one of many beautiful buildings in downtown Winchester,
which has a mostly Victorian commercial district that is listed on the National
Register of Historic Places. It's a very comfortable area to stroll around to shop for
antiques, or simply to sit on a city-provided bench while sipping the ubiquitous
soft drink and watching the passersby.

■ MADISON COUNTY: SOUTH OF LEXINGTON

The drive south of Lexington into Madison County and south is scenic: I-75 traverses lovely open country; in summer the medians are abloom with wildflowers.

◆ WHITE HALL STATE HISTORIC SITE   *map page 105, Z-20*

This 13-acre estate on the outskirts of greater Lexington was the home of Cassius
Marcellus Clay, one of Kentucky's most fascinating historical figures.

White Hall State Historic Site.

Clay (1810–1903) was a lawyer who became an outspoken abolitionist early in his career. (In fact, he corresponded with abolitionist Rev. John Gregg Fee and donated 10 acres in Madison County that Fee used to found integrated Berea College. *See page 119.*) He supported the Union in the Civil War, becoming a friend and confidante of Abraham Lincoln, who appointed Clay ambassador to Russia. (Clay was instrumental in bringing about the purchase of Alaska from Russia.)

Clay was a bit of a fireball. It is said he participated in 200 fights and duels in his lifetime and that he fortified White Hall against attacks by opponents of his radical newspaper, *The True American.* A fiery man in more ways than one, at the age of 84 his wife divorced him, and he married the 15-year-old daughter of a tenant farmer—and *they* were divorced two years later. He died at the age of 93.

Clay's three-story brick mansion is a remarkable blend of Georgian and Gothic architecture with a smattering of Italianate flourishes. It is furnished in period antiques from the 1860s. *Take Exit 95 off I-75 and follow the signs; 859-623-9178.*

◆ VALLEY VIEW FERRY

The Valley View Ferry is Kentucky's oldest recorded business, in operation since 1785. It's fun to take the ferry to understand what was involved in crossing rivers before they were bridged and to experience the pace of travel before interstate highways were built. At one time workhorses pulled the ferry across a shallow spot in the the Kentucky River. These days, a century-old paddlewheel (now motorized) pushes the ferry, which can transport three cars at a time. The trip takes about three minutes. *Located on Hwy-169, approximately 10 miles northwest of Richmond. Open Mon–Sun; one-way fare is $2.50.*

◆ **FORT BOONESBOROUGH STATE PARK**   *map page 105, C-3*

Fort Boonesborough State Park is set on the banks of the Kentucky River on the site where Daniel Boone and Richard Henderson first built log huts among the sycamores in 1775. Sycamores still line the gentle slopes of the shore, which joins the pea-green water at the foot of the park's campground. It's easy to slip a canoe in the river here and drift along imagining yourself an explorer or an Iroquois.

Sitting back from the river on a slight rise is the reconstructed fort. It served as a strategic garrison during the Revolutionary War when the British used the Indians to harass settlers, and it was a stopping point on the way into the Bluegrass for the next 50 years. The stockade with its blockhouses is surrounded by dense woods that 200 years ago might well have hidden Indians hostile to white encroachment, as well as bears and wolves. You get the feeling that settlers could never have been very much at ease.

Today the park is staffed by craftspeople in period costumes (including buck-

A tobacco crop inside Fort Boonesborough State Park.

skin—probably pretty uncomfortable on hot summer afternoons) who carry out the everyday activities of pioneers, from blacksmithing to butter churning. Watching people work at these necessary and time-consuming tasks, you'll gain a greater appreciation for being able to pick up dinner ingredients at the corner grocery.

The park contains a museum housing many pioneer artifacts and displays on the history of the area, including the life of Boone. It also has a campground open to tents and RVs. There are interpretive trails too, with labeled geologic and native plant sites.

The 1778 Siege of Boonesborough by Indians is reenacted on the last weekend of May. Watching this, I wondered again at the courage and self-reliance of the settlers who chose to carve out a living in the wilderness. *Reached via KY-627 off I-75; 859-527-3131.*

◆ RICHMOND   *map page 105, C-3*

Richmond was one of the state's earliest towns, settled in 1785 by Virginian John Miller, who had served as a colonel in the Revolutionary War. Miller named the new town after his city of birth, Richmond, Virginia. After the Civil War, the city grew steadily after a branch of the Louisville & Nashville Railroad connected it commercially to the rest of the state. Today it serves as a bedroom community for nearby Lexington and is the seat of Madison County. It is a charming town with a slightly Southern touch, with handsome tree-lined streets of 19th- and early 20th-century houses.

Richmond is also the home of **Eastern Kentucky University.** The predominately Colonial-style campus adds to the city's feel of "College Town, U.S.A." **Hummel Planetarium**, located on campus, shows the sky as it would look from each of the planets in the solar system. *Kit Carson Dr.; 859-622-1547.*

Maps for tours of the battle route and/or the historic district, including the centerpiece 1850 Greek Revival Courthouse, can be obtained from the visitors center housed in the **Irvington Mansion;** *345 Lancaster Ave.; 800-866-3705.*

◆ BEREA   *map page 105, C-4*

Berea was founded when abolitionist Rev. John Gregg Fee came to this site at the base of the Cumberland foothills and the edge of the Bluegrass plains in the 1850s. He named the town (which he envisioned as a settlement for people of all races and classes) after a city mentioned in the New Testament. The Biblical Berea was described (in Acts 17:11) as a place where citizens "were more noble than those of Thessalonica in that they receive the Word with all eagerness of mind and searched the scriptures daily...."

Berea College: Reverend Fee started this church and a school whose mission was to educate children of all races from nearby mountain communities. The school initially served young children but had evolved into a college by 1869. Kentucky's notorious Day Law of 1904, which segregated the state's schools, overrode Berea's racially inclusive policy for the first half of the 20th century. But after the U.S. Supreme Court's ruling on *Brown v. the Board of Education* overturned school segregation, the college once again admitted black students.

There is no tuition at Berea. Low-income students from the Appalachian region earn their way through the liberal arts college by working on the campus 10 hours a week in a variety of jobs.

Of interest on this picturesque campus with buildings overlooking the Cumberland is the Log House Sales Room, featuring student-made furniture and crafts (859-985-3226). Berea College visitors often stay at the **Boone Tavern Hotel** on Main Street; its dining room serves traditional Southern fare, family style *(see page 271).* Free tours of campus, led by students, leave from the Boone Tavern *Mon–Sat; 859-985-3018.*

Town of Berea: The town of Berea has become a craft center for the state and the region. **Churchill Weavers,** which opened in 1922, is one of America's foremost hand-weaving studios, its products featured in elegant national stores (it's cheaper to buy directly from the Berea shop!). *Located on Lorraine Court; 859-986-3126.*

Furniture makers, jewelers, potters, quilters, and other artisans have workshops and showrooms along Berea's Broadway and Main Streets. If you are in the market for a traditional folk musical instrument, shop here. Dulcimers and fiddles are crafted with exceptional care and skill.

Good times to visit the town are May and October, when the semi-annual Kentucky Guild of Artists & Craftsmen Festival is held, and in July, when the Berea Craft Festival takes place.

■ HISTORIC BOYLE AND MERCER COUNTIES

These two counties, at the very geographic center of the state, are rich in 18th- and 19th-century history. Take scenic US-68 southwest from Lexington for a more leisurely drive than the interstate can offer.

◆ **SHAKER VILLAGE OF PLEASANT HILL**   *map page 105, A/B-3*

Shaker Village (or Shakertown) constitutes the largest restored Shaker settlement in the country. On its 2,700 acres of breathtakingly beautiful countryside are 30 meticulously restored limestone buildings.

The Shakers, originally called the Society of Believers, were a religious community founded by dissident English Quaker Anna Lee in the 1770s. (The nickname "Shaker" was given to the members because of the shivering dances they performed during devotional services.)

Lee and a small group of followers emigrated to America in 1774 and founded communities from New England and New York to Ohio, Indiana, and Kentucky. Men and women in the Shaker communities lived "as brothers and sisters," working together but not marrying and procreating. This segregation of the sexes is reflected in the architecture of the buildings, which have separate men's and women's entrances and stairways.

The Centre Family Dwelling in the Shaker Village of Pleasant Hill.

The spiral staircase in the Trustees Office exemplifies the Shaker tradition of exquisite carpentry.

This photograph of Mary Settle, then the oldest living Shaker, was taken in 1923.

The exquisitely crafted furniture and wooden implements of the Shakers are prized by collectors for their beauty and simplicity. (You may recall that the famous American folk hymn *Simple Gifts*—as in, " 'Tis a gift to be simple, 'Tis a gift to be free…"—is of Shaker origin.)

Visitors to Pleasant Hill can dine in the **Trust House Dining Room,** where Shaker fare is served family-style. Leave room for the tart-and-sweet Shaker lemon pie. The staff in the restaurant wears period costumes, as do the artisans working in the village who make reproductions of Shaker furniture for sale.

It's also possible to stay overnight in one of several buildings that have been furnished with Shaker reproductions. Popular as a retreat from spring until fall, Pleasant Hill is also quite beautiful during the winter off-season when the overnight accommodations with working fireplaces are supplied with wood and kindling. It's a magical place year-round with its quiet, pastoral setting, but especially when dusted with snow. *Off US-68; 859-734-5411 or 800-734-5611.*

◆ **OLD FORT HARROD STATE PARK**   *map page 105, A-3*

The centerpiece of the town of Harrodsburg on the Kentucky River is Old Fort Harrod State Park with its log stockade (rebuilt in the 1920s). Founded by settlers led by pioneer long hunter and marksman James Harrod, Harrodsburg was the first permanent white settlement west of the Appalachians. Tragedy and mystery surrounded the town's namesake in nearly equal measure.

Harrod was born in Pennsylvania sometime between 1742 and 1746. His father's first wife and later his own brother were murdered in Indian raids. Harrod and his mother fled their home for points south as buildings were burning in an Indian attack.

While participating in Indian wars in the Northwest Territory, Harrod learned several Indian languages as well as French. This quick-study frontiersman inspired trust in others, and a band of settlers in the Inner Bluegrass elected him their leader, establishing "Harrodstown" in 1774.

Harrod, who became a prosperous landowner, married young widow Ann Coburn McDonald, whose husband had been killed by Indians in 1778. His wife already had a son, and the Harrod marriage produced a daughter. In 1787, Harrod's stepson was abducted by Indians and burned at the stake. This seems to have been Harrod's breaking point. He started going on longer and longer hunting expeditions and eventually disappeared on one such trip in 1792.

The fort contains several tiny log cabins that give a graphic idea of the living conditions of the pioneers. The site is peopled by staff in period costume who recreate the day-to-day activities of frontier life. Kitchen gardens are planted with herbs and other plants that would have been used in the late 18th century.

Fort Harrod also has an amphitheater where outdoor productions are staged in the summer, highlighted by the historic play *The Legend of Daniel Boone*.

The Woodwright exhibit at Old Fort Harrod State Park.

INNER BLUEGRASS

In addition to the fort, the state park has a history museum housed in the oldest Greek Revival mansion in the state (started in 1813); a memorial to explorer George Rogers Clark, founder of Louisville, who lived in Harrodsburg for a time; and the log cabin (moved from Washington County) in which Abraham Lincoln's parents, Thomas and Nancy Hanks Lincoln, were married. *Intersection of US-127 and US-68 in downtown Harrodsburg; 859-734-3314.*

❖

The **Abraham Lincoln Heritage Area** is just to the west. Information on this area begins on page 203.

◆ **PERRYVILLE BATTLEFIELD STATE HISTORIC SITE**   *map page 105, A-4*

Perryville Battlefield State Historic Site was the scene of Kentucky's biggest and bloodiest Civil War engagement. On October 8, 1862, 16,000 Confederate troops commanded by Gen. Braxton Bragg engaged a 58,000-strong Union force under Maj. Gen. Don Carlos Buell. Up to this point in the war, the Confederates had been gaining control of border state Kentucky. But Bragg's army was overwhelmed at Perryville (510 killed, 2,635 wounded) and forced to retreat to Tennessee. The Federal army also suffered grievous loses, with 845 killed and 2,851 wounded, but had started the battle with a far greater number of men.

Re-enactment of the Battle of Perryville, Kentucky's bloodiest Civil War engagement.

Although historians do not consider Perryville to be one of the war's major battles, it effectively ended the Confederacy's Kentucky campaign and the lingering threat of secession.

The 100-acre battlefield site is open from April to October. A museum is on the site, and Civil War re-enactors stage the Battle of Perryville each year on the anniversary of the conflict. *Seven miles southwest of Harrodsburg on US-68; information and museum: 859-332-8631.*

◆ **DANVILLE**

map page 105, A-4

Danville is a quietly pretty Bluegrass town. Founded in 1783, it was the site of a series of meetings, held in a log courthouse, convened to draft the constitution of Kentucky.

McDowell House and Apothecary, where Ephraim McDowell performed the first abdominal surgery in 1809.

Downtown is dominated by the Greek Revival campus of **Centre College,** founded by Presbyterians in 1819 and one of the most highly regarded private liberal arts colleges in the United States. Its **Norton Center for the Performing Arts,** a facility designed by an architect from the Frank Lloyd Wright Foundation, hosts top performing arts ensembles from all over the world. Thousands of visitors converge on the broad lawn of Centre College and the surrounding tree-lined streets the second weekend of June for the Great American Brass Band Festival. This old-fashioned event is a hot-dogs-and-root-beer sort of celebration, since Danville is the seat of dry Boyle County. *For festival information, call 800-755-0076.*

Medical history was made in Danville in 1809 when physician Ephraim McDowell, who had grown up in Danville and studied medicine at the University of Edinburgh, performed the world's first successful abdominal surgery. Jane Crawford, who was thought to have an overdue pregnancy, was diagnosed by McDowell as suffering from an ovarian tumor. Crawford rode 60 miles on horseback to McDowell's office in Danville where he removed the tumor—without the aid of as-yet-to-be-invented anesthesia, while the patient sang hymns. She recovered and survived well into her 70s.

The McDowell House and Apothecary was built in stages from 1792 to 1820. It features period furnishings and the physician's apothecary shop. Medicinal herbs and wildflowers grow in the restored gardens. *125 S. Second St.; 859-236-2804.*

■ INNER BLUEGRASS DISTILLERIES: WEST OF LEXINGTON

It may no longer be made in its eponymous county, but bourbon, Kentucky's native whiskey, is a product of the Bluegrass, where the region's sweet-tasting limestone water (bourbon and "branch," or water from local creek or branch, is the preferred mix) is as important to bourbon distillation as it is to the building of racehorses' bones. Distilled from corn as well as barley, wheat, or rye, bourbon can

Woodford Reserve Distillery: bourbon fermenter casks.

be lusciously smooth. It tastes of vanilla and has fruity aromas such as those of apples or figs. The finest bourbons are beautifully balanced and as snifter-worthy as fine cognacs.

Four of the state's 10 remaining distilleries are located in the Inner Bluegrass, and those four produce a *lot* of bourbon. (Annual production of Kentucky bourbon is just under 10 million cases a year, or approximately 23.7 million gallons.) Kentucky law now allows limited tastings at the distilleries, and each visitor age 21 or older can buy a one-fifth (750-ml) bottle of bourbon per visit.

Woodford Reserve's distinctive copper stills.

◆ BOURBON DISTILLERIES

Woodford Reserve *map page 105, A-2*
This complex of handsome blue-gray limestone buildings (the oldest dating from 1812) and rose-brick aging warehouses is tucked into a hollow along the banks of Glenn's Creek. Woodford Reserve uses copper pot stills, introduced by Scottish chemist, physician, and distiller James Crow, to make its Woodford Reserve bourbon. (This is the type of still used for making Scotch. No other bourbon is made with this equipment.) The orientation center has a fine short film on the history of bourbon followed by an excellent tour.

Go west from Lexington through Versailles (pronounced "Ver-SALES") on US-60. On the left, just past KY-1685, you'll see the sign for Grassy Spring Road and a marker for Woodford Reserve. You'll travel along the two-lane road, lined by horse farms, for about 10 minutes until it ends at McCracken Pike. Turn right and the entrance to the distillery is only 200 yards away on your left; 859-879-1812.

Wild Turkey–Austin Nichols
map page 105, A-2

The metal-clad distilling houses where Wild Turkey is made may not be as aesthetically pleasing as the buildings of other bourbon makers, but they have a certain industrial dignity reminiscent of a schloss (a castle) overlooking the Rhine or the Danube. The distillery is perched dramatically on a precipitous cliff overlooking the Kentucky River.

Legend contends that this has been a site for whiskey making since the first settlers came to Kentucky. It is certainly protected, by virtue of its location, from both revenuers and whiskey thieves. The tour takes visitors through each step of bourbon making. *Located on Rte-1510 off US-62 East, which is west of Versailles; 502-839-4544.*

Four Roses *map page 105, A-2*

The Spanish colonial architecture of Seagram's Four Roses is more appropriate to a California winery than to a Kentucky distillery. So it's probably fitting that virtually all of the bourbon made here is exported abroad. (California counts as "abroad" to most Kentuckians, but in this case, the whiskey goes to Europe and Japan.) Tours are by appointment only. *1224 Bonds Mill Rd. in Lawrenceburg; 502-839-3436.*

Buffalo Trace *map page 105, A-2*

The former Ancient Age Distillery has recently been renamed, rather preciously, Buffalo Trace for its site on the Kentucky River near Frankfort where herds of bison grazed long ago. In addition to Ancient Age, Blanton's, and Elmer T. Lee bourbons, a bottling named Buffalo Trace was released in 1999. And while the spin is a tad hokey, the muscular whiskey is anything but. Grounds include a log clubhouse, stone mansion, and old railroad depot. The world's smallest whiskey warehouse contains a single barrel of Buffalo Trace's millionth. *1001 Wilkinson Blvd., five miles west of US-60; 502-696-5926.*

These distillery workers hold the tools of their trade, ca. the late 1800s.

The capital of Kentucky lies along a double bend in the curving Kentucky River.

■ FRANKFORT, STATE CAPITAL   *map page 105, A-1/2*

When Kentucky became a state in 1792, the cities of Lexington and Louisville each made a claim to become the capital. So the newly elected legislature decided to open up the selection process to bidding: The city that offered the sweetest deal would get to be the seat of government.

Frankfort landowner Andrew Holmes came forward with an offer that included several town lots, building materials dedicated to constructing the new capitol and courthouses, a percentage of rents from tobacco warehouses, and even a hefty sum of cash ($3,000) collected from local citizens. The legislature decided this was an offer not to be refused.

Frankfort is located on a double bend in the Kentucky River, just upstream from the spectacular Palisades scenic area. The first white visitor to the site on which the city now stands was Ohio Company surveyor Christopher Gist, who had followed a buffalo trace to its crossing at the river.

The name of the capital was derived from an incident in its pioneer past. In 1780, a salt-making party from Bryan Station near Lexington was working at a ford in the river when it was attacked by a band of Indians. A pioneer named Stephen Frank was killed, and the site became known as Frank's Ford, evolving into "Frankfort."

Today, Frankfort is a small city (pop. 27,000) with elegant architecture, both official and residential, and a large historic district. Maps are available at the **Visitors Center,** *100 Capitol Ave.; 800-960-7200.*

◆ FRANKFORT SIGHTS

State Capitol

The centerpiece of the city is its Beaux-Arts capitol, opened in 1910. The soaring dome is a copy of that on the capitol in Washington, D.C. The building's exterior, supported by 70 Ionic columns, is made of Indiana limestone built on a Vermont granite base. Interior features include several marble murals (two depicting episodes from the life of Daniel Boone), a rotunda modeled on the one above Napoleon's tomb, and a staircase inspired by that of the Paris Opera House. The State Reception Room is a copy of Marie Antoinette's drawing room at Versailles (the room of the queen whose arrogance brought on the French Revolution). *Capitol Ave.; 502-564-3449.*

Floral Clock

A notable attraction located directly behind the capitol is an outdoor floral clock—a 34-foot clock with a flower-bed face. The plantings are changed seasonally. The clock is tilted toward a reflecting pool so that the 530-pound minute hand and 420-pound hour hand can be easily read.

Governor's Mansion

Completed in 1914, the governor's mansion was designed to match the capitol, so the architectural connection to France's notorious queen continues. Made of Kentucky limestone, the mansion is a copy of Petit Trianon, Marie Antoinette's Versailles play place. *Located just east of the capitol on Capitol Ave. Individuals may visit Tues or Thurs 9–11 A.M.; group tours by appointment; 502-564-3449.*

(opposite) Interior of the State Capitol.

Kentucky History Center

Frankfort is a center for historical research. Exhibits trace the history of the state from the pioneer era to the present. The building houses the Kentucky Historical Society's Genealogical Research Library, too; *100 West Broadway; 502-564-1792.*

Kentucky Military History Museum

Appropriately housed in the Old State Arsenal Building, the museum contains displays of weapons (including the legendary Kentucky long rifle), photographs, and uniforms. *125 E. Main St. at Capitol Ave.; 502-564-3265.*

Other Attractions

Within an easy walk of one another along Broadway downtown are the **Greek Revival Old State Capitol;** the **Georgian Old Governor's Mansion** (420 High Street), which currently serves as the lieutenant governor's residence; and the **stores and restaurants** housed in 19th-century buildings.

　　Daniel Boone's Grave, containing the remains of Boone and his wife, Rebecca, is located on a hill in the tree-shaded **Frankfort Cemetery** on Main Street, overlooking the city and the Kentucky River. On Coffee Tree Road, next to the State Library and Archives, is the **Kentucky Vietnam Veterans Memorial.** It is constructed in the shape of a giant sundial with the names of Kentuckians killed in action etched in granite. It was designed so that the shadow of the gnomon points to the name of the veteran on the anniversary of his death.

*An aerial view of the Palisades of the Kentucky River at Polly's Bend,
just south of Nicholasville.*

■ PALISADES OF THE KENTUCKY RIVER

Where the meandering Kentucky River has cut through limestone on the Lexington Plain rise spectacular tall cliffs in the 460-million-year-old Ordovician-era rock. Known as the Palisades, the tree-lined heights towering over the river are most beautiful between Frankfort and Boonesborough. No one road runs along it, and the best way to enjoy the view is from a boat on the river itself. In the fall, the cliffs are ablaze with color as the leaves of maples, hickories, and oaks turn red, orange, and gold. Excursions run from both Frankfort and Boonesborough State Park. Private watercraft are allowed on the river as well. Call **Canoe Kentucky** at *800-K-CANOE-1.*

*Paul Sawyier painted this view of a covered bridge near Frankfort.
(The Speed Art Museum, Louisville)*

■ SHELBYVILLE   *map page 185, D-1*

Located halfway between Louisville and Frankfort is Shelbyville, the seat of Shelby County. While Thoroughbreds populate the Inner Bluegrass, most of the horse farms lining US-60 (which runs through the town) are home to American saddlebreds, the high-stepping horses that compete in dressage shows.

This is a very pretty little Kentucky town (pop. 6,954), in spite of some of the suburban sprawl that has sprung up along US-60. Many of the houses in the center of Shelbyville are carefully maintained Victorian homes with gingerbread trim and wraparound porches. A four-block stretch of Main Street between Third and Seventh Streets is a designated landmark on the National Register of Historic Places. Tucked in among the 19th-century storefronts is a tiny log cabin built by one of Shelbyville's earliest residents, Squire Boone, brother of Daniel.

The main attraction here is the **Wakefield-Scearce Antiques Gallery.** Located a block north of Main Street, it is part of a complex of mellow, redbrick Georgian buildings that once housed Science Hill, a prestigious girls' school, in operation from 1825 to 1939. Wakefield-Scearce is an antique hunter's dream. It's filled with beautiful (and very expensive) English and American antique furniture, artwork, and accessories, all displayed in room settings. If you need a brass fireplace fender for the antebellum mansion you're restoring, this is the place to come. The flatware and teapots in the cellar's silver vaults gleam like the treasure in Aladdin's cave. *525 Washington St.; 502-633-4382.*

The Science Hill property also includes a **restaurant** where traditional Kentucky food is served, and, in the school's former classrooms, a series of shops where upscale clothing, silver, and fine linens are sold.

NORTHERN TRIANGLE
O H I O   R I V E R   T O W N S

Food & Lodging *page 264*
Also see map page 136, towns in yellow.

■ TRAVEL BASICS

Area Overview: The Ohio River forms the northern border of this region, and huge, vital Cincinnati, Ohio, is just across the bridge from Covington, Kentucky. Some flat land edges the river, but steep bluffs rise above it. The banks of the river are heavily industrialized from Cincinnati to Louisville. Southwest of Covington, the landscape is quite hilly, gradually turning into the rolling meadows of the Bluegrass.

Travel: If you are traveling to the Bluegrass State from a distance (including from the other side of the globe), you will likely land at the Cincinnati/Northern Kentucky International Airport—the only airport in the state with direct international flights. There are no shuttles, per se, from the Cincinnati/Northern Kentucky Airport to Louisville or Lexington, but there are connecting flights to these cities (either flight will take about 20 minutes). And it's easy to rent a car at the airport for the one-and-a-half-hour drive to Louisville or Lexington.

This is a heavily urbanized area, and traffic gets very congested the closer you are to Cincinnati. Interstates and bypasses seem always to be under construction, which adds to delays. (Between April and December you'll also want to be aware of the schedules of the Cincinnati Reds baseball team and the Bengals football franchise. On afternoons and evenings of games, the roadway jam is even worse.)

Outside of Kenton and Boone Counties, traffic is generally much less of a problem. But if you are headed along KY-9 from Covington to Maysville, it's possible to get stuck behind slow-moving farm vehicles on the two-lane highway.

Interstates 71 and 75, which go south to Louisville and Lexington, respectively, are lovely drives, with densely wooded, hilly vistas. But there's one navigational mistake that's easy to make: I-71 and I-75 are the same road south out of Covington for about 20 miles. Then the highway forks; I-71 is marked as an exit. If you want to go to Louisville, not Lexington, keep your eyes open for the sign. More than one unwary driver has accidentally headed due south instead of southwest and taken a very time-consuming, 150-mile detour!

Weather: Summers are hot and muggy, with temperatures in the high 80s and 90s; humidity is always high. Coal-burning fuel plants along the Ohio River contribute to summer smog, although their emissions are less dense than they once were thanks to environmental cleanup legislation. Winter temperatures typically dip into the teens at night, then rise into the 30s and 40s during the day. Snow and bitter cold are infrequent, but it's always a bit damp. Fog is common.

Food & Lodging: In the picturesque towns along the Ohio, you'll find some nice little restaurants that are good especially for lunch. Bed-and-breakfast inns are a good bet if you're looking for atmosphere.

The historic Licking River area of Covington is a quiet neighborhood of 19th-century mansions, many of which now house bed-and-breakfasts and inns, and downtown Cincinnati is five minutes away across the graceful Roebling Suspension Bridge. Cafes and interesting little shops are springing up in the Licking River neighborhood, making it a good place for a quiet evening's stroll.

Refer to the **Food & Lodging map,** page 265; toll-free numbers for chains on page 266. Towns are listed in alphabetical order beginning on page 267. For charts relating towns to chapters see page 311.

■ ALONG THE OHIO RIVER

The Ohio River marks the 665-mile length of Kentucky's northern boundary (and in spite of its name, the river is the property of the Bluegrass, not the Buckeye, State). During the 18th century, white settlers traveled into this part of Kentucky by canoe, flatboat, and keelboat along the Ohio River. With the invention of the steamboat and budding commerce of early 19th-century America, Kentucky cities along the Ohio flourished. Abundant coal-powered factories and ships brought industrial goods and agricultural products to market.

In the middle of the 20th century, the Army Corps of Engineers built a series of locks and dams along the river, effectively turning the waterway into a series of giant pools. Today more tonnage passes through these locks than passes through the Panama Canal. Most of the freight consists of agricultural products and industrial commodities such as coal, sand and gravel, crude oil, and steel. These goods are transported on huge barges pushed along by tiny tugboats. On misty spring

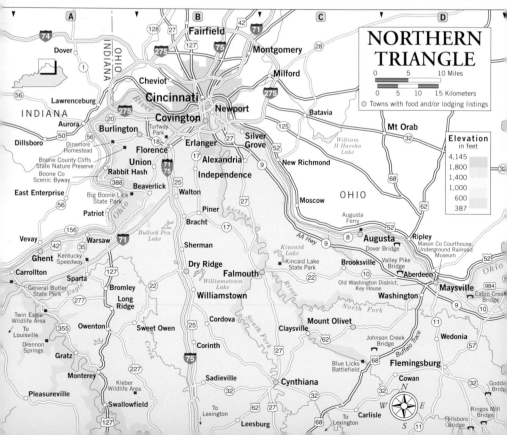

Throughout the 1920s and '30s, the Ohio River frequently flooded Covington and other riverside communities. A WPA plan finally brought the river under control in 1938. (Underwood Photo Archives, San Francisco)

and fall nights their foghorns moan to one another, and the sound echoes along the riverbanks.

Coal-burning electric plants are situated along the river, too, since the fuel can be brought by barge. Their smoke contributes to smog in the hot, humid summers, although installation of smokestack "scrubbers" in recent years has improved the air quality somewhat. But population growth and the concomitant multiplication of automobiles mean that the skyscrapers of downtown Louisville and the church spires of Covington are obscured by a gray-yellow cloud when summertime temperature inversions trap the smog. (The Ohio Valley in August or September can resemble a huge sulfur-scented outdoor sauna.)

South of the Ohio River, the land is defined by the horseshoe-shaped ring of Appalachian foothills known as the Knobs. They stretch southeast from the banks of the Ohio at the tip of Jefferson County (which contains Louisville) through Nelson, Marion, and Lincoln Counties and then swing northeast, and back to the river, in Lewis County.

Outside of the large urban areas on the Ohio, the counties comprising the Northern Triangle, with their gently rolling countryside, are largely devoted to agriculture.

Farms in Nelson and Spencer Counties provide much of the corn for the bourbon distilled in Bardstown and Louisville. Tobacco is still an important crop, and the region is home to large beef and dairy cattle farms. Near Louisville and Covington, however, farmland is being steadily overtaken by suburban development.

■ COVINGTON

The triangularly shaped portion of the state wedged between Ohio and Indiana is virtually a suburb of Cincinnati, Ohio. Four bridges span the Ohio River at Cincinnati, enabling a significant portion of the people living in Covington to

(opposite) Covington Landing and Cincinnati as seen from Covington at night.

commute to jobs in the larger city. But the distinctive character of the Kentucky side, with charming river towns and the gracious, tree-lined streets of Covington, reflects a Southern sensibility not found on the opposite shore.

Modern Covington, Kentucky's fourth-largest city (population 43,700), stands on a site once known as The Point, where the Licking River joins the Ohio, a favorite staging area for 18th-century explorers paddling into Kentucky's Bluegrass interior. In 1780 a soldier named George Muse traded his military allotment of 200 acres of land here for a keg of whiskey. The new owner swapped it for some buffalo meat, and the land changed hands again and again until it was surveyed and, in 1801, sold to Thomas Kennedy for $750. In 1815 a town was chartered and named for Leonard Covington, a hero of the War of 1812.

By the 1830s the town was a trade center, with early settlers coming from over the Appalachians and bringing plantation culture with them. In the mid-19th-century, Covington experienced a population explosion when a wave of German and Irish immigrants settled in the city.

Main Strasse Village in Covington.

German engineer John A. Roebling invented the high-strength cable necessary for the design and construction of suspension bridges. In 1856, he designed a 1,057-foot suspension bridge connecting Covington to Cincinnati; the bridge is heavily used today (above photo). Roebling later used this suspension bridge as a prototype when he was asked to design the Brooklyn Bridge.

The German influence on the city is strong—and visible. The immigrants invested money and labor in large churches, the steeples and domes of which vie for prominence on the skyline with Bavarian-style buildings that were once breweries, now preserved as entertainment complexes. In recent times, tasteful brick townhouses designed to blend with the historic architecture have been constructed and have helped fuel gentrification, as have new restaurants and cafes in the heart of the city and along the riverfront. Office complexes have sprung up along the river too, attracting businesses from throughout the region whose employees wish to be close to the Cincinnati/Northern Kentucky International Airport—15 minutes' drive from downtown.

John A. Roebling Suspension Bridge

map page 139, B-1

German émigré John Augustus Roebling was a civil engineer who came to the United States in 1831. He first tried to earn a living in western Pennsylvania as a farmer, but he was an inventor, not a cultivator. He eventually landed a job as an engineer for the state. Roebling revolutionized bridge construction when he invented high-strength, woven-wire cables. These allowed the design and building of suspension bridges. In 1856, Roebling was commissioned by the Covington and Cincinnati Bridge Company to design a bridge over the Ohio River connecting the two cities.

Construction was interrupted by the Civil War, but the bridge finally opened in 1867. Its span of 1,057 feet made it the longest suspension bridge in the world. This was later bested by Roebling's most famous design, New York's Brooklyn Bridge, opened in 1883 with a span of 1,595 feet, for which the Covington Bridge had been a prototype.

At one time the Roebling Bridge carried horse and streetcar traffic. The massive arched pillars of stone and the graceful cables connecting them are now strung with lights, and the bridge accommodates automobiles on KY-17, providing a fast route between downtown Covington and Cincinnati.

Licking Riverside Historic District

map page 139, B-1/2

Bounded by Eighth Street and Riverside Drive, this is one of the original residential areas of the city. Along its narrow, tree-lined streets enormous antebellum homes

were built. Their architectural styles include Italianate, Second Empire, Queen Anne, Romanesque, and Greek Revival. In the past decade many of these houses have been restored as single-family homes.

If you stay in one of the handful of bed-and-breakfast inns that operate out of these mansions *(see page 278 for ideas)*, you'll be struck by the contrast between the peaceful tone of the neighborhood and its close proximity to real hustle and bustle. The neighborhood backs up to the tree-lined banks of the Licking, but the view across the Ohio, where the horizon is filled by the big-city skyline of Cincinnati, is an almost shocking reminder that a major metropolis is only two minutes away over the John A. Roebling Suspension Bridge.

To get to the historic district take the Pike Street exit from I–71/75 and follow Pike northeast to Washington Street. It then becomes Seventh Street, which you follow three blocks to Greenup Street. Turn left and go north into the historic district.

Coming from the Cincinnati side of the Ohio River, take Vine Street across the Roebling Bridge, which will bring you right into the district as soon as you've crossed into Covington.

George Rogers Clark Park

map page 139, B-1

Kentucky's pioneer/settler heritage is commemorated in the George Rogers Clark Park, a tidy block of grass and trees tucked into the Licking River Historic District. It's equipped with several comfortable benches so you can linger and gaze at Cincinnati's skyline. It's also a great vantage point for the annual Tall Stacks event, held in mid-

October. Some dozen or so riverboats from throughout the Ohio and Mississippi Valleys rally on the river in a Mark Twain–ish version of New York City's Tall Ships festival. *Corner of Garrard St. and Riverside Dr.*

Main Strasse Village

map page 139, A-2

The half-timbered storefronts of this historic area of downtown, west of the Licking River district, are left over from the wave of German immigration to the city in the mid-1800s.

Twice a year, in spring and fall, the pedestrian-only streets are the site of traditional Maifest and Oktoberfest celebrations. The 100-foot **Carroll Chimes Bell Tower** in the center of the village contains a 43-bell carillon that plays on the hour from 9 A.M. until dark. In addition to the carillon, the bell tower features an animated clock with 21 performing figures acting out the story of the Pied Piper of Hamelin. (One would think the legend of Daniel Boone or Simon Kenton would be reenacted, but the German heritage pushed out the pioneers for once.)

The village is worth a day's exploration and browsing in its variety of shops, restaurants, and cafes. *Located along Philadelphia St. between Fifth and Ninth Sts. Reached via Exit 192 off I-75 N.*

Cathedral Basilica of the Assumption

map page 139, B-2

Covington's German and Irish Catholic immigrants poured their money and building skills into erecting beautiful, incense-perfumed churches, the domes and spires of which are easily visible from I-75, routed along the western edge of the city.

The Cathedral Basilica of the Assumption was begun in 1894 and completed in 1910. The interior, with ribbed Gothic vaults rising 81 feet above the floor, was largely copied from St. Denis in Paris. The Cathedral of Notre Dame in Paris also provided architectural inspiration, particularly for the west facade. The cathedral contains 82 stunning stained-glass windows, including a copy of the famous Rose Window in Notre Dame de Paris. Measuring 67 feet high and 24 across, it's among the largest stained-glass windows in the world.

Originally called St. Mary's Cathedral, it was designated a basilica in 1953 by Pope Pius XII. *1140 Madison St.; 859-431-2060.*

Mother of God Church

map page 139, B-2

The Mother of God Church dates from 1870. The Italian Renaissance Revival church is an unmistakable building with its 150-foot-tall dome flanked by a pair of 200-foot-tall bell towers. The church is a repository for an impressive collection of religious art and sculpture.

German craftsmanship is everywhere in this church: the stained-glass windows were fashioned by the Munich firm of Mayer and Company; the oak altars were hand-carved by artisans of Cincinnati's Schroeder Brothers; the tile floors came from Germany, as well as England; and Covington sculptor Ferdinand Muer designed and crafted the crucifix above the altar. *119 W Sixth St.; 859-291-2288.*

NORTHERN TRIANGLE

Newport Aquarium

map page 139, C/D-2

Covington's neighbor across the Licking River is the city of Newport, a place notorious in the first half of the 20th century for mob-controlled gambling and houses of ill repute. In the 1960s, the citizens got fed up with the sleaze and mounted a successful campaign to clean up their city. Today it's the home of the Newport Aquarium. The state-of-the-art facility, located near the banks of the Ohio River, contains 16 galleries of various aquatic environments.

King penguins waddle around in a snow-laced 8,000-gallon pool. At the other end of the habitat spectrum, a hot, humid wetlands exhibit is home to a swarm of American alligators. Also on hand are octopi, stingrays, poison frogs, and piranhas.

Futuristic acrylic tunnels make you feel more like a scuba diver at a coral reef than a visitor in sneakers. As you walk through one 84-foot tunnel, you'll see nurse, sandtiger, and sandbar sharks flashing through the water just inches from your nose. *One Aquarium Way, off Third St.; 859-491-3467 or 800-406-3474. www. newportaquarium.com*

(above) Sharks surround visitors in the Newport Aquarium's 84-foot tunnel.

(opposite) The interior of the Gothic-style Cathedral Basilica of the Assumption in Covington. The cathedral was funded largely by the city's German and Irish immigrants.

■ BOONE COUNTY

The county just to the west of Covington is Boone. Several small towns and cities in the county have become bedroom communities for the Greater Cincinnati area, and the interstate highways and bypasses that cross the county always seem to be under construction. The Cincinnati/Northern Kentucky International Airport is located here, off of I-275 at Erlanger. Unlike Louisville's so-called international airport, which only has direct flights abroad for UPS packages, the Northern Kentucky Airport has daily direct flights to London, Paris, Frankfurt, and Rome.

Burlington *map page 136, A-1*
Burlington is a mecca for antique hunters. To reach it, drive five miles along KY-18 from the I-75 exit through traffic lights and suburban sprawl to the courthouse at the intersection with Jefferson Street. Turn right. The street is lined with buildings dating from 1830 to 1850 that contain cafes, shops, and galleries. One of the most interesting is **Burlington Antiques,** located inside the 1837 Methodist Church, which was built with separate doors for men and women. *5952 Jefferson St.*

Dinsmore Homestead

Dinsmore Homestead *map page 136, A-1*
Built in 1842 by James Dinsmore, the farm was worked and managed until 1988 by five generations of his descendants. The site is fascinating because of all the period furniture and historic farming equipment that was preserved. (The Dinsmores seem to have preferred the technology of the 19th century to that of the 20th.)

Politically well-connected, the family was acquainted with several U.S. Presidents. The huge trophy elk in the main house was a gift from Teddy Roosevelt. *Located on KY-18, 6.5 miles west of Burlington; 859-586-6117.*

**Boone County Cliffs
State Nature Preserve** *map page 136, A-1*
This 75-acre preserve protects an old-growth forest and habitat for several species of plants and animals uncommon in the state. A long-loop trail and a short-loop (but more difficult) trail pass high cliffs and meander through forests of sugar maple (which dominates), redbud, and dogwood. Wildflowers here include yellow celandine poppies, blue phlox, and wild ginger.

Because of the fragile nature of the cliffs, stay on the marked trails. The preserve is open year-round during daylight hours. There are no facilities. *Take KY-18 west (from Burlington) to Middle Creek Rd. Go left two miles to a small parking lot on the left; 502-573-2886.*

A field of cosmos flowers near Union.

Boone County Scenic Byway

Kentucky Highway 18 at Dinsmore is the point of origin for the Boone County Scenic Byway, which winds for about 20 miles through wooded ridges and hills opening onto panoramic views of the Ohio River. *Turn off KY-18 at KY-536 to head 11 miles west to Rabbit Hash.*

Rabbit Hash   *map page 136, A-1/2*

Kentucky has more than its share of colorfully named wide spots in the road. Examples of these include Monkey's Eyebrow, Krypton, Thousandsticks, Black Gnat, Hi Hat, Bugtussle, Asphalt, and Paint Lick. Don't bother asking about the name ori-

gins; no one ever seems to know (though you may have a colorful yarn spun just for your benefit if you query a local).

Rabbit Hash is a historic riverside village with a fine old general store dating from 1831. Listed on the National Register of Historic Places, it looks like a spot where characters from a Fannie Flagg novel shop. It's a great place to buy authentic, salty Kentucky country ham, not to mention tractor caps with "Rabbit Hash, KY" embroidered on the crown.

The store is located on Lower River Road, along with a row of antique shops selling items ranging from beautiful locally made quilts to tacky bric-a-brac.

■ BIG BONE LICK STATE PARK   *map page 136, A-2*

The scenic byway leads to Big Bone Lick State Park, where massive ice age mammals—mastodons, giant sloths, wooly mammoths, and shaggy bison—roamed 12,000 to 20,000 years ago. The site attracted animals to its exposed salt licks. Marshy ground, what the pioneers referred to as "jelly land," was characteristic of the area, and hundreds of animals became trapped in muck and died, leaving their huge bones behind.

In 1744, Indian trader Robert Smith came to the site and started removing the bones. Other explorers followed, including Lewis and Clark, who shipped fossils to President Thomas Jefferson. Jefferson donated the Kentucky specimens to the Academy of Science in Philadelphia and the Paris natural history museum.

Mary Draper Ingles (thought to have been the first white woman in Kentucky) was captured by Shawnee Indians and brought here on a salt-making expedition. She escaped in 1756 and walked hundreds of miles back to her home in what is now West Virginia. She recalls that when she escaped, a Frenchman in the party was "sitting on a giant bone, cracking walnuts."

The salt licks are gone now but some of the sulfur springs that turned the area into a resort in the 19th century still flow, and their eggy scent adds to the place-out-of-time atmosphere. A herd of bison roams the rolling land, and there's a small museum with an exhibit about the prehistoric animals. The centerpiece is a 10-foot-long tusked mastodon skull, excavated in 1955. The park has picnic and camping facilities, including sites that overlook pastures and hillsides. *Off KY-338 at 3380 Beaver Rd.; 859-384-3522.*

■ SPEED TRACKS

South of Boone County, the shopping malls and apartment complexes lining the road gradually give way to open countryside and wooded hills. Towns and farms are just out of sight on the other sides of the slopes. Also tucked in between the hills are wide, flat areas that are well-suited to racing of both horses and cars.

Turfway Park   *map page 136, B-1*

This 1950s Thoroughbred racetrack has none of the architectural charm or distinction of Churchill Downs or Keeneland, but the racing cards have become more exciting in the past decade with more valuable purses for winners and with an important Derby prep race, the Jim Beam Stakes, held in late March.

Racing dates from the end of November to early April provide turf action in the winter. This isn't like attending a football game in Green Bay. Only the jockeys have to wear long underwear, since the grandstand and clubhouse are glass enclosed and heated. *Located at 7500 Turfway Rd., just north of Florence off I-75, Exit 182; 859-371-0200 or 800-733-0200.*

Kentucky Speedway   *map page 136, A-2*
This one-and-a half-mile oval track accommodates both stock and open-wheel racing cars. Events include races in the NASCAR and Indy Racing League series. The track is especially striking at night, since the four-score 70-foot-high light stanchions ringing the stadium make it glow like a giant UFO that's landed in the middle of Gallatin County farmland. *Located near Sparta, 35 miles south of Cincinnati and 55 miles north of Louisville on KY-35, a quarter mile off I-71, Exit 57; 888-652-7223 or 859-647-4309.*

NORTHERN
TRIANGLE

A stock car race at the Kentucky Speedway.

■ AUGUSTA *map page 136, C-2*

Highway 8 follows the Ohio River from Augusta to Covington (or take the newer "AA" Highway 9 to Foster and catch Highway 8 there). Following the river on the Ohio side, Highway 52 is a scenic byway and offers the prettiest approach to Augusta, which comes into view across the river.

Augusta, set high on a bank of the Ohio River, was founded in 1798. In 1862 the town was the site of a Civil War battle, and it retains the feel of the rural South. The riverfront of this once-bustling port remains active and inviting, with fishermen on the banks, barges and pleasure boats going by, and ferries coming and going. The **Augusta Ferry** began operation in 1798, the year of the town's founding. It crosses the river between Augusta and Boudes Landing, Ohio, during daylight hours most of the year, and the captain will make trips by request as well; *dock at the end of Main St.; 859-756-3291.*

Historic buildings constructed in pioneer, Federal, and Victorian styles line **Riverside Drive**. A walking tour map lists 54 buildings.

■ MAYSVILLE *map page 136, D-2*

Maysville (population 7,200) is perched on the banks of the Ohio River. Simon Kenton and John May made the first land claim where the town now stands.

May, after whom the town is named, was a surveyor and clerk of the Virginia Land Commission, which sent him to Kentucky in 1779. Other Maysville founders included Daniel Boone and his cousin Jacob, who were among its first trustees. In the mid-1780s, Boone and his wife operated a tavern and inn here. (She did the work; he went hunting.) Until the Battle of Fallen Timbers in 1794, when the local Indians were finally defeated badly enough to be driven away, most settlers lived in tiny Washington, on the hill overlooking Maysville.

The invention of the steamboat and the resulting river traffic turned Maysville into a hopping spot in the early 1800s. Brick row houses that make up much of the downtown residential district are trimmed with elaborate ironwork reminiscent of the architecture of New Orleans, with which Maysville had commercial ties. Romanesque church steeples and the gold cupola of the 1846 **Greek Revival Mason County Courthouse** at 29 W. Third Street dominate the skyline.

The view across the river is of the tree-covered hills of Ohio, which was a free state in the mid-1800s, unlike Kentucky where slavery was legal. Because of its

MAYSVILLE MEMORIES: ROSEMARY CLOONEY

The late singer Rosemary Clooney was born in Maysville, Kentucky, in 1928. She made her first public appearance there at the age of three. Later, she had her own television show and sang with the likes of Bing Crosby, Frank Sinatra, Marlene Dietrich, and Tony Bennett.

In the 1990s she enjoyed a comeback, with two albums topping the Billboard *charts and four Grammy nominations in six years.*

$\mathcal{F}$rom the porch, the river looked smoky brown sometimes, rosy and lavender when the sun was going down, then slate gray, just before it turned pitch black.

From the porch, the lights of the *Island Queen* beckoned, like reachable stars.

From the porch, the river promised better times coming, far-away places just around the bend.

From the porch, the river was a wide tranquil ribbon, no hint of a dangerous current. All you could see from the porch were possibilities, not perils.

❧   ❧   ❧

$\mathcal{T}$he porch was at my grandmother's house in Maysville, Kentucky, on the Ohio River. Although Maysville was called a port city, it was a classical small town, its life centered in a few downtown blocks between the train station and the bridge: Magee's Bakery, Merz Brothers Department Store, the diner with the swinging EAT sign and six stools at the counter, where we sat and watched our hamburgers—the size of half dollars—frying on the grill.

—*Girl Singer,* Rosemary Clooney with Joan Barthel, 1999

Rosemary Clooney christens a street named in her honor.

proximity to Ohio, Maysville was an important stop on the Underground Railroad, the escape route for thousands of slaves fleeing north. Visit the **Underground Railroad Museum,** located inside the Maysville Visitors Center. *115 E. Third St.; 859-564-6986.*

Maysville's modern economy is based on tourism and light manufacturing. **Excursion steamboats,** including the *Delta Queen* and the *Mississippi Queen,* make the town a port of call. Maysville is particularly proud of two of its native daughters, the late singer Rosemary Clooney and Miss America 2000, Heather French, wife of a former Kentucky lieutenant governor.

◆ MAYSVILLE'S OLD WASHINGTON DISTRICT

Head east on Third Street, past the Maysville historic district and the bridge, and turn right on US-68 into what was once the separate town of Washington and is now incorporated in the city of Maysville as Old Washington. (It is a little area, well marked, off the AA Highway, just three and a half miles from the Ohio River.) The pioneer town was founded in 1785 on land bought from Simon Kenton for 50 cents an acre.

Romanesque church steeples contrast with the gold cupola of the Greek Revival–style Mason County Courthouse in Maysville.

SLAVE SALE: WASHINGTON, KENTUCKY

In the 1840s, Harriet Beecher Stowe observed a slave auction on the steps of the Washington Courthouse, and in her novel, Uncle Tom's Cabin, *she describes the scene. Stowe's book became a rallying point for the Abolitionist movement when it was published in 1852, and some Union soldiers carried it into battle. Kentucky, half slave and half free at the outbreak of the Civil War, remained with the Union.*

EXECUTOR'S SALE,—NEGROES!—Agreeably to order of court, will be sold, on Tuesday, February 20, before the Court-house door, in the town of Washington, Kentucky, the following negroes: Hagar, aged 60; John, aged 30; Ben, aged 21; Saul, aged 25; Albert, aged 14. Sold for the benefit of the creditors and heirs of the estate of Jesse Blutchford, Esq.

SAMUEL MORRIS,
THOMAS FLINT, EXECUTORS.

❖   ❖   ❖

*A*bout eleven o'clock the next day, a mixed throng was gathered around the court-house steps, —smoking, chewing, spitting, swearing, and conversing, according to their respective tastes and turns,—waiting for the auction to commence. The men and women to be sold sat in a group apart, talking in a low tone to each other. The woman who had been advertised by the name of Hagar was a regular African in feature and figure. She might have been sixty, but was older than that by hard work and disease, was partially blind, and somewhat crippled with rheumatism. By her side stood her only remaining son, Albert, a bright-looking little fellow of fourteen years. The boy was the only survivor of a large family, who had been successively sold away from her to a southern market. The mother held on to him with both her shaking hands, and eyed with intense trepidation every one who walked up to examine him.

"Don't be 'feared, Aunt Hagar," said the oldest of the men. "I spoke to Mas'r Thomas 'bout it, and he thought he might manage to sell you in a lot both together."

"Dey needn't call me worn out yet," said she, lifting her shaking hands. "I can cook yet, and scrub, and scour,—I'm wuth a buying, if I do come cheap;—tell 'em dat ar,—you'll tell 'em," she added, earnestly.

—Harriet Beecher Stowe, *Uncle Tom's Cabin,* 1852

In 1833 a young author named Harriet Beecher (later Beecher Stowe), who had moved with her family from her native Connecticut to Cincinnati, visited Maysville and Washington. She observed a slave auction at the Marshall Key House in Washington and was so affected by the inhumanity of the proceeding that she was moved to write *Uncle Tom's Cabin*. The chilling account of a slave auction in the novel was based on her experience (*see page 153*).

When the novel, set in Kentucky and Louisiana, was published in 1852, it became the first international best-seller by an American writer and the rallying point for the anti-slavery movement. Some Union soldiers allegedly marched into battle with copies of the book in their backpacks. President Abraham Lincoln is reputed to have said when he met Stowe, "So you're the little woman who wrote the book that started this great war."

The 1807 **Key House** is now the home of the **Harriet Beecher Stowe Slavery to Freedom Museum**. At the **Paxton Inn** is a hidden stairwell, a site on the Underground Railroad that moved escaped slaves up north to freedom. The place where

Beecher saw the slave auction is also marked here. Parts of Washington are so unchanged that it's easy to imagine Simon Kenton himself stepping out of a doorway, long rifle slung over his shoulder. *Guided tours daily; 859-759-7411.*

Harriet Beecher Stowe, who saw a Maysville slave auction. The scene was included in Uncle Tom's Cabin, *one of the most popular novels of the 19th century. (Library of Congress)*

■ COVERED BRIDGES

At one time Kentucky had more than 400 covered bridges; today there are 13. Many were destroyed during the Civil War. There are several in the Maysville area.

Valley Pike Bridge   *map page 136, D-2*
The only privately owned covered bridge in Kentucky. From Maysville take Highway 10 west to Valley Pike Road.

Dover Bridge   *map page 136, D-2*
On KY-3113 (Tuckahoe Road) near the junction with KY-8 at Dover.

Cabin Creek Bridge   *map page 136, D-2*
In Lewis County. From Maysville, take Highway 10 east to Plumville and turn onto KY-984 (Spring Creek Road).

South of Maysville are three covered bridges: the Goddard (or White), the Ringos Mills, and the Hillsboro.

Goddard (White) Covered Bridge
map page 136, D-3
The only surviving example of Ithiel Town truss design (a lattice-like design that uses rigid, triangularly placed beams as supports) in the state. A country church can be seen through the bridge. From Maysville, take Highway 11 south to Flemingsburg, then take Highway 32 east to Goddard.

Ringos Mills Bridge   *map page 136, D-3*
An 86-foot bridge built in 1867, once part of a large gristmill. Follow Highway 32 a bit from Goddard and turn west on Highway 1895.

Hillsboro Bridge   *map page 136, D-3*
Roofed and sided with corrugated tin, the abutments are made of "red stone." Construction is of the burr truss design with multiple king posts. On Highway 111 south of Hillsboro.

Johnson Creek Covered Bridge near Mt. Olivet.

Johnson Creek Covered Bridge
map page 136, C/D-3
This covered bridge was built in 1874 just north of Blue Licks Battlefield State Park, and crosses the creek on the route of the original buffalo trace *(see following page for more)*. From US-68 take Highway 2505 north to Highway 1029. Head north and watch for the bridge (closed to traffic).

■ BUFFALO TRACE: SCENIC US-68

The Buffalo Trace, now US-68, was the route followed by huge herds of buffalo between watering holes at the Ohio River and salt deposits at Blue Licks. Settlers arriving at Limestone Landing (later Maysville) on the Ohio used the route, as the Indians had before them, finding that the buffalo herds had chosen the easiest and most direct path inland.

Today the route is a scenic byway. As you head southwest and approach Lexington, you'll enter horse country.

■ BLUE LICKS BATTLEFIELD STATE PARK   *map page 136, C-3*

"The Last Battle of the Revolutionary War," the Battle of Blue Licks (August 19, 1782), was indeed among the frontier skirmishes that took place before word of Cornwallis's surrender had reached the more remote outposts of the new United States. The intensely fought battle between 182 buckskin-clad Kentuckians and 26 redcoats backed up by 300 Indians lasted about 16 minutes.

The frontiersmen suffered a terrible defeat: one-third of them, including Daniel Boone's son Israel, were killed. If you visit on the anniversary of the battle, you'll be able to watch a re-enactment of the battle. The grounds have both wooded areas and rolling meadows where the rare Short's goldenrod blooms in late summer and early fall. The park is nestled within the meandering bends of the Licking River, and it's a fine place to rent a canoe and paddle between the tree-lined shores.

A stone house that now functions as a museum contains pioneer-era household items, including antique kitchen implements, clothing, toys and dolls, and long rifles. The area's salt-making history, as well as an account of the period when a mineral springs and spa were on the site, is also part of the exhibit.

Blue Licks has a campground and cottages in case you want to linger a day or two. *In Mt. Olivet on US-62, 48 miles northeast of Lexington; 859-289-5507.*

In this engraving, Aaron Reynolds helps Capt. Robert Patterson escape at the Battle of Blue Licks.

APPLE FARM IN WALLINGFORD, KENTUCKY

I was raised surrounded by apples.

My earliest memory is of the swaying limbs atop a row of Golden Delicious trees. It was summertime and the Kentucky sky hung hot behind those high twigs, their leaves leathery-green on top, soft as down underneath. Rows of Goldens stood next to a dirt road that separated the orchard from our front yard. Beyond the top row an acre of apple trees marched down the slope toward the gravel highway, the ground beneath them blanketed by rye and fescue and orchard grass, Queen Anne's lace, orange milkweed, and buttercups. The apples, a little bigger than shooter marbles, played hide-and-seek with a child's eyes unless, on a June afternoon, a late thunder shower drenched them and the last golden sunlight showed them off like Christmas balls. They were in that way both ordinary and magical, as common as toast, as elusive as dreams.

🍃 🍃 🍃

As a practical matter, Sunday was the only day most of the country people were free to come buy apples. Until the 1960s, few women drove cars, and their husbands were busy workdays. Farmwork started at six-thirty or seven o'clock in the morning and ended well after sundown. Inside the household, there were also strict regimens. Monday was wash day. Saturday was town day, and each square (there were only two) was packed with men in denim overalls standing around jawing while their wives bought groceries. Saturday night was bath night. Sunday after church and chicken dinner, was the time "to drive out to the mountain" to get apples. City people who had come from Lexington or Cincinnati took the day as an autumn outing; they usually bought anywhere from a peck to a bushel and a half of fruit. Country people, who were most of our customers, packed off from two to ten bushels, and often they returned a month later for a like amount. So Sunday was the practical day to buy apples. Still, there was something else; because it was Sunday, and because the apples were both wholesome and primordially forbidden, the whole experience bore just a trace of an illicit adventure. Driving up that scary mountain road with the steep cliffs (maybe 150 feet down), spending money just after the sermon was over, letting the kids loose to romp in the orchard, looking over the city folk in their fancy hats and polished Pontiacs (or, for the city folk, pointing at the pickups and listening to the hillbilly twang), and complaining politely about how the prices seemed "awful high this year": all this made coming to get apples unlike any other shopping experience.

—Frank Browning, *Apples,* 1998

LOUISVILLE
KENTUCKY DERBY

■ HIGHLIGHTS   *page*

Food & Lodging   *page 294*

■ TRAVEL BASICS

City Overview: Louisville is Kentucky's largest city and the nation's northernmost Southern city, the latter reflected by the unflagging hospitality of its residents and the town's relatively relaxed daily pace. People here love to entertain and to be entertained, and the restaurant scene is lively, especially at Derby time, when a party atmosphere prevails.

Louisville is known for its handsome homes and tree-lined streets. The city is especially beautiful in the spring when the dogwoods and the pink redbud trees blossom, and tulips and daffodils bloom in the city's gardens. Louisville's lush greenery is augmented in three city parks designed by Frederick Law Olmsted that define the areas of the city: Cherokee, Iroquois, and Shawnee.

Getting Around: You'll need a car to get around in Louisville. All the areas of the city are connected by expressways and parkways leading out from downtown. If you arrive by air, you'll find plenty of car rental companies at the Louisville Airport at Standiford Field. Even though TARC (Transit Authority of River City) provides bus service throughout Louisville and into surrounding Jefferson County, it's only convenient along a handful of routes. A 15-mile trip outside the city center, which would take about 20 minutes by car, can take over an hour on a TARC bus. Outside of the rush hours, traffic moves pretty steadily for a metro area of a million people. At any time of day, beware of

(opposite) The skyline of Louisville at dusk, as seen from Clarksville.

Spaghetti Junction, the tangle of ramps and looping lanes at the downtown riverfront where Interstates 65, 71, and 64 converge. It's easy to think you are headed to Churchill Downs and find that you have wound up in southern Indiana instead.

Coming for the Derby: Derby Festival time, late April to early May, is in many respects the best time to visit. The city parties for weeks. But during Derby Week (the seven days right before the first Saturday in May) many hotels and restaurants jack up their prices. Plan ahead and shop around a bit so as not to pay more than necessary.

Weather: In the summertime temperatures in Louisville are in the 80s and 90s and air quality can plummet as temperature and humidity rise. Some rain falls in spring, but both spring and fall are lovely. This location is protected from heavy snowfall in winter. Temperatures may drop to the 20s or teens. Unfortunately, Louisvillians are lousy winter drivers. If an inch or so of snow accumulates on the roads, it causes traffic chaos.

Food & Lodging: The restaurants are varied and generally quite good. A wide choice of lodging is offered—from well-known hotel and motel chains to historic inns and B&Bs. Louisville listings begin on page 294.

■ CONTRADICTIONS

Natives of Kentucky's largest city can't seem to agree on how to pronounce its name. "LOO-uh-vuhl" is common, as is "LULL-vuhl." Only mail-order-catalog sales clerks and salespeople at catalog 800 numbers pronounce it "LEW-is-ville," which is *all* wrong, since the city was named after Louis XVI, the French king, by veterans of the American Revolutionary War in gratitude for the help France gave the colonies. The King of France helped the rebels to vex his longtime English enemies; he was hardly a champion of freedom himself. After all, a few years after Louisville was named for him, Louis XVI lost his head at the hands of his *own* subjects during *their* revolution. Ironically, Louisvillians named their city for an ally who, despite fighting for their democratic ideals, held none of them himself.

Today many residents call their city the "Gateway to the South"; older families whose fortunes were made in, say, bourbon might cultivate a magnolas-and-mint-julep image. But in truth, a Midwestern sensibility pervades the city. With its sprawl of suburbs, Louisville might as well be across the Ohio River in Indiana.

Home of the Kentucky Derby and birthplace of boxing champ Muhammad Ali, Louisville has no major league sports team, but fans consider the University of Louisville's basketball and football teams worthy substitutes. Professional minor league teams are the Bats baseball team and the Panthers ice hockey team.

Certainly the city can boast some sophisticated performing artists whose adventurous programs are downright impressive for a city of this size. The Louisville Orchestra is admired in classical music circles for its half-century of commissioning, performing, and recording works by new composers; the orchestra also plays for the city's opera and ballet. Actors Theatre is known for the annual Humana Festival of New American Plays, which won the theater a special regional Tony Award, and for premiering major new works that go on to Broadway and London stages.

■ NEIGHBORHOODS: AN OVERVIEW

Metropolitan Louisville, encompassing Jefferson and surrounding counties, is home to just over one million souls, but Louisville proper, made up of a patchwork of neighborhoods, still has much of the small town about it. Make a new acquaintance over bourbon-and-branch aperitifs at a dinner party, and he or she will ask you where you went to school—*high* school, that is, not college—in order to place you accurately in Louisville's social strata.

A statue of George Rogers Clark, founder of Louisville.

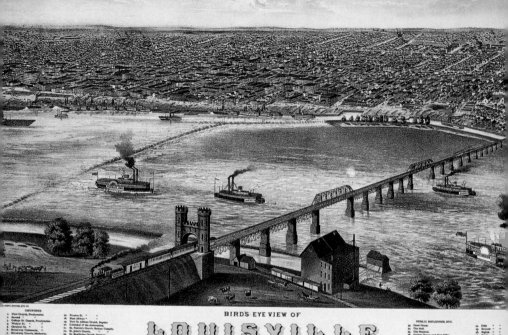

A bird's-eye view of Louisville circa 1876. (Library of Congress)

◆ **DOWNTOWN**   *map page 163, B-2*

Bounded to the north by the Ohio River is the central business, medical, technology, and arts district. Several blocks of Main Street contain five-story buildings with ornate cast-iron facades that look very much as they did when Charles Dickens strolled past them in 1842. The Victorian structures and Greek Revival government buildings along Jefferson Street were joined in the late 20th century by a handful of skyscrapers, creating a modest but interesting skyline. Two notable buildings are Michael Graves's pink granite **Humana Building,** at 500 W. Main; at Fourth and Market stands the state's tallest building, John Burgee's Art Deco– esque **Aegon Tower,** whose dome sparkles with red and green lights at Christmas. A marble statue of Louis XVI stands in front of the Jefferson County Courthouse.

◆ **EAST END**   *map page 163, D-1/2*

The elegant streets of **Cherokee Triangle** (bounded by Cherokee Park on one side and restaurant-lined Bardstown Road on another) are graced with stately mansions and lovely trees. Farther east on Frankfort Avenue and River and Brownsboro Roads lie **Butchertown, Crescent Hill, St. Matthews,** and **Glenview.**

◆ **WEST END**   *map page 163, A-2*

Just west of downtown and bounded by the river on its west side, the West End has long been a residential area for many of the city's African Americans. Portions of the West End still suffer from poverty and crime, but Portland, Shawnee, and Chickasaw, among others—are seeing an influx of new businesses and the restoration of 19th-century homes. Just south of western downtown, the city of **Shively** was incorporated in 1938 so that distilleries headquartered there could sidestep Louisville city taxes. Brown-Forman still has a corporate office and distillery here; their water tower (a giant Old Forester bottle) can be seen from offices downtown.

◆ SOUTH END *map page 163, C-4*
The South End can be broadly described as the working-class center of the metro area. Major employers include General Electric, United Parcel Service (at the airport), and Churchill Downs, home of the Kentucky Derby. Concentrated here are subdivisions built after World War II on former farms; once autonomous villages, towns such as Fern Creek, Valley Station, Okolona, and Pleasure Ridge Park are now part of the Greater Louisville area.

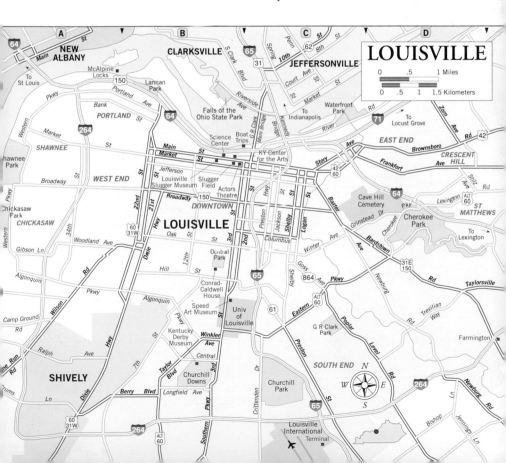

LOUISVILLE'S CASSIUS CLAY—MUHAMMAD ALI

*R*unning west down Greenwood Avenue in heavy, steel-toed boots, the teenager flashed jabs and combinations, emitting a loud pop with every punch. He looked and sounded motorized. His smile was playful, but he carried a deadly serious preoccupation. He was just 15, but he was training, appearing out of the darkness, almost every night. It was 1957, in Louisville, Kentucky, and Cassius Clay was an obscure, black, Baptist youngster in the city's West End, running alone down Greenwood Avenue toward Chickasaw Park, the Ohio River—and his destiny as the greatest boxer of all time.

The story of Cassius Clay's introduction to boxing is better than fiction. It all began when the 12-year-old rode his new bicycle to the annual convention of the Louisville Service Club, and the new bike was stolen. In tears, the child was led to the nearest cop, who was officer Joe Martin, the boxing coach at the Columbia Gym. The boy told Martin he would "whip" the person who stole his bike. "Well," Martin told him, "you'd better come back here and learn how to fight." Clay, who weighed in at 89 pounds, became a fixture in Joe Martin's gym. Christine Martin, Joe's widow, remembers driving groups of teenagers to boxing tournaments, rolling from town to town in a Ford station wagon, staying in motels with no screens and no fans.

"I was about as involved as Joe, except for the actual training," she said. "I would drive those boys everywhere. Indianapolis, Chicago, Toledo. In those days, the black boys couldn't go into the restaurants, so I didn't take any of the boys in. I'd just go in myself and get what they wanted, however many hamburgers per boy, and bring it back to the car.

"Cassius was a very easy-to-get-along-with fellow. Very easy to handle. Very polite. Whatever you asked him to do, that's what he'd do. His mother, that's why. She was a wonderful person. On trips, most of the boys were out looking around, seeing what they could get into, whistling at pretty girls. But Cassius didn't believe in that. He carried his Bible everywhere he went, and while the other boys were out looking around, he was sitting and reading his Bible."

He also was gaining weight and developing every bit of his talent. The first newspaper story about him appeared on October 27, 1957, three years after he started boxing. It was three paragraphs: "Cassius Clay established himself as the No. 1 contender for the light-heavyweight title in the Golden Gloves competition next January when he scored a fourth-round technical knockout over Donnie Hall in last night's WAVE-TV fight show main event."

In 1959 the 18-year-old Cassius Clay was to lead nine boxing titlists to the Olympic trials in San Francisco. But there was a problem. Clay was afraid to fly. Boxing officials declared that, if he made the Olympic team, he'd have to fly to Rome, so he might as well get used to it. Clay finally agreed to fly—but then he went to an army surplus store and bought a parachute and actually wore it on the plane. It was a pretty rough flight, and companions said he was down in the aisle, praying with his parachute on.

At the Olympics, Clay blossomed. He defeated stronger, heavier opponents from Belgium, Russia, Australia, and Poland on his way to the light-heavyweight gold medal and developed a reputation as an "audacious" fighter. He also was one of the most popular athletes in the Olympic village.

After Clay won an Olympic gold medal in 1960, he was met at Louisville's Standiford Field by Mayor Bruce Hoblitzell, six Central High cheerleaders, and about 200 friends and fans. He rode in a 30-car motorcade to a welcome-home party at the school. But, as Cassius Clay became Muhammad Ali, Louisville's response to him became strangely muted. Maybe it was the loudmouth routine—"I am the greatest!"—that sabotaged his popularity. Ali's conversion to the Muslim faith and his refusal to fight in the Vietnam War were unpopular, too. It seemed for awhile that he was less loved in Louisville than he was in the rest of the world. In 1978, the city decided only grudgingly, by a 6-5 vote, to change the name of Walnut Street to Muhammad Ali Boulevard. Today, though, Louisville and Kentucky seem to recognize and value the worldwide humanitarian influence the young, black boxer from the city's West End has demonstrated throughout his adult life. Plans for a new interactive Muhammad Ali Museum are well under way in the city of his birth.

—Hunt Helm, adapted from
an article in the
Louisville Courier-Journal,
September 14, 1997

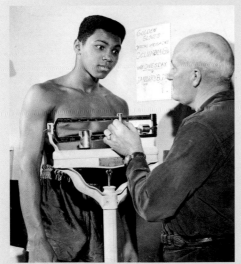

A young Cassius Clay weighs in at the Columbia Gym in 1958 under the watchful eye of his trainer and mentor, Joe Martin. (Courier-Journal, Louisville)

LOUISVILLE

■ LOUISVILLE SIGHTS

Riverfront and Waterfront Park
map page 163, B-1/2

Louisville's original commercial district was along the riverfront. Today people go to the shoreline for leisure and entertainment.

From the Waterfront Park's **Great Lawn,** a green apron jutting out into the Ohio River, you can enjoy a fine view of the city skyline, fly a kite, or in summer take in an outdoor concert. Also in Waterfront Park (River Road at Bingham Way) are a playground and numerous fountains offering relief from summertime heat and humidity.

The fountains of Waterfront Park.

To explore Louisville's river heritage, set aside some time to walk the 6.9-mile **River Walk,** which stretches west from Waterfront Park to Chickasaw Park. In some spots the paved pathway is right down by the water. In others the path winds through bosky parkland: you'll forget you're so close to a city. Best, though, is the overlook near 26th Street of the McAlpine Lock & Dam: here coal-laden barges and passenger-laden boats are eased around the Falls of the Ohio. The 1913 ***Belle of Louisville*** paddle steamer, a beloved city symbol, takes passengers on daily two-hour trips up and down the river. *Docked at the foot of Fourth St. at River Rd.; 502-574-2992.*

Belle of Louisville.

Falls of the Ohio Fossil Beds
map page 163, B-1

Cross the Second Street Bridge to Clarksville, Indiana, to visit The Falls of the Ohio State Park, site of the world's largest exposed Devonian fossil bed. An inland sea full of flora and fauna 400 million years ago, today this layer of limestone contains the fossil record of 600 plant and animal species, such as corals and armored fishes, who lived here. Best to visit in late summer, when the water level is low. *201 W. Riverside Dr., Clarksville, IN; 812-280-9970.*

Actors Theatre *map page 163, B-2*

Actors Theatre is housed in a distinguished 19th-century Greek Revival building that started life as a bank and now serves as an architectural anchor on Main Street. The complex contains three auditoriums, a restaurant and bar, and spacious lobbies.

Actors Theatre is recognized as one of the finest regional theaters in the country. Some 200 plays that have debuted here are still being performed all over the world, including 'Night Mother, by Louisville native and Pulitzer Prize–winner Marsha Norman. Performances are given year-round. Summer brings musicals and comedies; the Humana Festival of New American Plays is hosted in March. *Downtown at 316 W. Main St. between Third and Fourth Sts.; 502-584-1205.*

Kentucky Center for the Arts.

Kentucky Center
map page 163, B-2
Home to Louisville's orchestra, opera, and ballet, the center also hosts touring Broadway companies. For its Kentucky Authors Forum, perhaps the city's most notable intellectual/cultural feature, the center invites' writers for onstage interviews. Participants have included John Updike, John Glenn, Jane Goodall, Katherine Graham, and Elie Wiesel. Modern sculptures here include works by Louise Nevelson and Jean Dubuffet. *5 Riverfront Plaza; 502- 584-7777.*

The echo dish at the Louisville Science Center.

Louisville Science Center
map page 163, B 2
This refurbished dry goods warehouse, sporting a brightly painted cast-iron facade, contains hands-on natural history and technology exhibits. Highlights include a space gallery with a replica of an Apollo capsule and an exhibit on human anatomy and physiology. There's separate admission for the four-story IMAX theater, which shows a changing selection of nature-based films. *727 W. Main St.; 502-561-6100.*

Louisville Slugger Field.

Louisville Slugger Field *map page 163, B-2*
The AAA-International League Bats (affiliated with the Cincinnati Reds) play ball in

LOUISVILLE

this comfortable new stadium a block from the river. Fans enter the 13,200- seat ballpark through a handsome century-old redbrick building that was once a train shed, which gives the state-of-the-art facility a nostalgic character. A bronze statue of Louisville native and Baseball Hall of Fame shortstop Pee Wee Reese graces the entrance. *401 E. Main St.; 502-212-2287.*

Louisville Slugger Museum.

Louisville Slugger Museum
map page 163, B-2
Ever wonder what it would be like to face a Major League pitcher? You can step up to the plate at the Slugger Museum's Virtual Pitch exhibit. No batter's helmet is necessary, but the experience is realistic enough. The exhibits honor baseball history from the batter's perspective, since it's bats, not balls, that are made in the Hillerich & Bradsby factory next door. (You can tour the assembly line, too.) It's an easily identified building, with the six-story-tall bat leaning against its side, handle jutting into the sky. *800 W. Main St.; 502-588-7228.*

Conrad-Caldwell House
map page 163, B-3
The residential neighborhood of imposing Victorian mansions just south of downtown is known as Old Louisville, and there's no more imposing edifice than the massive Romanesque Revival Conrad-Caldwell House, at the corner of St. James Court and Magnolia Street, overlooking Central Park. The opulent home of Theophilus Conrad, who made his millions in timber, has elaborate exterior stonework and intricate interior woodwork. It's furnished in Victorian antiques. Alas, visitors aren't allowed to light up their stogies on Conrad's smoking balcony, located on a turret at the top of the three-story house. *1402 St. James Court; 502-636-5023.*

Conrad-Caldwell House.

Speed Art Museum   *map page 163, B-3*
Over 6,000 years of art history are represented in this extremely accessible museum located at the edge of the University of

Speed Art Museum.

Louisville's campus. Notable exhibits include the Satterwhite Gallery of Renaissance and Baroque tapestries and textiles, European and American paintings, a modern sculpture court, and an interactive gallery for children called ArtSparks. The Speed regularly hosts traveling exhibits of national and international significance. *2035 S. Third St.; 502-634-2700.*

Kentucky Derby Museum.

Kentucky Derby Museum
map page 163, B-4
The horse race itself lasts only two minutes, but the exhibits at the Derby Museum will keep you enthralled for hours. *The Greatest*

Race—a heart-pounding movie shown on a 360-degree screen—depicts the drama and traditions of training a Thoroughbred to race in the Derby. Interactive exhibits encourage you to place a bet, shoe a horse, even mount a scale-model racehorse with a "jockeycam" to show you a rider's perspective. *Entrance at Gate One of Churchill Downs, 704 Central Ave.; 502-637-1111.*

Bedroom at Locust Grove.

Locust Grove
About 15 minutes' drive east of downtown on River Road (a Kentucky Scenic Byway), you'll come to a stoplight at Blankenbaker Lane and see signs pointing to Locust Grove. The Georgian mansion, one of the area's earliest residences, was built in 1790 by William Croghan, who was married to George Rogers Clark's sister, Lucy. Situated on 55 rolling acres, the plantation's restoration includes a formal garden and several outbuildings. The house is furnished with period antiques and contains an impressive ballroom, a marvelously elegant space in this very civilized frontier house. *561 Blankenbaker Lane; 502-897-9845.*

Farmington *map page 163, D-3*
Just off the Watterson Expressway at Bardstown Road stands this 1810 Federal-style house built by the Speed family from a design by friend Thomas Jefferson; note the octagonal rooms. The Speeds grew hemp, which today may be reintroduced to help the state's struggling tobacco farmers. In 1841, Joshua Speed's friend Abe Lincoln stayed here. *3033 Bardstown Rd.; 502-452-9920.*

Cave Hill Cemetery *map page 163, C/D-2*
At the intersection of Baxter and Broadway is the grand entrance to Cave Hill Cemetery, final resting place for the city's most prominent families. City founder Gen. George Rogers Clark is buried here, as is KFC founder Col. Harlan Sanders. Chartered in 1848, the park-like cemetery is a bird sanctuary and a national arboretum with some 300 labeled tree species. In one

The bust of Col. Sanders at Cave Hill.

portion, both Union and Confederate dead are buried: Cave Hill is the only federally funded Civil War cemetery. *Bardstown Road briefly becomes Baxter Avenue, then meets the foot of Cherokee Road and the head of Broadway. 701 Baxter Ave.; 502-451-5630.*

The midway at the Kentucky State Fair in Louisville.

Alexander Helwig Wyant painted Falls of the Ohio and Louisville *in 1863.*
(The Speed Art Museum, Louisville)

■ DRIVE ALONG RIVER ROAD

Louisville's River Road follows the Ohio River for seven miles from the downtown waterfront to stately mansions perched on bluffs overlooking the water. You can start from the foot of Third Street, where, unless she's out on a cruise, you'll see the city's *Belle of Louisville* paddlewheel steamboat docked. This is also where the *Delta Queen,* a sternwheeler owned by the city of Cincinnati, and the *Mississippi Queen,* a modern luxury excursion paddlewheeler the size of an ocean liner, also dock when they stop in Louisville.

Heading east out of the city you'll wind around the back of Louisville Slugger Field and past the fountains and tree-dappled walkways of Waterfront Park. River Road is lined with trees and recreational parks, from those sporting soccer fields, softball diamonds, and driving ranges to Cox's Park, stretching along the riverfront, where people picnic or launch boats.

At Zorn Avenue, just before Cox's Park, a long lawn reaches down to the river and the old pumping station for the Louisville Water Company; the building's graceful white tower is easy to spot; it's now home to the Louisville Visual Art

Summer: A field of mustard flowers, near Brownsboro.

Fall: An early snowfall dusts the carnelian leaves of a maple tree.

Winter: A record snowstorm transforms the landscape in a Louisville park.

Spring: The pink blossoms of an Eastern redbud stand out against the chartreuse of new oak leaves.

Association and a gallery of changing exhibits. Access to many of Louisville's wealthiest suburban enclaves is off River Road. Exclusive country clubs and estates don't advertise their presence, however, and, as with such places everywhere, if you don't know how to get to them, you don't belong there.

The **Glenview area,** between Blankenbaker Lane and Lime Kiln Lane, boasts enormous mansions in styles ranging from Italian Renaissance to Greek Revival. Many have gardens and grounds designed by the landscape architecture firm of famed architect Frederick Law Olmsted. You can spot some of them from River Road in the winter when the trees surrounding them are bare. These houses were built in the early 20th century by industrialists and businessmen who made their money in bourbon, coal, hardware, and newspaper publishing.

If you're touring between spring and fall, stop at the **Chick Inn** or **Captain's Quarters,** restaurants with outdoor seating by the water. The food may not be exciting, but the terrific views will make a soda-and-sandwich lunch a pleasure.

Head back toward town along River Road and enjoy the view of the city skyline as you approach. Just going out to Glenview and back takes only about 40 minutes, but stops along the way to watch the river traffic, to have a meal, or to tour Locust Grove—only a five-minutes' drive up Blankenbaker Lane *(see page 171)*—could stretch your River Road tour to a morning or an afternoon.

(opposite) Bradford pear trees bloom in Seneca Park.
(above) A full moon rises above Interstate 264 and Breckenridge Lane.

KENTUCKY DERBY BASICS

Location
Churchill Downs, Louisville
see map page 163, B-4.

Date
First Saturday in May.

Information
502-636-4446. www.kentuckyderby.com

Tickets
The day of the race, seats for the following year, go on sale. Price range is from $40 for general admission to $525 on millionaires' row. Getting a seat where you can actually *see* the track on Derby Day is a task that can take years. Box seats cost hundreds of dollars and there's a long waiting list. However, you can get on the list by writing to Reserved Seating, Special Events, Churchill Downs, 700 Central Ave., Louisville, KY 40208. Don't try to phone or send e-mail. Only written requests are accepted.

Another method is to place a Tickets Wanted ad in the *Courier-Journal* a month or so before the Derby. Be prepared to pay top dollar.

Traffic and Parking
Predictably, these are a mess. Several shuttles from local hotels. The *Courier-Journal* publishes extensive maps and schedules.

Betting
You can bet the Derby at the track any day of Derby Week at the Advance Betting window, which are clearly marked. Minimum bet is $2; there is no maximum.

The Oaks Race
This is the famous fillies race on the Friday before the Derby; see page 179.

Dress
People *dress up* for the Derby. Race fans are outfitted in silk and linen. Think Easter Sunday Best at a tony Episcopal church. Women glory in hats, both fashionable and facetious. Men sport brightly colored blazers they wouldn't be buried in any other time of year.

Of course, there are less dressy types. They wear hats shaped like horse's heads (worn by both men and women) and fringed outfits that would be the envy of a performer at the Grand Ol' Opry. The infield is the territory of the 20-somethings, who have been known to shed most of the clothes they are wearing if the day is warm and sunny.

Atmosphere
Whatever the sartorial taste and income level of the spectators, by the time the horses come on the track on Saturday afternoon and the band strikes up the opening bars of "My Old Kentucky Home," emotions are running high.

The twin spires rise behind this view of the turn at Churchill Downs.

Thoroughbred horses race at Churchill Downs.

Chances are that most of the fans have had at least one or two mint juleps' worth of bourbon and they've bet a fair amount on the race.

What's at Stake

The horse owners, trainers, and jockeys all have hopes and reputations riding on the outcome. The payoff is a gold trophy, the famous garland of roses that is draped over the neck of the winner, a $1 million purse, and racing immortality. The winner of the Kentucky Derby joins the ranks of racing's elite. Of the 35,000 Thoroughbreds foaled each year, only one's name will join the list that began with Aristides in 1875 and has included Sir Barton, Gallant Fox, Count Fleet, Whirlaway, War Admiral, Citation, Seattle Slew, and Secretariat.

In other words, ask anyone involved in racing and he or she will tell you that the material gain is secondary to being able to say, "My horse won the Kentucky Derby."

DERBY FESTIVAL EVENTS

Dates

Kentucky Derby Festival events begin in April, a fortnight before Derby Day, which takes place the first Saturday in May. They continue until Derby Day.

Locations

In and around Louisville.

Festival Information

Events require little or no advance planning, and big public events are free as long as you are wearing a Pegasus Pin. This is a plastic lapel pin that can be purchased for $2 virtually anywhere in town, from grocery stores to gas stations. You'll see racks on the counters. Sales help fund the annual festival. **Information phone:** 502-584-6383. www.kdf.org

Thunder Over Louisville

The city of Louisville kicks off the annual two-week Kentucky Derby Festival with a literal bang the Saturday night two weeks before the Derby. This pyrotechnics extravaganza of colorful, ear-splitting fireworks takes place on the city's riverfront. There's no charge to view the show from Waterfront Park in Louisville or from riverside vantage points on the Indiana shore; **parking** can set you back $10.

Several new restaurants have sprung up along the riverfront, many of which take reservations and are even willing to host parties. And many downtown hotels have rooms facing the river.

If you plan to attend this festival opener, go early in the day and take in the air show overhead and free concerts on the Great Lawn in order to secure a good vantage point. **Caution:** Do not claim a space under the highway. You can still see, but the noise, which gets trapped between pavement and ground, is deafening.

Spring Meet

During Festival time it sometimes seems like everyone and everything is engaged in some sort of race. And the Festival kicks into high gear the Saturday before the Derby, which also happens to be the date that the Spring Meet (racing season) opens at Churchill Downs.

Derby Mini-Marathon

The Derby Mini-Marathon—a mini-marathon for humans—is held the Saturday before the Derby. It starts at 8 A.M. in Iroquois Park and finishes downtown.

Hot Air Balloon Race

This is a stately, colorful event. Citizens of Louisville and surrounding county are treated to the sight of hovering, practicing balloons for several weeks before the actual race. The balloons lift off from the Kentucky Fair and Exposition Center shortly after dawn on the Saturday before the Derby.

Run for Rosé

This race pits local restaurant servers against one another. They race around the bases at Louisville Slugger Field balancing filled wineglasses on trays. This takes place at noontime the Tuesday of Derby Week. And like many festival events, has free admission if you are wearing a Pegasus Pin.

Run for the Rodents

Run for the Rodents is sponsored by a local university. Students enter lab rats in a maze race for a garland of Fruit Loops. Day and time depends on students' final exams schedule. Call Spalding University; 502-585-9911.

Wednesday Boat Race

The *Belle of Louisville* paddle steamer take on Cincinnati's much larger riverboat, the *Delta Queen*. (And if you don't think the race is rigged to keep the home-town favorite's record even with that of her up-river rival, you probably think World Wrestling Federation contests are actual sporting events, too.) Both boats sell passenger tickets; call the Derby Festival number, 502-584-6383, for details.

You can watch the race from the shore using the same vantage points that are good for Thunder (see page 177). The race begins at 5 P.M. The Louisville Visual Arts Association hosts an annual race-watching party that includes dinner. Tickets $35-40; call 502-896-2146 for reservations.

Derby Parade

The annual Derby Parade takes place downtown on Broadway, the Thursday afternoon before the Derby. Contact the Derby Festival about reserved bleacher seats, or take a lawn chair and stake out a space on the sidewalk. If you are happy to stand, it's also easy to watch from just about any vantage point along the route.

Locals host party after party. These range from celebrity-encrusted black-tie affairs to backyard picnics where everyone puts a buck in a betting pool and pulls a horse's name out of a hat.

Kentucky Oaks Horse Race
This race for three-year-old fillies is run on the day before the Derby. Oaks Day is for the locals. That's the day most of Louisville race lovers celebrate the season at Churchill Downs, since the Kentucky Derby itself has become more of a national and international event. Even the schools and courts close for Oaks Day.

The race track is located south of downtown at 700 Central Avenue. General Admission to the Oaks is around $35, which doesn't guarantee you a seat, but you can walk around the garden and paddock areas or camp out in the infield. The only way to see the race is on television monitors placed in strategic spots.

Robert Brammer and Augustus Smith's Oakland House and Race Course.
(The Speed Art Museum, Louisville)

CENTRAL KENTUCKY
HISTORY, WHISKEY & CAVES

■ HIGHLIGHTS   *page*

Fort Knox	184
Bardstown	189
Distilleries	196, 200
Abe Lincoln Birthplace	204
Horse Cave	210
Mammoth Cave	213
Dale Hollow SR Park	225
Green River Lake Park	225
Lake Cumberland Park	225

Food & Lodging *page 264*
Also see map page 185, towns in yellow.

■ TRAVEL BASICS

Area Overview: In south-central Kentucky it's not uncommon to see a tobacco or cattle farm with a modern barn and metal silo sitting next to an obviously 200-year-old redbrick farmhouse. The mix of the old and the new gives a feeling of continuity, of the generations of people who have cultivated the long stretches of fertile land nestled between knobby hills. In the north you'll find the rolling country where Abraham Lincoln was born; farther south lies Kentucky's spectacular cave region.

Roads leading to the numerous large lakes of this region are two-lane highways bounded by corn and tobacco fields that carry a steady stream of farm vehicles, as well as trucks and cars towing boats and trailers.

Travel: The main artery through this region is the north-south Interstate 65. It's a very heavily traveled highway, being a major route for truck freight, and it comes with the requisite fast food, gas stations, and chain lodgings.

If you want a more leisurely ramble through the countryside to attractions such as Abraham Lincoln Historic sites and the distilleries around Bardstown, take the Old

Kentucky Turnpike, US-31E, which runs south from Louisville to Nashville. The road takes more time, but you'll get a better taste of the countryside, from rolling hills to tidy farms tucked into creek bottomlands. Do take seriously the "reduce speed" signs you'll encounter as you go through small towns. Speeding tickets are often an important source of municipal revenue.

Mammoth Cave, the world's longest known cave system, spreads out beneath the limestone plain of the Pennyroyal. Above ground, the woodlands and wildlife preserves are as beautiful as the geological formations below.

You can get to Mammoth Cave and Bowling Green by picking up the Cumberland Parkway at Glasgow and heading west back to I-65. The roads around Mammoth Cave can become congested in summer.

Weather: The climate here is temperate. Winter lows are likely to be in the 20s at night and in the 30s and 40s during the day. But don't be surprised if the temperature drops into single digits or soars into the 60s. Summers are hot and muggy but rarely break 100 degrees. Spring and fall are characterized by cool nights with temperatures in the 50s. Spring days can be cool and rainy, or the sun can break out and the air will be crystalline and warm into the 60s and 70s. The heat of summer usually lingers on autumn afternoons, and the mercury can creep up to 80 before the sun sets, taking warmth with it. On occasion a tornado sweeps through this area between the end of March and the end of September. Usually, there's plenty of warning.

Food & Lodging: Bardstown and the surrounding area has many charming bed-and-breakfasts (mostly in historic properties) and reliable old-fashioned motels. Restaurants specializing in Southern fare are also to be found in Bardstown. In the lakes region, the lodges and cottages at state parks offer very comfortable accommodations. Be aware that most of the counties in this part of the state are dry, and restaurant choices are limited.

If you plan to spend time at Mammoth Cave, try to book lodging in the hotel on the grounds. Though the interstate doesn't go right into Bowling Green, it makes a good base of operations for the region, with reliable lodging and a small selection of non-fast-food restaurants.

Refer to the **Food & Lodging map** page 265; toll-free numbers for chains on page 266. Towns are listed in alphabetical order beginning on page 267. For charts relating towns to chapters see page 311.

■ OVERVIEW

Because of its fertile and well-watered land, central Kentucky was settled earlier than most of the rest of the state. (Bardstown, established in 1780, is the state's second-oldest city.) Both of Abraham Lincoln's grandfathers settled in this area; and the President himself was born in the region on February 12, 1809.

Dozens of rivers were available for impoundment to make the reservoir lakes that reach throughout the region's eastern portion. The abundance of spring-fed streams in central Kentucky is responsible for the formation of the caves and sinkholes that shape the underground landscape in the western part of the region.

South of the caves lies a part of the **Pennyroyal** region, some of which is discussed in this chapter. This diverse 11,500-square-mile region of south-central and western Kentucky takes its name from a rather weedy member of the mint family, the American pennyroyal, *Hedeoma pulegioides.* Called "pennyrile" by the locals, the plant grows abundantly in dry fields where limestone is barely covered by a thin layer of soil.

In late summer, the slender stems of the pennyroyal plant bear hundreds of tiny blue flowers arrayed along the leaf axils. The plant's pungent, minty odor attracted the attention of the early settlers to the region, who infused the leaves to make a tea drunk to relieve colds and flu. But don't try this at home. For one, pennyroyal tea has a history among practitioners of folk medicine, who prescribed it to young and unwed women in order to terminate an unwanted pregnancy—not exactly an endorsement of drinking pennyroyal tea to ameliorate minor cold symptoms. And pennyroyal has been linked to certain kinds of cancer. A compound called pulegone in the oil of pennyroyal is a very effective insect repellent, but don't try *that* at home either, as pennyroyal can be absorbed through the skin. In short, pennyroyal is pretty poisonous.

■ FORT KNOX   *map opposite, B-2*

South of Louisville, the Dixie Highway (US-31W) is lined on both sides with commercial development ranging from the brand new to the seedy. After about 30 miles, at Muldraugh, the buildings thin out to be replaced by rocky, tree-covered hills. The sudden appearance of a battle tank, standing like a sentinel on the west side of the road and ensconced on a stone platform carved out of a hillside, announces the approach to Fort Knox.

Gold Depository *map page 185, B-2*

As the home of the U.S. Bullion Depository, Fort Knox has passed into the American vernacular as a metaphor for security, and for good reason: the place is built to endure World War XV. From the road, you'll easily spot the concrete-and-steel gold vault, which sits atop a barren hill. In addition to housing the nation's gold reserves, the vault has been a safe house for other treasures. During World War II the original copies of the Declaration of Independence and the Constitution, as well as the Crown Jewels of Great Britain, were kept there. Not surprisingly, there are no tours of the facility.

Fort Knox Army Base *map page 184, B-2*

The 109,000-acre base at Fort Knox is the main training ground for the U.S. Army's armored force. All American soldiers who are going to drive, maintain, or otherwise be associated with tanks and/or armor spend a good chunk of their military careers here. That the woods and fields of Fort Knox are used as training grounds for future tankers and such is no secret to those who live nearby: the dull boom of artillery can be heard as far away as Louisville—especially on overcast nights, when the sounds echo off the cloud cover.

An aerial view of the U.S. Bullion Depository at Fort Knox circa 1940, prior to the construction of the army base now surrounding it. (Underwood Photo Archives, San Francisco)

Armor Memorial Park

If you drive through the main entrance to the base, you'll see the neatly trimmed lawns of Armor Memorial Park, where dozens of armored vehicles and tanks are displayed. Most are American, but you can also see German panzers, British Mark I battle tanks, and tanks from the Soviet M1 series.

Patton Museum of Cavalry

The adjacent Patton Museum of Cavalry, named after World War II General George S. Patton, Jr., has exhibits of tanks, half-tracks, jeeps, and other vehicles from World Wars I and II, the Korean and Vietnam Wars, and Operation Desert Storm. The armored car in which General Patton was killed is also on display, as well as a series of military uniforms. Kids often get a kick out of climbing down inside tanks (which for a claustrophobe is, quite frankly, not a whole lot of fun). *Chaffee Ave. off US-31W. 4554 Fayette Ave.; 502-624-3812.*

Tioga Falls National Recreation Trail

Located in Fort Knox, the Tioga Falls Trail follows the route of former Muldraugh Road, climbing an escarpment that divides the Salt River and Green River Valleys. The trail passes the site of early 1900s Tioga Railroad Station, a trestle bridge, and the ruins of a spring house and tannery. Natur-

Tioga Falls National Recreation Trail.

al features include limestone outcroppings, the 130-foot Tioga Falls, and forests of oak, poplar, maple, beech, shagbark hickory, as well as tulip trees. The two-mile hike is moderately difficult.

Nearby is the **Bridges to the Past Trail,** an easier, barrier-free trail that passes over several stone bridges built in the mid-19th century. Along the way you'll see wildflowers, limestone gorges, seasonal waterfalls, and caves.

From US-31W (Dixie Highway) take the old L&N Turnpike almost a mile to the small picnic area. For information, call *502-624-8674.*

■ SCENIC DRIVE ALONG THE OHIO RIVER

map page 185, A/B-1/2

Southwest of West Point and Fort Knox at Muldraugh, take KY-1638 west, which leads to Otter Creek Park (30 miles from Louisville, map page 184, B-2). At this point the drive becomes lovely, passing steep cliffs and wooded banks along the Ohio River. Take KY-448 north to Brandenburg. The main street runs straight to the Ohio River. Find Lawrence Road, near the river. It becomes Battle Road (KY-228) to Wolf Creek, looping through several small towns.

■ BARDSTOWN   *map page 185, C-2*

The "bard" in Bardstown (population 6,800) isn't a poet or balladeer: It's David Bard, who received a 1,000-acre land grant from Gov. Patrick Henry of Virginia in 1780 and, with his brother William, led the founding of Kentucky's second-oldest

(above) A tugboat pushes a coal barge up the Ohio River across from Otter Creek Park.
(opposite) Autumn colors frame Federal Hill in My Old Kentucky Home State Park.
(following pages) Sunrise over the Ohio River near Muldraugh.

city. The Nelson County seat's claims to fame do include a somewhat poetic one, however. In addition to being a center of bourbon making and the site of the first Catholic cathedral west of the Appalachians (St. Joseph's Proto-Cathedral), Bardstown has Federal Hill, the Georgian-style mansion reputedly visited by composer Stephen Foster. His sojourn in the Bluegrass apparently inspired him to write what was to become the state song, "My Old Kentucky Home."

Another famous resident of the community was monk and author Thomas Merton, who lived at the nearby Trappist Abbey of Gethsemani.

Bards and monks aside, what the area is famous for is the hard stuff. Early settlers quickly discovered that the water running through the streams and from the numerous springs in the area was uncommonly pure and sweet. Naturally, not wanting to waste a precious resource, they immediately started using it to distill whiskey. The bourbon industry grew steadily over the next century and a half, and at the time just before Prohibition there were 26 distilleries in Nelson County. Today there are four: Heaven Hill, Jim Beam, Barton Brands, and Maker's Mark. The whiskey heritage is celebrated in Bardstown every September during the annual Kentucky Bourbon Festival.

The city center looks like a movie set for Small Town, U.S.A, and over 200 of its buildings are listed on the National Register of Historic Places. Log houses survive, as well as Greek Revival, Federalist, and Georgian mansions. (Distiller emeritus and grandson of Jim Beam, Booker Noe, lives with his wife, Ennis, in one of the white-columned edifices on Main Street.)

Looming at the town hub is the Richardson Romanesque **Nelson County Courthouse,** looking like a giant piece of brick gingerbread. It's not at all difficult to orient yourself to the town from the spokes thrusting out from the square toward several interesting places, including antique shops located within walking distance of the square.

Bardstown is a comfortable base of operations for touring this part of Kentucky. It offers easy access to cave country, as well as to historic sites associated with the early life of Abraham Lincoln. And it's an interesting town in which to linger for a couple of days.

◆ BARDSTOWN SIGHTS AND DISTILLERIES

Old Talbott Tavern

In the block directly west of the courthouse are two Bardstown landmarks, the Old Talbott Tavern and the Old County Jail. The former is a brick-and-stone tavern, restaurant, and inn dating from 1779. Among its illustrious visitors were Daniel Boone and Jesse James. A fire in 1998 temporarily closed the tavern. Restoration work uncovered murals painted by Louis Philippe of France during his stay here in 1797 that had been hidden under layers of paint.

Louis Philippe lived abroad during the reign of Napoleon (1796–1814) and in Philadelphia from 1797 to 1800. (As king, he was overthrown by a citizens' revolution in 1848, abdicated, and escaped to England.) As for his visit to Bardstown, here's the WPA guide, 1939:

A doubtful legend, cherished by the citizens, is that Louis Philippe, Duke of Orleans, later King of France, was a resident of the little town for a time, during which he taught French and dancing to the children of the gentry and worked at the watchmaker's trade. Louis Philippe and two brothers, on their way from the capital to New Orleans, crossed the Salt River at Pitts Fork with difficulty on October 16, 1797, and spent the night at Captain Bean's tavern here. Though the Duke became very ill, he was left alone because the first company of stage troupers had come to town—an event causing much excitement.

The inn has been furnished in antiques and reproductions, but the tavern part itself would be unrecognizable to Boone. Cocktail tables are made from bourbon barrels, and several large-screen televisions are impossible to avoid. Nonetheless, there's a terrific selection of bourbons—so forget the lack of period charm and enjoy the goods. *Located at 107 W. Stephen Foster Ave.; 502-348-3494.*

Old County Jail

Directly next door to the tavern is the imposing Old County Jail, a medieval-looking limestone fortress built in 1820 that actually housed miscreants as late as 1988. (Note the stocks on the front lawn.) The jail has been converted to an unusual bed-and-breakfast called the Jailer's Inn. A windowless upstairs room has been kept as it was, complete with iron rings in the floor to which prisoners were shackled. There are still bars on the bedroom windows. One room is actually a cell, complete with bunks, but updated with a water bed, which gives new meaning to "overnight lock-in." It's actually somewhat unnerving.

You don't have to be a guest to take a tour: just knock on the door and someone will walk you around for a small fee. *111 W. Stephen Foster Ave.; 502-348-5551.*

Oscar Getz Museum of Whiskey History
Spalding Hall is the location of the Oscar Getz Museum of Whiskey History, a fine place to visit if you are trying to bring some scholarly justification to your love of bourbon. Displays include an exhibit detailing the steps of bourbon making, old bottles and barrels, and several stills. And you'll learn how Kentuckians coped during Prohibition: for example, doctors prescribed bourbon, which is why drugstores in the state stock alcoholic beverages to this day.

The people behind the bottles are given much exhibit space, with displays about Jacob Beam (founder of Jim Beam Distillery), the Samuels family (of Maker's Mark), and others. There's even an exhibit devoted to women in the bourbon industry. Don't miss the incredible photographs of the terrible fire that swept through Heaven Hill in 1997, destroying the main warehouses. Flaming bourbon streamed down hillsides, creating a river of fire in the creek by the distillery. *114 N. Fifth St.; 502-348-2999.*

My Old Kentucky Home State Park
map page 185, C-2
One mile east of the courthouse on US-150 is Federal Hill, the redbrick Georgian mansion that was home to Judge John Rowan, who built the house in 1815 on land that had been a wedding present from his father-in-law. Rowan was a native of Pennsylvania, and his Pittsburgh cousin, Stephen Foster, made occasional visits. Foster was the composer of such nostalgic tunes as "Beautiful Dreamer," "Camptown Races," and "Jeannie with the Light Brown

(above) The Stephen Foster Story *plays outdoors at My Old Kentucky Home State Park.* *(opposite) The Oscar Getz Museum of Whiskey History.*

Hair." The Rowan house is said to have inspired "My Old Kentucky Home."

The mansion sits on 285 wooded acres. Tours of the interior are given by guides in antebellum costume. Since this is a state park, there are a small campground, a nine-hole golf course, and tennis courts, all discreetly out of sight from the mansion. In summer the ongoing costume musical *The Stephen Foster Story* is presented in an amphitheater on the grounds. *502-348-3502.*

Heaven Hill Distillery *map page 185, C-2*
This bottling plant is just south of the city. You might be surprised to see tequila and gin being bottled along with whiskey, but the company owns several beverage brands. Bourbons here are Heaven Hill, Evan Williams, and Elijah Craig. Daily tours. *1064 Loretto Rd. (KY-49); 502-348-3921.*

NOTE: For information on nearby **Lincoln Homestead State Park,** *see page 208.*

Maker's Mark Distillery *map page 185, D-3*
Continue driving along KY-49 for about 20 minutes from Heaven Hill through densely wooded, hilly countryside and follow the signs to Maker's Mark. Nestled on rolling meadows surrounded by hills, the 19th-century distillery is listed in the National Register of Historic Places. The handsome frame-and-brick buildings are painted black, the shutters and trim bright red. (It's the same shade of red as the wax that seals the bourbon bottles.) During tours, you can walk right up to the sides of the unique cypress vats in which the sour mash is fermenting. *3350 Burks Rd., Loretto; 270-865-2099.*

Scenes at Maker's Mark Distillery: (above) a large wooden fermenter and (opposite) bourbon bottles being sealed by hand with melted wax.

BOURBON: A SHORT HISTORY

Scotland has its single malts. Russia has its vodka, and Mexico its tequila. The United States has Kentucky bourbon, our own native whiskey.

The original whiskey, distilled from corn using backwoods methods, evolved into bourbon when someone stored it in white oak barrels that had been charred on the inside, thus imparting an amber color and sweet vanilla/caramel flavor. The charring was probably an accident. For the wooden staves of barrels to be bent, they have to be heated. Somewhere along the way, one or a few barrels got too toasted, and the distillers liked the results. So charring became standard.

Origins: One legend has it that a Baptist minister and businessman, Elijah Craig, invented the process in 1789 at his mill near Georgetown in Owen County. The whiskey was named for neighboring Bourbon County because it was shipped in barrels from small ports along the Kentucky River, which runs through Bourbon County.

Whatever its origins, bourbon became a beverage identified with Kentucky for several reasons. The limestone water of the state's streams is good for whiskey making. Corn, one of bourbon's main ingredients, was plentiful. The white oak trees used in making the barrels were also widespread. And hot Kentucky summers facilitate the aging process, in which the whiskey leaches in and out of the lining of its barrels.

What Bourbon is: Bourbon, by law, is distilled from fermented grain that cannot be less than 51 percent corn. Other grains, in combinations that differ from one brand to another (and the reason why bourbons are distinctive) are combinations of malted barley, rye, and/or wheat. During distillation, proof (twice the percentage of alcohol) cannot go higher than 160 and when put in the barrel for aging, proof must be no higher than 125. The distillate must be aged for at least two years, though better bourbons are aged five and more. And they must be aged in charred white oak barrels that haven't been used before. Upon bottling, the proof is lowered by the addition of limestone spring water or distilled water.

Before Prohibition there were hundreds of distilleries scattered across the Bluegrass. Today only about a dozen distillers remain, but they make over a hundred brands of bourbon.

Famous bourbon drinkers: They include in their noble ranks Andrew Jackson, Walt Whitman, Henry Clay, Daniel Webster, Ulysses S. Grant, and Mark Twain—who once wrote that "too much good bourbon is never enough."

How to drink bourbon: Most Kentuckians simply drink bourbon with a little water (the classic "bourbon and branch"). The very best stuff is drunk straight, in a snifter, warmed slightly. From my bourbon collection I can choose between Pappy Van Winkle 23-Year-Old (a rare and expensive bourbon) to Woodford Reserve (so smooth and creamy that it's like a vanilla sundae with caramel sauce, but better, because all of the calories come from alcohol).

This author is occasionally asked by friends from other states about popular bourbon drinks. I tend to grow faint at the thought of "bourbon drinks," and must have a bracer in order to recover. Few Kentuckians drink mint juleps, believing they taste like mouthwash. Well, maybe on Derby Day we drink them, just as eggnog must sometimes be drunk at Christmas.

Manhattans and Old Fashioneds are the best bourbon drinks if one really must add anything at all to the Life's Blood.

Civilized taste: Even (mostly) teetotalling Kentuckians have been known to indulge in bourbon as an addition to dessert. It's hard to imagine that classic Southern, sweet bread pudding without traditional warm bourbon sauce made of bourbon whiskey, caramelized brown sugar, and butter. And a very civilized way to indulge in a taste for bourbon is in the splendid combination of bourbon and chocolate to be found in "bourbon balls"—candies marketed by nearly all distilleries as well as the Rebecca Ruth candy makers of Frankfort.

Browns Mill and Bardstown Square in scenic Bardstown.

Jim Beam Distillery   *map page 185, C-2*
Use another day to venture to the Jim Beam Distillery and Bernheim Forest, both in Clermont on KY-245, about 12 miles northwest of Bardstown. There are no tours of the distillery proper, but a complex called the Jim Beam American Outpost has a museum, complete with an elaborate exhibit on the making of bourbon barrels. You can also tour the 1911 Beam family home, furnished with period antiques. *149 Happy Hollow Rd.; 502-543-9877.*

Bernheim Forest and Arboretum
Owned and operated by a private foundation, huge Bernheim Forest and Arboretum is situated on land donated by bourbon magnate and German native, Isaac W. Bernheim. The entrance is almost directly across from the Jim Beam Distillery. The 1,500-acre center of the property is devoted to a fine, landscaped arboretum and is home to 1,800 species of cultivated and native woody plants.

You can often spot several species of ducks and geese on the lake situated among the clumps of ornamental shrubs. The rest of Bernheim is forested and looks much as it probably did when the first settlers arrived here.

The 35 miles of scenic, well-marked hiking trails (most of medium difficulty) loop through knobs, ridges, valleys, and hollows. **Jackson Hollow Loop** is a short, fairly easy hike (follow the red blazes) that passes through hardwoods, over hills, into hollows, and under a tunnel of sassafras. You might see turkeys strutting around. NOTE: There is an unbridged creek crossing; you'll have to wade. *502-955-8512.*

Gethsemani Farms Trappist Monastery

map page 184, C-2

The Gethsemani Monastery is the largest and oldest Order of Cistercian Monks (also called Trappists) in the United States. Founded in 1848, the monastery was later home to author and Cistercian brother Thomas Merton, best known for his autobiographical work *The Seven Storey Mountain.*

These days, Gethsemani serves as a retreat house and is probably best known for the fruitcakes and cheese the monks produce. Although you can try to make a room reservation, there's usually a long waiting list. There is no set charge; donations are made on a volunteer basis.

If you stop just for a day, you can attend church services or walk that part of the grounds open to the public—a thousand acres of meadows and woods. If you're lucky you'll hear the chanting of monks echoing from the church.

From Bardstown, take Hwy-31E south to Culvertown and turn onto 247. Watch for a blinking light on top of a hill three miles south and turn right. A sign on the road points the way. 502-549-3117.

The Monastery of Gethsemani, once home to Cistercian brother and author Thomas Merton.

CENTRAL KENTUCKY

SOUTH OF ELIZABETHTOWN, 1938

If you plan to visit the Abraham Lincoln Heritage Area, you'll likely want to take US Highway 61 from Elizabethtown—as did this Federal Writers' Project author in 1938.

South of Elizabethtown [on US-61] the road winds between the knobs; some of these lumpy outcroppings are denuded of everything except grass, others have small stands of timber near their crowns. In summertime the light green of tall cornstalks blends with the darker green of the tiny tobacco patches and rough fields; but with fall's coming, dun-colored wigwams of shocks stretch across the fields of stubble, the truncated tobacco plants make a dark brown stain upon the clay, and large plots of broom sage ripple over the fields and hillsides.

South of the Nolin River 62.5 *m.*, is a small area of livestock farming with substantial houses and multiple fodder ricks bunched in the fields that are separated from the highway by dense clusters of honeysuckle.

The thick, dark shadow of a sizable evergreen woods falls across US 31W as it winds up and around hills to Upton, 69.8 *m.* (402 pop.), a trading center that looks to the Louisville & Nashville R.R. for its life. Some quarrying is carried on in the vicinity.

Just south of Upton a few ramshackle frame houses appear—one-story affairs with one or two rooms, feebly lit through small-paned windows. They suggest a farm's outbuildings rather than dwelling places. The small plots surrounding these places are littered with sundry articles, and the hand plow is sometimes seen in use. Here live poor white families who eke out a borderline existence. They are not representative of the region, and their number is small.

The highway dips up and down as it penetrates a cheerless country with jumbled contours, veined by steady erosion. Cornfields and pasture lands are plotted irregularly over the terrain; here and there a bared stretch of dark red soil stands on a drab hillside. The railroad tracks along the road seem like an intruder in this nearly primitive landscape where the dwellings are log cabins and big, black mules take the place of horses.

—*Kentucky, A Guide to the Bluegrass State,*
Federal Writers' Project, 1939

(opposite) The Sara Johnston Bush Lincoln Memorial in Elizabethtown.

■ LINCOLN HERITAGE AREA

In the early 1800s, young Abraham Lincoln often helped his stepmother do her shopping in the Green-Helm store in **Elizabethtown.** They were served there by a man whom Lincoln later described as "the first man I ever knew who wore store clothes all the week"—an indication of the austere life settlers lived in this part of Kentucky 200 years ago. Lincoln once wrote of his early life, "It can all be condensed into a simple sentence and that sentence you will find in Gray's *Elegy*— 'The short and simple annals of the poor.'"

Abraham Lincoln's antecedents had come to the New World from England almost 200 years before he was born, and each generation had moved—from Massachusetts to New Jersey to Pennsylvania to Virginia. In 1782, Lincoln's grandfather moved his family to Kentucky, following Daniel Boone's Wilderness Road. Lincoln's father, Thomas, saw his own father killed by Indians; later he may have worked as a hired laborer alongside slaves. Like many struggling white subsistence farmers, he was anti-slavery, identifying with the hardscrabble life of the settler rather than that of the comfortable Southern gentleman.

◆ ABRAHAM LINCOLN BIRTHPLACE
NATIONAL HISTORIC SITE   *map page 185, B-3*

On February 12, 1809, the American President who emancipated the nation's slaves and preserved the Union, Abraham Lincoln, was born in a one-room log cabin near Hodgenville, Kentucky. The cabin had a dirt floor and one small window. Its corncob bed was kept warm with bear skins.

The cabin was built in the stony, green countryside, on his father's farm, Sinking Spring, a remote and self-sufficient place. Life was hard and the food was plain, but the family was energetic and well-respected in the community. When Abe Lincoln was two-and-a-half years old, the Lincolns moved to a nearby farm, where they hoped the soil would prove more fertile.

Today a replica of the cabin in which Lincoln was born sits in a grand stone monument not unlike the Lincoln Memorial in Washington, which makes for an

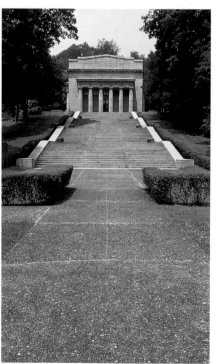

odd juxtaposition. But the motives of those who built this were excellent; notable Americans, including Mark Twain and William Jennings Bryan, helped to raise money for the site.

To reach the entrance to the monument, you climb 56 steps, one for each year of Lincoln's life. Carved over the entrance is a famous quote from his Second Inaugural Address in 1865:

With malice toward none,
with charity for all.

This address was given by Lincoln at the end of the Civil War. A visit here will remind anyone that great human beings can arise from humble circumstances. *Three miles south of Hodgenville on US-31E; 270-358-3137.*

Abraham Lincoln Birthplace National Historic Site.

ABRAHAM LINCOLN

*O*n the Knob Creek farm the child Abraham Lincoln learned to talk, to form words with the tongue and the roof of the mouth and the force of the breath from lungs and throat. "Pappy" and "Mammy," the words of his people meaning father and mother, were among the first syllables. He learned what the word "name" meant; his name was Abraham, the same as Abraham in the Bible, the same as his grandfather Abraham. It was "Abe" for short; if his mother called in the dark, "Is that you, Abe?" he answered, "Yes, Mammy, it's me." The name of the family he belonged to was "Lincoln" or "Linkun," though most people called it "Linkern" and it was sometimes spelled "Linkhorn."

The family lived there on Knob Creek farm, from the time Abe was three or so till he was past seven years of age. Here he was told "Kaintucky" meant the state he was living in; Knob Creek farm, the Rock Spring farm where he was born, Hodgenville, Elizabethtown, Muldraugh Hill, these places he knew, the land he walked on, was all part of Kentucky.

Yet it was also part of something bigger. Men had been fighting, bleeding, and dying in a war, for a country, "our country"; a man couldn't have more than one country any more than he could have more than one mother; the name of the mother country was the "United States"; and there was a piece of cloth with red and white stripes having a blue square in its corner filled with white stars; and this piece of cloth they called "a flag." The flag meant the "United States." One summer morning his father started the day by stepping out of the front door and shooting a long rifle into the sky; and his father explained it was the day to make a big noise because it was the "Fourth of July," the first day the United States called itself a "free and independent" nation.

—Carl Sandburg, *Abraham Lincoln, The Prairie Years, Vol. I,* 1928

◆ **HODGENVILLE LINCOLN MUSEUM** *map page 185, C-3*

The Lincoln Museum, located on the Hodgenville town square, is an oddly old-fashioned little museum but rather endearing in its lack of sophistication. Its dioramas are populated by wax figures that recreate incidents from the President's life. The square outside, dominated by a bronze statue of a rather somber-looking Lincoln, is the site of the annual Lincoln Days Celebration, held in October, where you can try your hand at rail splitting. The President was also famed for his skills as a speaker and debater, but, alas, there's no oratory contest. *Hodgenville town square; 270-358-3163.*

ABRAHAM LINCOLN

With malice toward none; with charity for all...
let us strive on to finish the work we are in....

*A*braham Lincoln, born in a one-room cabin on the Kentucky frontier, became one of our greatest Presidents, leading the Union through the Civil War and freeing the nation's slaves. In his great speeches at Gettysburg and his second inaugural address, he invoked charity in the face of division and urged the country to go forward in freedom and unity. Lincoln, assassinated in 1865, didn't live to see completion of the "work we are in."

The President's father, Kentuckian Thomas Lincoln, had grown up as a hardscrabble pioneer, working as a day laborer and a carpenter. In 1806 he married a young woman of unknown family background, Nancy Hanks. They moved with their first child, Sarah, to a small farm near Hodgenville, Kentucky, where their second child, Abraham, was born February 12, 1809. Not long afterward they moved to a second Kentucky farm, Spring Hill, and in the winter of 1816 to Indiana. There the family "squatted" under a rude temporary shelter and eventually built a cabin and bought the land.

Later in his life, Lincoln recalled frontier life as "pretty pinching at times" and

Abraham Lincoln was born in Kentucky in 1809.

noted, "It's best described in [Thomas] Gray's *Elegy [Written in a Country Churchyard]*, 'The short and simple annals of the poor.'" Lincoln's mother died in the fall of 1818 and was buried in the forest. Before the winter of 1819, Lincoln's father remarried a widow he had courted unsuccessfully some years earlier. Sarah Bush Johnston, who Abraham called his "angel mother," already had three children, but raised all the siblings with an abundance of affection and energy, seeming to have extra fondness for Abraham. Although they owned a Bible, both his parents were illiterate; his early schooling was "by littles"—a little here and there; and he readily admitted that he "could read, write, and cipher to the rul of three; but that wasll" by the time he came of age.

In 1830, the Lincoln family moved to Illinois. Abraham passed the bar in 1836 and began to practice law. He moved to Springfield, becoming one of the most successful lawyers in the state. Known for shrewdness, fairness, and honesty, he was elected to the Illinois State Legislature in 1834.

In November of 1842, Lincoln married Mary Todd, who came from a distinguished Lexington family. The early years of the Lincoln's marriage were marked by affection, but tragedy hit them as well. Of their four sons, Edward Baker died at four years and William Wallace at 11. Mary became despondent after the death of William and after the Civil War began, making her Kentucky relatives enemies of each other. Her son "Tad," his father's favorite, died after Lincoln was assassinated, and only Robert Todd, the eldest, survived to adulthood. After her husband's death, Mary accumulated debt and became insolvent, and, in 1875, she was declared insane.

Lincoln represented Illinois for one term in Congress, 1847-49. The years found him enmeshed in challenging President James Polk's stance on the Mexican War and supporting war hero Zachary Taylor. After a five-year hiatus from politics, he again entered the fray in opposition to his rival Stephen A. Douglas. He lost the Senate election in 1858, but after having gained national recognition in arguments regarding slavery, he was considered a prime Presidential candidate of the newly formed Republican, anti-slavery, party.

Lincoln won the 1860 election, and on April 12 of 1861, Confederates fired on Fort Sumter in the first act of what was to be the Civil War. Lincoln was re-elected in 1864. On April 9, 1865 the war ended with the surrender of the Confederacy's great general, Robert E. Lee, at Appomattox. Less than a week later on April 14, 1865 John Wilkes Booth assassinated Abraham Lincoln, as he attended a performance at the Ford's Theater in Washington D.C.

Walt Whitman's poem *When Lilacs Last in the Dooryard Bloom'd* reflected his and the nation's grief. It begins:

When lilacs last in the dooryard bloom'd
And the great star early droop'd in the western sky in the night,
I mourn'd, and yet shall mourn with ever-returning spring.

The poem ends:

For the sweetest, wisest soul of all my days and lands—and this for his dear sake,
Lilac and star and bird twined with the chant of my soul,
There in the fragrant pines and the cedars dusk and dim.

◆ ABRAHAM LINCOLN BOYHOOD HOME   *map page 185, C-3*

Lincoln's family moved to a farm on nearby Knob Creek in 1811, which Lincoln recalled in his 1859 autobiography as the place of "my earliest recollection." The farmland was fertile and Abe's parents, Thomas and Nancy Hanks Lincoln, achieved a certain degree of financial and social success here. (Thomas was appointed by the Hardin County Court as supervisor of the Nolin-Bardstown Road which passed though his farm.)

This log cabin is another replica, surrounded by a split-rail fence of the type "Honest Abe" was known for building when he helped his father on their farm. While living at this farm, Lincoln slipped and fell into Knob Creek when it was at flood stage. Luckily, his schoolmate, young Austin Gollaher (an unsung American hero), grabbed a long tree branch and held it out. Abe gripped the branch and was pulled to safety. (The guides at the homestead love to tell this story, and because the cabin is right by the creek, the incident is easy to envision.)

When Abe Lincoln was seven years old, his family's title to the farm was disputed and they were forced to move away. They settled next in Indiana.

Seven miles north of Hodgenville at 7120 US-31E; 502-549-3741.

◆ LINCOLN HOMESTEAD STATE PARK   *map page 185, D-2*

This park, near Springfield, has yet another replica log cabin where Lincoln's grandmother raised her three sons, Thomas, Josiah, and Mordecai. Thomas was a woodworker, and many pieces of furniture he made are displayed here. The park also contains a blacksmith shop and the Francis Berry House, the two-story home in which Abe's mother, Nancy Hanks, lived while she was being courted by Thomas Lincoln. (It was moved here from a site a few miles away.) The 120-acre park, in addition to a gift shop and picnic area, contains an 18-hole golf course on its rolling pastureland. (Hard to know why, except the land naturally lends itself to a course, and several Presidents after Lincoln certainly have been avid golfers.)

5079 Lincoln Park Rd., off KY-528; 859-336-7461.

In town, the **Washington County Courthouse** still contains the records of Lincoln's parents' marriage.

■ CAVE COUNTRY *map page 185, A/B-4*

The prettiest route into Cave Country from Lincoln Land is to go south on US-31E, take KY-88 west, and join up with I-65 heading south. Two-lane roads pass fields of corn, tobacco, and soybeans, as well as historic farmhouses (some impressive in size, but most simply modestly pretty) and occasional small towns that are just big enough for a gas station and a post office.

Exit 58 off of I-65 takes you to a tourist attraction you'd expect to encounter in Australia. But the name seems appropriate in cave country.

Kentucky Down Under displays aspects of life in Australia. It includes an open-air zoo for animals native to Australia, and on a field a mile east of the interstate on KY-218, kangaroos, wallabies, and emus roam about.

Among the attractions are aviaries, where colorful tropical birds fly about, including cockatoos and crimson rosellas. There's also collection of exotic reptiles, including some impressively large snakes.

Australia's human culture is represented in displays of Aboriginal art and musical instruments, and in demonstrations of Australian sheep farming. Guides (wearing bush hats) show kids how to tilt a sheep onto its rump for shearing—the sort of smelly, hands-on experience that makes you appreciate the fact that you work elsewhere.

Underneath the zoo lies **Kentucky Caverns**—caves with colorful onyx formations. Guided tours of the onyx caves are pleasant on hot summer days, since the caverns stay at a constant 60 degrees F.

Golden orange stalactites and stalagmites glow eerily in the half light of the chambers, accessible by stairs carved out of the living rock. When you emerge from underground, take the wooded path to an observation deck where you can gaze over a pasture that's home to a herd of American bison, an animal that roamed Kentucky by the millions just a few centuries ago. *KY-218 off I-65 at the Horse Cave exit; 270-786-2634.*

CENTRAL
KENTUCKY

■ TOWN OF HORSE CAVE   *map page 185, B-4*

There's some debate over the origins of the name of Horse Cave. Some townspeople claim that Hidden River Cave, over which the town is built, was used by Indians and horse thieves in the 19th century to hide their equine acquisitions. Others say there was a story about a horse that actually fell into the cave. And (perhaps lamest of all) it was common slang at the time of the town's settlement in the 1840s to refer to anything outsized as being "as big as a horse." At any rate, the large cave was the focal point for the town's growth, and the river that carved it provided energy for an electric generator in the late 1800s.

In 1925, explorer Floyd Collins was trapped in nearby Sand Cave while looking for a link between it and Mammoth Cave. A boulder fell and landed on his legs, pinning him in a narrow tunnel. Word spread of Collins's plight, and what ranks as the nation's first news-media circus resulted as reporters came from as far away as Europe to cover the rescue effort.

Collins was trapped for over two weeks, during which time he was interviewed by Louisville *Courier-Journal* reporter William Burke Miller, who called down the shaft to him. The resulting story netted the newspaper its second Pulitzer Prize. But workers trying to reach Collins by digging a lateral tunnel couldn't go fast enough. When they finally reached him, he was dead.

By the late 1970s, industrial runoff and sewage had polluted the cave so badly that animals indigenous to the cave, such as blind cavefish and eastern pipistrelle bats had all been killed or driven away. The town reeked of the stench.

The Environmental Protection Agency, the National Park Service, and concerned citizens of Horse Cave agreed to tackle the problem. A 10-year cleanup effort, which included a new sewage treatment plant, resulted in a notable restoration of the cave's ecosystem. *(See American Cave Museum, page 212.)*

◆ SIGHTS IN THE TOWN OF HORSE CAVE

Horse Cave is a plain little town with a huge, fenced hole, the entrance to the cave, in the town center.

The **American Cave Conservation Association** opened a museum here in 1993 because Hidden River Cave is a model for underground ecosystem restoration. You can take a tour of a two-story cave model, which you can view from both the lobby at street level and from one story down, and which features all the salient

(opposite) Kentucky Caverns near the town of Horse Cave.

points of cave anatomy—including stalactites and stalagmites. (You can remember that the stalactites "stick tight" to the ceiling, so the stalagmites are the ones pointing up from the floor.) The tour provides a great introduction to features you'll encounter in real caverns such as Hidden River and Mammoth Caves. How humans have used caves—as a water source, food storage, mining, shelter, and even as cemeteries—is another feature of the museum.

After learning about Floyd Collins, the explorer trapped in a cave for two weeks, you may be reluctant to venture into Hidden River Cave, four stories below the museum. But the journey by lighted elevator to the entrance is reassuring. (No ropes tied around the waist here.) After you reach the opening, from which crisp, cool air blows, there are 174 steps down to the water level of the cave, where the sound of the rushing water fills the chilly air. The guided tour includes the story of the cave's pollution and cleanup and a walk past the old waterworks and electricity-generating plant that served Horse Cave for decades.

The cave museum's gift shop has an array of books on geology, natural history, and caving that would be hard to find all under one roof anywhere else. *119 E. Main St.; 270-786-1466.*

The town of Horse Cave offers live theater from June to October. **The Horse Cave Theatre** presents a season of half a dozen plays by nationally known and regional playwrights. You might see a revival of a popular play like *Arsenic and Old Lace* or a world premiere of a work written by an up-and-coming Kentucky playwright. The venue is the intimate (343 seats) and beautifully renovated **Thomas Opera House,** which dates from 1911. *107 Main St.; 800-342-2177.*

■ MAMMOTH CAVE NATIONAL PARK

Getting There: Take the Park City exit (48) off I-65 and follow the signs to the main entrance to the park, where the crush of ticky-tacky souvenir shops and tourist traps lining the road comes to an abrupt stop. The pristine park grounds constitute an oasis in the midst of commercial chaos, although commercial exploitation has been a part of Mammoth Cave for the past two centuries.

◆ NATURAL HISTORY

The cave system under the park is the longest in the world. Nearly 350 miles of passageways have been mapped, and the deepest level is 379 feet below the surface.

By comparison, the world's next longest cave system, Optimisticeskaya in Central Asia's Republic of Georgia, extends for 113 miles and is 66 feet deep.

Today the surface of the park includes over 53,000 acres (about 80 square miles), divided into northern and southern halves by the picturesque Green River, a tranquil waterway that's wonderful to canoe.

Formation of the Cave System: The formation of the multilevel cave system started 350 million years ago when what is now the southeastern United States, including Kentucky, was located 10 degrees south of the equator and was covered by a shallow tropical ocean. The sea was teeming with Devonian crustaceans. As they died and sank to the sea floor, their shells dissolved, leaving behind sediments of calcium carbonate, the mineral component of limestone. Over the next 70 million years, about 700 feet of limestone and shale were deposited.

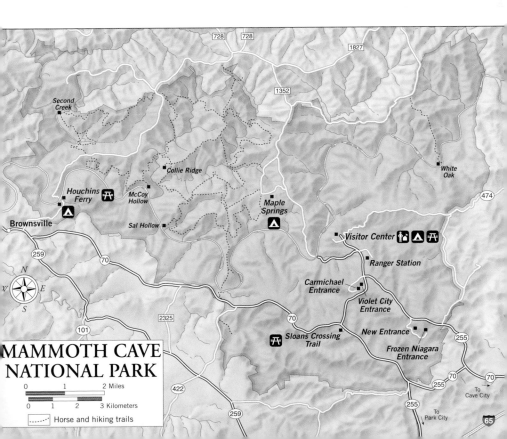

The sea levels started dropping about 280 million years ago and the continents formed. The ancient layers of limestone, often capped by sandstone, were exposed. As the plates of the earth's crust shifted, Kentucky moved northward and the rock layers were raised and twisted, creating cracks in the stone.

The channel for the Green River formed. Rain fell on the limestone, reacting with the calcium carbonate to produce carbonic acid, which in turn eroded the rock. Draining water flowed into the river, and the labyrinth of caves grew.

Types of Formations: Water dripping through cracks in the rock leaves mineral deposits behind, too. That's how stalactites and other cave "decorations," properly called speleothems, are formed.

Many of the chambers in passageways in Mammoth Cave are rich in speleothems. Perhaps the most beautiful and bizarre are the gypsum flowers. Bunches of flat strips of white gypsum curl out from the cave walls like strange stone chrysanthemums. Precursors of stalactites, called soda straws because of their thin, bent shape, occur frequently as well.

(above) Popcorn gypsum formations at Mammoth Cave National Park.

(opposite) Stalactites in the Drapery Room at Mammoth Cave National Park.

Fauna: The caves are also home to over 40 species of troglobites, or animals that have evolved to live their lives entirely in caverns. These include beetles, crayfish, and the blind fish *Amblyopsis spelaea.* Living in the pitch blackness of the lower reaches of the cave, these animals are pale and ghostly counterparts to their cousins who dwell on the surface. The cavefish, for example, has tiny, blind eyes. It negotiates its environment by means of a bristling network of tactile organs covering its body that allows it to feel its surroundings.

Among the animals that use the cave for shelter are a dozen species of bats, including the endangered gray and Indiana bats. In the mid-1800s, millions used the passageways of Mammoth Cave for hibernation and breeding. They number only a few thousand today, but conservation efforts are intense. Human activity in the cave and its popularity as a tourist attraction destroyed the bat habitat.

◆ HUMAN HISTORY AT MAMMOTH

Archeological digs in the cave have uncovered spear points made by Paleo-Indians 12,000 years ago. Other evidence suggests that later Archaic Indians ventured into Mammoth Cave as well, probably to collect gypsum and selenite, which they may have used medicinally.

White settlers discovered the cave in the late 1700s. The story (challenged by some historians) goes that a hunter pursuing a wounded bear chased the animal into the opening now known as the Historic Entrance. By 1798, claims were made on the property, and a land certificate was issued to Valentine Simmons for 200 acres and a pair of saltpeter caves. Simmons surveyed the land and sold it. It changed hands several times in the next two decades.

The owners in 1812 were Charles Wilkins of Lexington, and Hyman Gratz of Philadelphia, who mined over half a million pounds of saltpeter from the cave and sold it to E. I. Dupont de Nemours and Company. Dupont manufactured gunpowder from the Mammoth Cave saltpeter to supply the United States Army in the War of 1812 against the British. Records show that the Kentucky mineral accounted for about three-quarters of the army's munitions for the conflict, so the odds are that "the bombs bursting in air" over Fort McKinley, immortalized by Francis Scott Key, had their origin in soil dug from Mammoth Cave.

Mining stopped around 1815, but by that time the cave had become a popular tourist attraction. Franklin Gorin of Glasgow, Kentucky, purchased the cave and

200 acres around the entrance in the 1830s. He made improvements on an existing log hotel and built a road.

In 1839, Dr. John Croghan, a Louisville physician whose family had built Locust Grove, bought Mammoth Cave. Along with the property, Croghan acquired several of Gorin's slaves, including Stephen Bishop, who was the most celebrated guide to the cave.

Bishop is credited with exploring more miles of passageways than any other guide. Accounts by contemporary visitors mention him more often than any other guide: apparently he was charming and entertaining as well as knowledgeable.

Bishop was the first to cross an intimidating chasm known as the Bottomless Pit (it was too deep for the lanterns of the time to illuminate to its floor). He also explored as far as the lowest level of the system, where the Echo River continues to carve out the cave, and was the first to see some of the animals that are unique to the cave habitat, such as blind fish and crawfish.

Mammoth Cave, Kentucky, as drawn by an unknown artist in 1850.
(The Speed Art Museum, Louisville)

In addition to maintaining Mammoth Cave as a tourist attraction, Croghan made it the site of a rather curious medical experiment. In 1842, nine huts were built inside the cave to house tuberculosis patients, on the theory that the air, which remained at about 54 degrees year-round, would be conducive to a cure. Not surprisingly, no one was healed by this treatment. In fact, a few of the patients died. The huts were abandoned the following spring.

Ironically, Croghan himself died of tuberculosis in 1849. He had no children and he willed the cave to nieces and nephews. When the last of their descendants died in 1926, a movement was started by concerned citizens to acquire the cave and the surrounding land for a national park.

In July of 1941, after 48,000 acres had been acquired, Congress established Mammoth Cave as America's 26th national park. In 1981 it was declared a World Heritage Site by UNESCO, joining such others as Egypt's Pyramids at Giza and India's Taj Mahal. In 1990 it was designated an International Biosphere Reserve.

◆ TOURING THE CAVES

Basics: If you stop to visit the park, you'll want to go in a cave. Cave tours begin at the visitors center. Reservations are recommended. If you visit during the peak season in summer, it's essential to book a tour early. There are various modest fees, based on the length of the tour. *270-758-2328* or *800-967-2283*.

The vast system of underground rooms, tunnels, striking rock formations, and waterways with fanciful names—there's a River Styx—take more than one visit to truly appreciate. But there are several tours in which you can (often literally) get your feet wet. They range in difficulty from easy-on-the-feet to very strenuous, and they last from one-and-a-half to six hours. Outings for serious spelunkers, which wind through cramped passageways, require that participants wear kneepads and helmets and have a chest size of no more than 42 inches.

The park rates tours from "easy" to "very strenuous" and the guides are very serious about making sure that the people who sign up for the latter are in good physical shape. (Take the warnings to heart.) They also caution visitors about fears of heights and closed spaces. That said, there are tours designed for everyone—even the timid.

Travertine Tour

The quarter-mile, hour-and-15-minute Travertine Tour is an easy introduction to the wonders of Mammoth Cave. "Travertine" is the general name for calcium carbonate that has been deposited by water and has left distinctive formations like stalactites. The tour includes a visit to the cave's most famous formation, the Frozen Niagara. A vast curtain of stalactites that seems to have been poured from the high ceiling of the cave almost seems to move like fabric if you stare at it long enough.

And one of the most startling aspects of being underground becomes apparent when the guide stops talking and your fellow visitors stop shuffling and whispering. The utter silence makes your ears tingle. Close your eyes and rely on your sense of smell. You'll discover that stone has a distinctive odor.

Violet City Lantern Tour

The three-mile, three-hour Violet City Lantern Tour is among those rated "strenuous," but it could also be rated "fascinating." Illuminated by coal-oil lanterns, the route follows that taken by many of Mammoth Cave's early explorers. When the tour stops in a large room, the guides, just as their 19th-century predecessors did, lob kerosene flares onto high ledges to illuminate the chamber. Along the route you'll see prehistoric Indian artifacts, the remains of the mining operations, and the ruins of the misguided tuberculosis hospital huts. Some of the system's largest domed rooms and passageways with scalloped rock walls are included in this tour.

Tours for the Mobility-Impaired

This tour lasts a little over an hour and takes you through tube-shaped passages lined with intricate gypsum formations.

◆ ABOVE GROUND AT THE PARK

Hiking

The surface of the park is worth exploring, too. It is covered in woodlands and crisscrossed by 70 miles of scenic trails. Almost all the wildflowers (over 800 species) can be viewed throughout the spring, summer, and fall. The woodlands offer great opportunities for birders, too, with everything from tiny finches to herons that glide along the banks of the Green River.

CENTRAL KENTUCKY

Canoeing

If you are a keen observer of wildlife, hire a canoe and paddle along this clear, peaceful river. (It appears green from the reflected foliage of overhanging trees.) The river has a thriving population of freshwater mussels, and on bright days their shells glisten in the riverbed. To hire a canoe or kayak, try Green River Canoeing, 270-597-2031; Barren River Canoeing, 270-796-1979; or Mammoth Cave Canoe and Kayak, 270-773-3366.

Riverboat Trip

If you'd rather be a passenger than a paddler, take the hour-long tour on *Miss Green River*, a 63-foot riverboat. Deer and occasionally foxes can be spotted along the wooded shore. Wood ducks, with their distinctive bright coloring, are common on the water. Beavers make burrows in the banks. Frog and insect choruses fill the air from late March to late October. Be on the alert in the fall for the distinctive gobble of wild turkeys.

(above) A male northern bobwhite, and (opposite) a female northern cardinal among hawthorne berries.

■ BOWLING GREEN *map page 185, A-5*

The largest city in southern Kentucky, Bowling Green (pop. 41,000) is located off of I-65 about 25 miles southwest of Mammoth Cave. The rolling limestone-karst land is devoted to agriculture. From the road, you'll spot fields of tobacco, corn, and soybeans, as well as beef and dairy cattle grazing in green pastures. (I once saw a sign on a fence facing the highway that read "Used Cows for Sale" with a phone number. I was tempted to call and find out exactly what a used cow was, but in the end, I was afraid to find out.)

Bowling Green was founded in 1798 on two acres donated for a town by brothers Robert and George Moore, who had arrived from Virginia in 1794. There is some disagreement about how the city got its name. It may have been named after Bowling Green, Virginia. On the other hand, early records show the spelling to be Bolin Green and, sometimes, Bowlingreen. Robert Moore maintained a grassy "ball alley" near his house on which the locals played games of bowls.

The Barren River flows past the city. This was important to commercial growth in the 1820s and 1830s, when locks were built both on it and the Green River, opening the city to river commerce on the Ohio. When a dam broke near one of the locks in 1965, river traffic was no longer of economic importance, and the lock was not repaired.

As you drive southwest into the city along US-31W from the interstate, you'll see the CSX railroad yard, as well as a multitude of warehouses along the riverbank. The city center is relatively quiet. Many of the three-story, century-old buildings that surround the open green space known as Fountain Square are empty. Business and factory growth has stretched south of the city along US-231. Lined with shopping malls, motels, and chain restaurants, it's basically "Shopping Strip Anywhere, U.S.A."

The city's best-known resident was food writer Duncan Hines (1880-1959) who assigned his personal "seal of approval" to restaurants around the country in the 1930s and '40s. Restaurants here still proudly display the sign "Recommended by Duncan Hines." (Mr. Hines sold the rights to his name to Procter & Gamble in 1956, which uses it for a brand of cake mixes.)

Given Bowling Green's size and proximity to destinations in western Kentucky, it can make a good overnight stop or "center of operations" for touring the region. If you are a sports car buff, you'll want to drop by the National Corvette Museum across the street from the General Motors assembly plant.

National Corvette Museum

map page 185, A-5

The building—an asymmetrical, almost cone-shaped structure with a red spike—is rather odd-looking. But apparently, if you were to get a bird's-eye view, you'd see that it's roughly shaped like a silhouette of the car. Inside, you can watch a short film on the history of the car and walk along a series of dioramas that place different models in historical settings (parked in front of a 1950s barber shop, at the pump of a 1960s gas station, tooling along Route 66 in Arizona). There are also displays of every model of the car ever made, including one-of-a-kind and experimental models. The tour concludes in the 140-foot Skydome, where 16 different cars are on view. What you'll see depends on which vehicles in the collection have been chosen for the Skydome that month. *Take Exit 28 off I-65; 350 Corvette Dr.; 270-781-7973.*

Western Kentucky University

Bowling Green is also the home of Western Kentucky University, whose campus stands on several hills just south of the business district. Given the location, it's not too surprising that the department of cave studies is world-renowned. The journalism school has become prominent nationally in the past decade as well. The university's Hardin Planetarium features sky shows that change seasonally. And there's a small museum of Kentucky pioneer artifacts housed in a log cabin at the center of the campus. *College and 15th Sts.; 270-745-0111.*

Capitol Arts Center

Bowling Green's cultural life is headquartered downtown at the Capitol Arts Center, a restored art deco movie theater dating from 1939. Seating 840 patrons, it's a busy venue for concerts and plays. It also houses an art gallery. *1416 E. Main St.; 270-782-2/87.*

The National Corvette Museum.

■ LAKES AND FISHING

The Cumberland Parkway traverses the south-central portion of Kentucky, from west to east, starting at I-65 just south of Mammoth Cave and continuing for 90 miles east to Somerset, near the edge of the Daniel Boone National Forest.

The parkway (a toll road) is the main route into some of the state's loveliest lakes and rivers. Though all the lakes were formed behind dammed rivers, their shorelines are varied and scenic, ranging from sandy to wooded. Lots of people rent houseboats or pontoon boats for touring the lakes. Anglers are attracted to populations of large- and smallmouth bass, crappie, bluegill, rainbow trout, and walleyed pike.

The eastern half of the region is known as "the Barrens," since when the early European explorers first arrived the rolling countryside was relatively unwooded. Most of the water in the region was underground, so the fertility of the land that later made agriculture profitable wasn't at first apparent.

On the other hand, hints of the potential bounty were given by the native flora. Writing in 1802, French explorer and naturalist F. A. Michaux described the Barrens in the early days of settlement:

> *I* was agreeably surprised to meet with a beautiful meadow, the abundant grass of which was from two to three feet high, and afforded excellent food for cattle; amongst it I saw a great variety of plants, but particularly gall of the earth [and] white plantain—I, however, collected and sent to France upwards of ninety species.

Travelers today will see grazing cattle, tobacco, and cornfields, with a backdrop of low, green hills.

◆ BARREN RIVER LAKE   *map page 185, A/B-5/6*

It's a short 10 miles or so south of US-31E from the Cumberland Parkway Exit 11, near Glasgow, to Barren River Lake. The state resort park surrounding the lake has excellent facilities for fishermen, including boat rentals, bait and tackle shops, and a fish-cleaning station.

Within the lake, you'll see lots of submerged stump fields (a result of the flooding of bottomlands when the river was impounded) and submerged creek beds. These provide habitat for large channel catfish and several species of bass.

Sailboats, motorboats, pontoon boats, and houseboats share the lake. The 140-mile shoreline is mostly lined with trees coming right up to the water's edge, but there's a narrow sandy beach near the park lodge.

◆ **DALE HOLLOW STATE RESORT PARK**   *map page 185, C/D-6*

It's a longer trip (a little over 50 miles) from Glasgow (Cumberland Parkway Exit 14) to Dale Hollow State Resort Park. As you wind southeast along KY-90 toward Dale Hollow, you'll pass through quaintly named tiny Kentucky towns: Eighty Eight, Summer Shade, and Marrowbone. Take KY-449 south, then KY-1206 even farther south, and you're there.

The lake straddles the Tennessee border. The water at Dale Hollow is wonderfully clear, and swimming off the side of a houseboat is a favorite pastime. There are innumerable little inlets around the 653-mile shoreline of the lake, so if you hire a houseboat you can find a private cove to call your own for the duration of your visit. Keep an eye open for the blue herons and, from November to March, bald eagles.

Fishermen may embrace the challenge of trying to best the catch of the world-record smallmouth bass (11 pounds, 15 ounces), which was landed way back in July, 1955. A record 43-pound silver muskie was hooked in 1978.

There are numerous hiking trails along the heavily wooded lakeshore.

◆ **GREEN RIVER LAKE STATE PARK**   *map page 185, D-4*

If you like to fish, to use your own boat, and camp near shore, the campground here is right by the lake, though the spaces are rather tightly packed.

At Green River Lake you'll find two sandy beaches: one for swimmers, the other part of the lakeside campground. *Take Cumberland Parkway Exit 49 at Columbia and go north about 10 miles to Green River Lake State Park.*

◆ **LAKE CUMBERLAND STATE RESORT PARK**   *map page 185, D-5/6*

The largest of the four lakes in the region is Lake Cumberland, set in its eponymous resort park. The park's rugged, wooded shorelines with steep bluffs and rocky outcroppings are little changed since explorer Dr. Thomas Walker and his party came through here in 1750.

CENTRAL KENTUCKY

Partly because of its size and depth (up to 90 feet), there are a dozen species of sport fish living here, including walleyed pike, crappie, white bass, striped bass, and rainbow trout. Among the lake whoppers was a 58-pound rockfish. (If you are interested in sport fish, visit the **National Fish Hatchery** near the Wolf Creek Dam, three miles south of the park entrance on KY-127.)

Park Basics: You can spend the night in campgrounds, at the lodge, or on a houseboat. For information call 270-343-3111.

Directions: There are many points of entry to the park. *From the Cumberland Parkway take Exit 62 at Russell Springs and go south five miles to Jamestown.*

(above) Burning bushes at Bernheim Forest in Clermont.

(opposite) The state dock at Lake Cumberland State Resort Park in Jamestown.

WESTERN KENTUCKY

■ HIGHLIGHTS   *page*

Food & Lodging *page 264*
Also see map page 231, towns in yellow.

■ TRAVEL BASICS

Area Overview: The Ohio River forms the northern boundary of this region. Bluffs rise above the water, and the shoreline is fairly rugged here as the river heads toward the Mississippi. The cities of Henderson and Paducah are fairly compact and take up little land along the shoreline. South of the river is a vast area of coalfields, much of the landscape strip-mined. Some of the surface has been replanted, but many of the little towns along the state roads, whose economies were closely tied to the now mostly closed mines, are shadows of their former selves. This is not a region of the state well-suited for meandering along country roads in pursuit of scenery.

Far western Kentucky is as flat as eastern Kentucky is mountainous. Broad, cultivated fields line either side of the highway. Trees crop up along fence rows. Known as the Jackson Purchase, this far western segment of the state is still a remote region. When you get onto two-lane roads here, you'll encounter farm vehicles (tractors and livestock trailers) and cars hauling boats to Reelfoot Lake or the wildlife management areas along the Mississippi River.

Land Between the Lakes is one of Kentucky's loveliest natural areas and a prime spot for hiking, fishing, and camping. While driving through the region you'll enjoy views of cypress swamps and of the Ohio River.

Weather: Summer and winter temperatures go to the same extremes as those in the rest of the state: from the teens and 20s in the winter to the 80s and 90s in the summer. In spring it can rain for two or three days at a time, so do keep an umbrella

(opposite) Sunset at Smith's Bay, part of Land Between the Lakes National Recreation Area.

handy. Rain is infrequent in August and September, usually falling no more than a day a week, sometimes less. From April to August tornadoes are a real possibility, so heed warnings on the radio. In winter, fast-moving weather fronts, including ice and snow, blow in from the Midwest.

Driving: The northern section of western Kentucky is well-served with Kentucky parkways—four-lane divided highways. Easy access to the south is via the Wendell H. Ford Parkway, which will take you to the northern tip of Land Between the Lakes. (If you are hauling a large boat to the recreation area, this is the route to take.) In winter, roads may not get salt trucks and snow removal crews quickly.

Food & Lodging: Many counties in this part of the state are dry, and the dampening effect this has on any restaurant scene, plus the relatively sparse population, means that often the only food a traveler can find is that offered at fast-food outlets around highway exits. Paducah, though, does have some nice restaurants.Refer to the **Food & Lodging map** page 265; toll-free numbers for chains on page 266. Towns are listed in alphabetical order beginning on page 267. For charts see page 311.

■ INTRODUCTION TO WESTERN KENTUCKY

From the low wooded hills of the Ohio River in the north, past the wooded ridges and cliffs of the Western Coalfield, the land spreads out into a flat Midwestern horizon. The coalfields themselves are denuded and economically depressed. In the far west, even though the landscape is beginning to look flat and Midwestern, the people have a twang in their speech that places them firmly in Kentucky. Outside of the towns, most people who live here are farmers, and virtually everyone hunts squirrel, duck, and deer. Near the Mississippi River, the landscape becomes swampy lowlands.

■ OWENSBORO   *map opposite, E-1*

Even though Owensboro fans out east, south, and west from a horseshoe-shaped bend in the Ohio River, the city site was chosen by an explorer who reached it from land rather than by river. In 1798, William Smeathers followed a buffalo trace to a watering site on the shore. He built a cabin nearby that became a trading post for travelers on the Ohio. The settlement was originally called Yellow Banks for the color of the mud along the shoreline, but when the town was laid out in 1816, the state legislature named it Owensboro in honor of Col. Abraham Owen, who was killed in the Battle of Tippecanoe.

The city grew in the 19th century as a river port, a shipping and receiving point for both goods and people. Tobacco, coal, and bourbon all have been traded in Owensboro, though all the bourbon distilleries here have now closed. Josiah Henson, who came to the city via riverboat as a slave in 1825, escaped to Indiana in 1830. (He was supposedly the model for Harriet Beecher Stowe's "Uncle Tom.") After he escaped from Kentucky he traveled to Canada, where he became a well-known abolitionist.

Owensboro Business District

Owensboro's original business district, only a few blocks square, is relatively quiet in the middle of a workday. An exception is the activity at the silos of Owensboro Grain Co. overlooking the riverbank just to the east of the only bridge crossing the Ohio into the city. Most companies are located in the industrial park at the southern tip of the city. To the west of the bridge is the **RiverPark Center,** home to the local symphony and host to Broadway musicals and bluegrass concerts; *101 Davies St.; 270-926-7891.*

WESTERN KENTUCKY

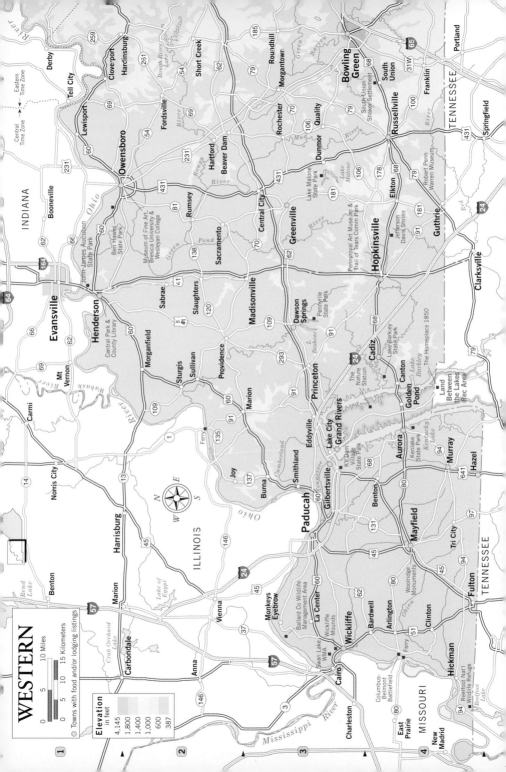

Also in the complex is the **International Bluegrass Music Museum,** which includes a Bill Monroe Gallery. Monroe, the acknowledged founder of bluegrass, was born south of Owensboro in Ohio County in 1911.

Second Street

The century-old, four- and five-story brick buildings on Second Street have been renovated as homes for antique shops and other businesses. But these are a relatively small part of Owensboro's commerce. Indus-trial and commercial growth are taking place at the southern end of the city.

Owensboro Barbecue

The city's big event is the **International Bar-B-Q Festival.** Held outdoors near the River-Park Center every May, it draws thousands of visitors who chow down on 20 tons of pork, beef, chicken, and mutton. The entire riverfront smells of smoking, roasting meat.

Owensboro's **Moonlite Bar-B-Q Inn** is known all over the state for western Kentucky –style barbecued mutton and burgoo *(2840 W. Parrish Ave. (also see page 303).* Burgoo is a thick meat stew made with lamb and other meat. Traditionally, western Kentucky burgoo contained squirrel, but faint-hearted health-department officials don't allow restaurants to use that particular ingredient these days.

(above) This mural, painted on a building next to the RiverPark Center, proclaims Owensboro the "Barbecue Capital of the World."

(opposite) A bass fiddle on display at the International Bluegrass Music Museum.

After manufacturers donated new
instruments to the rest of the Red
River Valley Boys on stage at IBMA
FanFest '91, attendees pooled their
money to purchase a new upright bass
for Victor Zadrozney. Unable to carry
two instruments of this size home,
Zadrozney deposited his old bass in
the museum's permanent collection.

Residential Neighborhoods

Tree-lined residential neighborhoods fan out from the small downtown, and it's in these that the character of the community lies. Owensboro may be the state's third-largest city with a population of about 54,000, but realistically it's Kentucky's largest small town. Sit in a restaurant or park and you'll hear residents constantly greeting one another by name. Small children under the supervision of day-care workers walk along sidewalks without being "roped together." More often than not, their adult caretaker will be leading them in a song.

The place feels very suburban mid-America, since 80 percent of the houses were built after World War II (though with little "urb" to which to be "sub"). It's the sort of place that you might want to live if raising a family were your number-one goal. The main north-south artery through Owensboro is Frederica ["FRED-ruh-ka"] Street.

Owensboro Museum of Fine Art

Housed in a Civil War–era mansion, this museum's permanent collection features paintings by American and European artists of the 18th, 19th, and 20th centuries. While there are no really famous paintings here, the combination of the high-ceilinged antebellum house and the artwork feels like a cultural oasis, where residents of the small city can be reminded of the wider world. *901 Frederica St.; 270-685-3181.*

Brescia University

The Ursuline Sisters of Mt. St. Joseph founded Brescia in 1950. The modern architecture of the buildings—many built of glass and yellow brick—gives the small campus an urban feel. *Seventh and Frederica Sts.; 270-685-3131.*

Kentucky Wesleyan College

Wesleyan's redbrick and white-columned Colonial-style buildings are spread out on a green, park-like campus that's a welcome respite from the development along the southern part of Frederica Street. The Methodists founded the college in 1858. *3000 Frederica St.; 270-926-3111.*

The Sassafras Tree

The landmark not to be missed is the sassafras tree on the grounds of the E. M. Ford & Company insurance firm at Frederica and 21st. Not your ordinary woody specimen, it's thought to be the state's oldest living tree (estimated at nearly 300 years old), as well as the largest of its species (150 feet tall) in the nation, according to an American Forestry Association statement on a nearby marker. The tree's girth is even more impressive: with a circumference of 19 feet, it's a sumo wrestler of a sassafras tree. The sassafras is especially striking in the fall, when its leaves turn gold, red, and russet. When Frederica Street was widened in 1957, the tree was going to be cut down, but an appeal was made to then-governor, A. B. "Happy" Chandler, who saved the sassafras by executive decree.

■ HENDERSON   *map page 231, D-1*

The charming river town of Henderson is perched on a bluff 70 feet above the waterline of the Ohio, about 25 minutes west of Owensboro via the Audubon Parkway. The city is more compact than neighboring Owensboro, being about half the size, with a population of about 26,000.

Founded in 1797, Henderson has retained its historic character. The downtown, with wide streets and stone-and-brick storefronts, has remained the commercial center. Located in the heart of the district is **Central Park** (between Main and Elm Streets), a gracious half-block greensward of large old oak and maple trees. It was part of the original town plan and is the oldest city park west of the Appalachians.

Standing at the Washington and Main corner of the park is the **Henderson County Library,** one of the famous Carnegie libraries. Its white stone facade gleams over the park like a beacon, the entrance supported by four tall Ionic columns.

The central residential area of Henderson consists of block after block of large, elegant 19th-century homes, with wide porches, gabled roofs, tall windows, and tidy gardens. If you stroll along the sidewalks on a summer evening, residents wave from their front porches, where they are seated on hanging bench swings or white wicker furniture.

Every June the small-town peace and quiet is broken by one heck of a party. Henderson boogies during the **W. C. Handy Blues and Barbecue Festival,** a week of concerts and picnics in venues all over town. Information: *270-826-3128.*

Known as the "Father of the Blues," composer/songwriter Handy lived in Henderson in the 1890s, when he was employed as a cornet player in the local Hampton Cornet Band. In his autobiography, Handy wrote about the influence of the city's African-American population on his music: "I didn't write any songs in Henderson, but it was there I learned to appreciate the music of my people. The blues were born because from that day on, I started thinking about putting my own experience down in that particular kind of music."

Henderson's other famous resident strolled the streets (and surrounding woodlands) from 1810 to 1818. Artist and naturalist John James Audubon came to Henderson from Louisville at the urging of his business partner. The two ran a general store that supplied goods and equipment to trappers and traders. The business operated out of the front of a log cabin. Audubon and his young family lived in the back.

WESTERN KENTUCKY

A red-tailed hawk.

Audubon loved being in Henderson because of the town's location on the busy Mississippi flyway, a major bird migration route. In springtime it's possible to see over 170 species of birds passing through the area. Audubon, whose unparalleled portfolios of American wildlife, including *The Birds of America* and *Viviparous Quadrupeds of North America,* gained him an international reputation, was not a successful businessman. For the first few years, the store was prosperous, but eventually Audubon and his family were forced to leave Henderson when an economic depression resulted in his bankruptcy.

◆ **JOHN JAMES AUDUBON STATE PARK**   *map page 231, D-1*

Audubon's association with Henderson and the state of Kentucky is commemorated year-round with a museum and nature center at John James Audubon State Park. The 692-acre park includes a lake and nature preserve and is crisscrossed by hiking trails. More than 20 warbler species arrive here in late March and early April. (It's not easy to tell one kind of these tiny brown-gray birds from another. They have such identifying characteristics as "small yellow streak over the eye.")

The centerpiece of the park is the **museum**—a replica of a Norman chateau that's constructed of buff-colored stone and blue slate, complete with a cobblestone courtyard and corner tower crowned with a conical roof. It was built in 1938 as a WPA project.

The museum features galleries that tell the naturalist's life story with quite realistic dioramas, and an outstanding collection of his drawings and paintings. If you are familiar with Audubon only through reproduction prints, you'll come to appreciate the exhaustive care he took in studying his subjects when you see the watercolors and oils of birds and mammals "in the flesh." Details of each feather and hair were captured by Audubon's brush.

The Observation Room in the **Nature Center** next door to the museum is a large, circular space with huge windows looking out into the woods. Pictures and descriptions of birds you'll probably spot are set on panels just beneath the tall glass panes. This is a great way to be introduced to birding, if you don't already happen to be hooked.

The park is off US-41, four miles north of downtown Henderson; 270-827-1893.

John J. Audubon's paintings of these birds can be seen in the museum at Audubon State Park. Both the blue-eyed yellow warbler (above) and the cardinal grosbeak (at right) are native Kentucky species. (images courtesy John J. Audubon State Park.)

■ WESTERN COALFIELD

Kentucky's Western Coalfield takes in nine entire counties and small portions of eight others. It's a roughly circular region of 4,200 square miles with its northern boundary defined by the Ohio River. The high-sulfur coal here has been a major economic factor in this region, the landscape of which changes from low, rolling hills in the east to plains farther westward along the river.

While there were underground coal mines built here, most coal seams were opened by stripping the surface off the land with enormous shovels resembling iron dinosaurs. These are still in use, and sometimes you may get a glimpse of the top of one peeking over one of the rises along the highways near Greenville. The combined activities of coal mining and timber harvesting in the first half of the 20th century ravaged the region. Thus the lyrics to John Prine's song "Paradise" in which a child asks his father to take him back to Muhlenberg County and hears in reply that Mr. Peabody's coal train has hauled it away.

Coal, coal, and more coal in Gilbertsville.

KENTUCKY BURGOO

"Who, excepting Kentuckians and their favored Southern friends and kinsmen, has ever really known the bliss of genuine burgoo?" asked a writer for the *Washington Post* in June, 1906. You might also ask just what "burgoo" *means*. The short answer is a meaty stew simmered with vegetables until it has the consistency of a thick gravy. The origin of the word is obscure, but it's believed to be a variant of "bulgur" (the wheat used in tabbouleh) erroneously used to mean "oatmeal." Food historian John Mariani writes in his *Dictionary of American Food and Drink* that by the mid-19th century, "burgoo" became the name for a Southern barbecue dish "made of hunters' contributions to a vast stew." Pretty much any game found in Kentucky—deer, rabbit, squirrel—was fare for the burgoo pot; native vegetables grown in the fields—corn, green beans, tomatoes—were added to the mix, too.

And because it could be made in huge quantities, this stew dish suited the South's tradition of generous hospitality. In 1895, Lexington chef Gus Jaubert cooked up a 6,000-gallon batch of burgoo for the Grand Army of the Republic. In the 1940s and '50s, fellow Lexingtonian James T. Looney (Kentucky's self-styled Burgoo King) regularly served gatherings of 10,000 people. He owned a 700-gallon, a 500-gallon and three "small" 75-gallon iron kettles for cooking his "heavenly stew from Dixie's dew."

You can try your own hand with the Moonlite Bar-B-Q Inn recipe below. Its relatively meager three-gallon yield will feed a group for dinner and leave enough for you to freeze for later, impromptu gatherings. You don't need to be a slave to the recipe, either; the *Moonlite Bar-B-Q Inn's Collection of Recipes* notes, "Some area cooks add dried or lima beans, tomatoes, and a little boiled shredded beef or wild game."

❀ MOONLITE'S BURGOO ❀

4 lbs. mutton	juice of 1 lemon
1 - 3 lbs. chicken	3/4 cup distilled vinegar
3/4 lb. cabbage, ground or chopped fine	1/2 cup Worcestershire sauce
3/4 lb. onion, ground or chopped fine	2 1/2 T. of salt, or more to taste
5 lbs. potatoes, peeled and diced	2 T. black pepper
2 cups fresh corn	1 t. cayenne pepper (more if you like)
3/4 cup tomato catsup	water
3 10 3/4-oz. cans of tomato puree	

Boil mutton in enough water to cover. Cook until tender, about 2-3 hours. Throw out broth and bones. Chop meat fine. Set aside. In a large kettle, boil chicken in 2 gallons of water until tender. Remove chicken; add potatoes, cabbage, onion, corn, catsup, and 1 gallon of water to chicken broth and bring to a boil. Meanwhile, chop chicken meat, discarding bones and skin. When potatoes are tender, add chicken pieces, mutton, lemon, salt, both peppers, Worcestershire sauce, vinegar, and tomato puree and simmer for 2 hours or longer, stirring occasionally as it thickens. Yield: 3 gallons.

There is a town called Paradise, though it was largely destroyed in the 1960s to make way for the largest coal-burning electric power plant in the state, operated by the Tennessee Valley Authority. At one time more coal was mined in Muhlenberg County than in any other part of the United States. Today only a few mines are open, and they employ less than a thousand workers. Most of the coal goes to the Paradise power plant.

Agriculture is an important part of the economy. Cleared forests made way for factory farms where millions of chickens, pigs, beef, and dairy cattle are raised. As is the case elsewhere in the state, many fields are planted in tobacco, corn, and soybeans.

Bluegrass music and barbecue are the region's main cultural assets. Merle Travis was born in Muhlenberg County, as were the Everly Brothers, Don and Phil. In addition to penning the song "Sixteen Tons" about the coal-mining industry, made famous by singer Tennessee Ernie Ford, Travis is credited with two musical innovations. He invented a style of guitar playing known as "thumb-picking" or "Travis picking," which involves using the thumb to maintain the bass line under the melody, and he designed the first solid-body, flat-topped guitar, the Fender. The Everly Brothers were the first country-singing duo to cross music genres and have a hit song that topped the pop charts, 1957's "Bye-Bye Love."

◆ PASSING THROUGH

A lot of people wind up driving through this part of Kentucky rather than stopping in it. Towns such as Greenville (seat of Muhlenberg County) and Madisonville (seat of Hopkins County) had their boom days during the height of coal operations and tobacco production. With both industries in decline, the once-bustling towns are relics, with little to interest visitors—though tenacious **antique buyers** may ferret a few gems in stores found in the small, 19th-century business districts of both towns. And there is the annual **Washer Pitching Contest** in Greenville the weekend after Labor Day, when hundreds of competitors assemble at the Masonic Lodge to toss metal washers 30 feet into a three-inch-wide hole. (There's a trophy and a cash prize for the winner.)

The human population of the Western Coalfield numbers around 320,000, about a third of which is concentrated in the cities of Owensboro and Henderson, both located on the Ohio River.

BLUEGRASS MUSIC

◆ FIRST, THE INSTRUMENTS...

Flatten the tortoiseshell back on that old mandolin for a more pungent sound. Put a fifth drone string on the West African banjo for a more rhythmic drive. Get the gut strings off that Spanish guitar and replace them with steel ones for more zing. Line up a fiddle, an acoustic bass, and if you are so inclined, one of those reworked Hawaiian lap steel guitars made by the Dobro Brothers. You're ready.

◆ NEXT, THE MUSICAL TRADITION...

Into your pot, throw in lots of Scots–Irish fiddle melodies, white Protestant church hymns and harmonies (make sure one is a sharp-and-high tenor line), some blues, and some raw folk songs about lost loves, leaving home, murders, railroads, and disasters of all kinds. Now stir all this for a century or more and see if any musical geniuses show up.

◆ THEN, THE GENIUSES...

Show up they did... around 1946. Their band was called "The Bluegrass Boys" in honor of Kentucky, home state of their leader Bill Monroe. Earl Scruggs was on the banjo. Listen and you'll hear him creating the sound we now associate with the instrument. The licks and bass runs of Lester Flatt still define what we expect to hear from a rhythm guitar. Chubby Wise's fiddle playing is brilliant. But the band's leader, Bill Monroe, towers above them all. A visionary with an original approach to the mandolin and a sharp tenor voice, he heard and shaped the Bluegrass sound to unrelenting clarity. Listen to some of his creations such as "Blue Moon of Kentucky," "Muleskinner Blues," or "Footprints in the Snow," and you'll hear a made-in-America music as unique as the blues or jazz.

—Richard Duane, of the "I'll Be Right Home Honey" Bluegrass band

Bill Monroe and the Bluegrass Boys, 1983. (Courtesy Ohio County Park, Hartford, KY)

■ WESTERN PENNYROYAL

The western Pennyroyal region curves south of the coalfields and west of Bowling Green *(see map page 25)*. Long ago, great herds of buffalo formed a trace here during their seasonal migrations between the Gulf of Mexico and the Great Lakes. Meriwether Lewis, who traveled in the area while governor of the Upper Louisiana Territory, noted that he and his company were so engrossed by the rugged beauty of the land that they relaxed their vigilance in looking out for Shawnee and Wyandot Indians.

Along US-68 west out of Bowling Green, the landscape levels out dramatically, and while it's Kentucky-green, it's Kansas-flat.

◆ SOUTH UNION SHAKER SETTLEMENT   *map page 231, F-4*

In 1809 a community of deeply religious people committed to a life of simplicity—Shakers—built a village at South Union on 6,000 acres. The settlement eventually had 200 buildings. The largest to survive is the handsome redbrick, 40-room Centre House built in 1824. It houses a Shaker Museum devoted to furniture and crafts, including weavings, baskets, and silver. The museum also features a journal kept by one of the eldresses of the community. She gave a detailed account of the feeding and accommodating of Civil War troops, both Union and Confederate. For years this was the only village for miles in an endless vista of corn and soybean fields that fanned out in all directions. *US-68, South Union; 270-542-4167 or 800-811-8379.*

Unique among the 24 Shaker villages around the United States is a commercial venture the South Unionists embarked upon in 1869. When the railroad came through the town, they built a hotel for "people of the world" in order to increase the income of the community. In contrast to the simple elegance of Shaker style, the hotel is high Victorian. It has been restored and under the name, the Shaker Tavern, operates as a bed and breakfast. *Hwy-73, one-and-a-half miles from the museum; 270-542-6801.*

◆ RUSSELLVILLE   *map page 231, E/F-4*

The Logan County seat of Russellville was founded in 1798. Its economy revolves around the tobacco market. (The flat, fertile soil of this part of western Kentucky makes this an important burley-growing region.) A notable town landmark is the Old Southern Deposit Bank at the corner of Third and Main Streets. Built in 1810 and now a private home, the bank was the site in 1868 of Jesse James's gang's first robbery. They got away with the not inconsiderable sum of $9,000.

WESTERN
KENTUCKY

◆ **ROBERT PENN WARREN MUSEUM**   *map page 231, E-4*

The tiny town of Guthrie, just north of the Tennessee border, was the birthplace in 1905 of three-time Pulitzer Prize winner, Robert Penn Warren. The Warren family house at Third and Cherry Streets is now the Robert Penn Warren Birthplace Museum, devoted to exhibits about the first U.S. poet laureate's life and work. Warren's most famous novel, *All the King's Men,* was based on the story of notorious Louisiana governor Huey Long. *270-483-2683.*

◆ **JEFFERSON DAVIS SHRINE**   *map page 231, E-3*

To get here from Guthrie, head back to US-68 going northwest on State Road-181. Rejoin 68 at Elkton and go west. The land becomes densely wooded. After some 10 miles rises a dramatic 351-foot concrete obelisk from a clearing to the left. You've arrived at the Jefferson Davis Monument State Shrine.

Davis, the first and only president of the Confederate States of America, was born in nearby Fairview in 1808. His family moved to Louisiana when he was an infant. He returned to Kentucky to attend Lexington's Transylvania University before going on to the U.S. Military Academy at West Point. Davis's political career included two terms as United States senator from Mississippi and, as a war hero in the Mexican War, a term as Secretary of War under U.S. President Franklin Pierce.

The shrine, which was not built with public money, hasn't stirred controversy as a monument to the Confederacy, as did displays of Confederate flags in some Southern states. Perhaps it's because the location is out-of-the-way. It's basically a picnic stop and a place to view the surrounding countryside. (You can ride an elevator to the top of the obelisk.)

Jefferson Davis, first and only president of the Confederacy, was born in Fairview, Kentucky. (Library of Congress)

WESTERN KENTUCKY

Driving west towards Hopkinsville, you enter a farming area owned by Amish and Mennonite families, many of whom relocated to Kentucky from Pennsylvania, Indiana, or Ohio.

◆ **HOPKINSVILLE**   *map page 231, D-4*

Christian County's seat, Hopkinsville (pop. 30,000) is a serene city 10 miles west of the Jefferson Davis Shrine. Its economy has become closely tied to the presence of Fort Campbell, 101st Air Assault Division of the U.S. Army, which is located on a large base about 13 miles south of the town and straddles the Tennessee border. Hoptown, as it's called by residents, is the location of the **Pennyroyal Area Museum**. This is a good place to stop to learn about Jefferson Davis and Robert Penn Warren if you didn't have time to visit their sites. There's also an exhibit devoted to alleged clairvoyant Edgar Cayce, who was born in Hopkinsville in 1877. History displays include an account of the infamous Trail of Tears of 1838 and 1839 in which some 15,000 Cherokee Indians were forcibly marched from their tribal lands in Georgia to reservations in Oklahoma. More than 4,000 died along the way. *217 E. Ninth St.; 270-887-4270.*

One of the stops along the route was on the southern edge of Hopkinsville, an area that has been designated the **Trail of Tears Commemorative Park.** The 12.5-acre park is one of the few documented campsites along the trail. On the grounds are a log cabin that serves as a visitors center and statues of two Cherokee chiefs, Whitepath and Fly Smith, who died and were buried here. Every September the national Trail of Tears Commission sponsors an intertribal powwow in the park. *US-41S; 270-886-8033.*

■ **LAND BETWEEN THE LAKES**   *map page 231, C/D-3/4*

Wildlife preserve, living history project, and recreational paradise, the huge inland peninsula known as the Land Between the Lakes (called LBL for short) is a successful combination of human engineering and nature.

In 1944, in order to generate hydroelectric power, the Tennessee Valley Authority impounded the Tennessee River, creating 160,000 acres of water surface and 2,380 miles of meandering shoreline that made **Kentucky Lake.** In 1965 the Army Corps of Engineers dammed the Cumberland River, and thus was born Lake Barkley, something of a little-brother body of water with a "mere" 58,000 aquatic acres.

If you are driving in from the east, a two-lane bridge spanning **Lake Barkley** takes you a couple of miles across water that seems to stretch out forever on either side. Sailboats with multicolored sails outnumber powerboats on the blue surface. Nonetheless, both lakes are famous among regional bass and crappie fishermen for the quality and quantity of their piscine populations.

When you finally make it to the far shore, you are in a heavily wooded finger of land that offers wildlife enthusiasts, especially birders, some fascinating opportunities.

◆ **WILDLIFE**

Land Between the Lakes has a thriving colony of nesting bald eagles. Since these birds favor the bare tops of dying trees, they are relatively easy to observe in spring. But they are only one out of some 250 species of birds that can been seen in the preserve. The ornithological runner-up for America's national symbol, the wild turkey, is abundant here, too. Other animals living in the dense oak and hickory woodlands include white-tailed and European fallow deer, coyotes, bobcats, otters, red-tailed fox, skunks, and raccoons.

Male wild turkey in courtship display.

◆ **GOLDEN POND**

In the middle of the peninsula is the wide spot in the road and former town of Golden Pond, which was infamous during Prohibition as a source of high-quality moonshine. The whiskey was peddled as far away as the speakeasies of St. Louis, Chicago, and Detroit. Today Golden Pond is the administrative headquarters of LBL, which is run by the National Forest Service. A visitors center contains a theater featuring a very informative multimedia show about the ecology of the area and a planetarium that orients you to the seasonal features of the night sky. Golden Pond should be your first stop because you get maps and information about the rest of the LBL features.

◆ **HIKING TRAILS**

Over 200 miles of hiking trails wind their way through the woods between the lakes. There are several campgrounds, too. You can be an RV driver or a bare-basics

(above) Young red fox kits play at the entrance of their den.

(opposite) Male bluebird at nest cavity.

backpacker. The long trails are multiuse, so look out for mountain bikes and horses. Day hiking trails for foot travel only surround **The Nature Station,** an educational facility devoted to teaching visitors about native wildlife and how to interact with the natural world.

For a short, easy walk, try the **Long Creek Trail,** a paved, barrier-free loop along a creek. **Woodland Walk** is slightly more difficult—a one-mile loop on an interpretive trail with lots of opportunities to spot wildlife. **Honker Trail** is also fairly easy, but it is 4.5 miles long, circling Honker Lake, where Canada geese can often be seen.

For a fairly easy hike that can be accomplished in just an hour and a half (or can take all day, if you're in a leisurely mood), try the **Hematite Lake Trail.** This is a 2.4-mile loop around Hematite Lake, and the wildlife on display is exceptional. The trailhead is at the far end of the lake picnic area, near the dam spillway. The lake is up the trail a bit and covered with lotus (a type of water lily), ducks, and Canada geese. There are several wooden bridges crossing creeks along the trail, and a boardwalk leading through bottomland hardwoods and marshy backwater (filled with wildflowers and river cane). Be on the lookout at about mile .55 (after the observation platform and bench but before the boardwalk); there's a beaver lodge below the trail.

◆ ELK AND BISON PRAIRIE

Kentucky history is given a nod at two notable sites within the peninsula. The 750-acre Elk and Bison Prairie is a place where you can watch the big, shaggy animals grazing on native grasses. (These are the plants that the famous bluegrass replaced.) At **The Homeplace 1850,** guides in homespun period clothes populate a mid-19th-century family farm. They will stop and talk to you about their activities, but always seem engaged in their chores, from gardening to tending sheep and chickens. If you really have a wanderlust, hire a houseboat on one of the lakes and putter around for a few days exploring the seemingly countless inlets that make up the shorelines. *Visitor information can be found at 100 Van Morgan Dr., Golden Pond; 270-924-2000 or 800-525-7077.*

■ JACKSON PURCHASE

When Kentucky became a state in 1792, its western boundary stopped at the Tennessee River. The natural barriers of the Ohio River to the north and the Appalachian Mountains to the east formed two other boundaries. Decades of activity by surveying parties cobbled together the southern boundary with Tennessee.

Today's westernmost tip of the state, known as the Jackson Purchase or simply the Purchase, was added in 1818. Isaac Shelby, who had been Kentucky's first governor, and Andrew Jackson, a Tennessean who was to become the seventh President of the United States, negotiated a sale of land with the Chickasaw. The tribe received $300,000. Kentucky and Tennessee added about 2,000 and 6,000 square miles, respectively.

The Kentucky region covers eight counties whose topography is dramatically different from that found in the rest of the state. Gently rolling farmland gives way to flat, swampy wetlands as you go west. The bottomlands make up much of the landscape, a large part of which was also profoundly reconfigured by the massive earthquakes of 1811–12. While the tree cover of the rest of Kentucky is characterized by oak, hickory, and maple, here the dominant trees are the swamp-dwelling water tupelo and bald cypress. Until land was drained for farming, virtually any flat surface (most of the region) was covered with water.

The Purchase is bounded on the east by the Tennessee River, on the north by the Ohio, and on the west by the Mississippi. There's an odd "island" of land called the New Madrid Bend that is part of westernmost Fulton County. It can be reached only by dipping south through Tennessee, then driving back north into the bend.

Most of the Purchase is agricultural. The fertile drained bottomlands are planted in wheat, corn, and soybeans. Some manufacturing takes place in the two urban centers, Paducah, in the northern part of the region on the Ohio, and Mayfield, near the geographic center of the region. There's also enough clay beneath the topsoil that clay mining is an important part of the economy. Murray, in the southeast corner, is the educational center of the region, home to Murray State University.

Visitors come to the region to look for antiques, and to photograph or hunt waterbirds in the wildlife management areas along the rivers. One can also view remnants of the earliest human inhabitants of the area, the prehistoric people who built the mounds being excavated near Wickliffe.

WESTERN KENTUCKY

◆ **MURRAY**   *map page 231, C-4*

This college town is the seat of dry Calloway County, and the food scene here tends toward pancake houses and sandwich shops.

You may want to use a motel in Murray as a base of operations for your antique and collectibles hunting in nearby Hazel.

◆ **HAZEL**   *map page 231, C-4*

Nine miles (less than a 15-minute drive) from Murray down US-641—barely north of the Tennessee border—this hamlet of 500 is an antique shopper's candy store. Almost every storefront on Main Street (US-641 in town) is a specialty antique shop.

Though you won't find any fine European or Early American treasures here, there are lots of very good country oak pieces, including tables, beds, and ladder-back chairs. Pie safes abound (those square cabinets with perforated tin doors and shelves for cooling baked goods), as do old farm implements, antique toys, lamps, china, silver, and glass. There's even a shop that has more recent "antiques"—vinyl, plastic, and aluminum furniture from the 1950s.

◆ **MAYFIELD**   *map page 231, B-4*

Mayfield is the hometown of novelist and *New Yorker* short story writer and essayist Bobbie Ann Mason, who lives with her family on a farm nearby. The movie of her novel *In Country* was filmed on location in and around Mayfield. The town's handsome **courthouse** has a striking hexagonal clocktower; another architectural landmark (though not as elegant) is Emma's restaurant—the building with a giant rooster on its roof, a tribute perhaps to the chicken-processing industry based here.

The town is a decidedly quiet little place. At Maplewood Cemetery (even quieter) look for the **Woolridge Monuments,** a collection of statues that are a testimony to eccentricity. In the 1890s, local horse breeder Henry Woolridge decided to create a family memorial of life-sized statues. The 15 figures clustered around what became his tomb include his dogs, a fox, various family members, and Woolridge himself, mounted on his horse, Fop. (The animals seem rather more animated than the humans.) While the attendant sandstone figures were carved in Mayfield and Paducah, Woolridge's is made of marble and was carved in Italy. The whole effect of the monument is more than a bit strange.

WESTERN KENTUCKY

The Woolridge Monuments at Maplewood Cemetery.

◆ PADUCAH   *map page 231, B-3*

Paducah, a city of about 28,000, is located at the convergence of the Ohio and Tennessee Rivers. In 1795, Gen. George Rogers Clark, who had led the first settlement at the Falls of the Ohio, laid claim to 37,000 acres on the site where the city now stands. Lengthy litigation with a rival claim (which went all the way to the U.S. Supreme Court) delayed development of the land. Clark prevailed, but died in 1818 and the claim went to his younger brother William, the Clark of the Lewis and Clark Expedition.

William Clark had a town platted at the mouth of the Tennessee in 1827 and wrote to his son, "I have laid out a town there and intend to sell some lots [in] it, the name is Pa-du-cah, once the largest nation of Indians known in this country, and now almost forgotten." Somehow this lost tribe was transmogrified by local lore into one Chief Paduke, who apparently loomed so large in the collective local imagination that there's even a statue of him, sporting long locks and a heroic gaze, at Jefferson and 19th Streets downtown. Historians agree that Paduke is pure fiction, but don't try to tell that to the otherwise-friendly natives of his namesake city. You'll get an earful about "interferin' know-it-alls."

In the 19th century, Paducah had a reputation as a rough-and-tumble river town where gambling and prostitution flourished. Today it is a commercial and regional arts center with a refurbished late Victorian downtown. Paducah's major employer for the past four decades has been the Uranium Gaseous Diffusion Plant on the western outskirts of the city, and revelations of safety violations at the uranium enrichment facility have been widely reported.

ENTERPISE ON HER FAST TRIP TO LOUISVILLE, 1815.

The Enterprise *on her first trip to Louisville, ca. 1815.*

GLAMOUR ON THE OHIO RIVER

*S*teamboat travel was both glamorous and squalid. The stately four-deckers, white as a wedding cake, had floral carpets, inlaid woodwork, and oil paintings on the stateroom doors. They provided a nursery, a barbershop, gaming rooms, and a gleaming bar. Their cabin passengers sat down to five-course dinners with orchestra music. But most of the travelers never saw the splendors of the grand saloon. Immigrants, woodsmen, and frontier farmers were crowded among cargo and livestock on the lower deck, cooking porridge on the boiler flues and drinking river water. They slept on bales and boxes. Living close to the engines and the waterline, they were the first victims of collision and explosion. The one inducement to deck passage was economy. For a dollar, a decker could travel five hundred miles—one fifth the fare for cabin passengers.

—Walter Havighurst, *Ohio,* 1975

Steamboats crowd the docks at Paducah in this photograph taken around 1900.

WESTERN KENTUCKY

◆ Visiting Paducah

You can spend a very pleasant day strolling on the brick sidewalks along the tree-lined downtown streets, meandering in and out of antique shops in the four- and five-story stone-and-brick storefronts. Boutiques, ice cream and coffee shops, and gift shops (some a tad on the precious side) are located between Seventh Street and Broadway in an area that extends to the Ohio River.

Down by the river the city flood wall is decorated with colorful murals by Louisiana artist Robert Dafford. The striking 15-foot-tall panels, somewhat reminiscent of Currier & Ives prints (albeit with bolder colors), depict the history of the city—there are scenes of riverboats docking on the shore and of horse-drawn carriages wheeling along unpaved streets. One of the murals pairs Paducah's two most famous native sons, Alben Barkley and Irvin Cobb. Alben Barkley (1877–1956) was Vice President of the United States under Harry Truman. A museum devoted to his life and career is housed in an antebellum 1852 mansion; *533 Madison St.; 270-442-7064.*

Robert Dafford painted downtown Paducah's murals—illustrations of the city's history.

St. Francis Catholic church in downtown Paducah.

Irvin Cobb (1876–1944) was a noted humorist and journalist who had a brief career in Hollywood as an archetypal, julep-sipping Southerner in several forgettable movies. Cobb quotes crop up on historical markers and signs around town. He was an unashamed local booster, whose folksy lines included the likes of "I'd rather be born an orphan in Paducah than be natural twins in any other city in the world."

A more contemporary painting shows the Market Place, a still-standing redbrick covered market at **Market House Square** (located on Second Street between Kentucky and Broadway). The market now houses shops that sell crafts, antiques, and handmade quilts. At the corner of Second and Broadway, from April to October, you can hire a horse-drawn carriage for a tour around the downtown. And when you need to refuel after a morning of browsing and buying, there are plenty of restaurants in the area. (My favorite is Jeremiah's, a brewpub on Broadway.)

WESTERN
KENTUCKY

The Museum of the American Quilters' Society, two blocks north of Market House Square, is a long, low contemporary building with a stunning collection of quilts. While there are some historical examples, the modern ones are more eye-catching. On some of the newer quilts, patterns of startling, brightly colored swirls look like kaleidoscopes made of fabric; other quilts contain portrayals of subjects ranging from airplanes to politicians, each finished in highly detailed needlework. If you are a quilter or a collector, visit the museum's book and gift shop, which offers a bonanza of information on the craft—over 400 specialist titles. Every April the American Quilter's Society hosts a juried national quilt show and contest that features over 400 quilts. *215 Jefferson St.; 270-442-8856.*

Quilts on exhibit at the Museum of the American Quiters' Society include Conway Album (I'm Not From Baltimore) *by Irma Gila Hatcher, 1992 (left) and* Corona II: A Solar Eclipse *by Caryl Bryer Fallert, 1989 (below).*

(Courtesy of the Museum of the American Quilters' Society)

In the evening, you might catch a performances at one of the following venues: **Paducah Symphony Orchestra** at Tilghman Auditorium *(2400 Washington St., 270-444-0065);* the **Paducah Concert Band** at various theaters *(270-443-7469);* and **Market House Theatre,** which produces live theater *(132 Market House Square, 270-444-6828).*

A peregrine falcon.

■ BALLARD COUNTY WILDLIFE MANAGEMENT AREAS
map page 231, A-3

US Highway 60 leads you west out of Paducah through Ballard County and the wildlife management wetlands areas along its Ohio River rim. The Ballard and Swan Lake WMAs are open from mid-March to mid-October, and both provide a glimpse of what this part of Kentucky was like before the white settlers arrived. The low-lying terrain includes prairie grasslands, swamps, and sloughs. Waterfowl such as egrets, herons, and bitterns nest near the shallow waterways. Bald eagles can be seen here surveying the land from the top boughs of tall trees. Other fauna include wild turkeys, mink, beavers, coyotes, foxes, and tree frogs.

At **Swan Lake** (so named by Audubon when he spotted trumpeter swans here in 1810), visit the observation tower. The view is over the lake, which is ringed with cypress trees, their knobby roots sticking out of the water like the knees of giants.

The **Ballard WMA** is an important overwintering site for migrating waterfowl. To get to it, you have to detour off of US-60 and meander just under six miles along state roads 1105 and 473, which will take you past low-lying fields, carpeted in summertime with wild aster. This has to be one of the quietest stretches of road in Kentucky.

WESTERN KENTUCKY

If you are looking at this area on a state map, you'll probably notice the curious name Monkey's Eyebrow. This tiny, mostly deserted little town (only a handful of isolated houses remain) got its name from a crescent-shaped ridge behind it, visible from the Ohio River. Tall grass growing atop it may have resembled a hairy eyebrow to a passing riverboat captain.

■ WICKLIFFE MOUNDS   *map page 231, A-3*

Eleven miles south of the entrance to the Swan Lake Wildlife Management Area on US-60 is the Ballard County seat, Wickliffe, built where the Ohio River flows into the Mississippi. If you pass though the center of town and onto US-51, in a few minutes you'll come to the clearly marked entrance to the state's most significant archaeological site. The **Wickliffe Mounds Research Center** preserves and studies the remains, in the form of several purpose built mounds, of a Mississippian-period Indian town that flourished from A.D. 1100 to 1350.

Excavation, supervised by faculty from Murray State University, is still very much in progress. Earthen mounds, once flat-topped, but now rounded by weather, lie in the middle of a low clearing ringed by tall hardwoods. A short orientation film shows the village layout and life a thousand years ago.

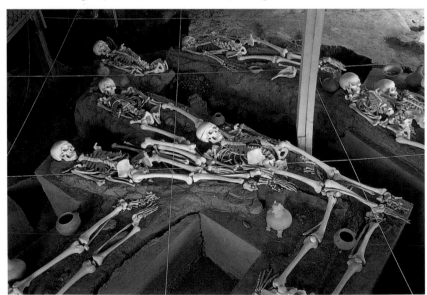

Excavation exhibit at the Wickliffe Mounds Research Center.

After the film, visit the Lifeways Building, a metal shed built over one of the mounds. Boards are laid across the soil for you to walk on so you can view the dig without disturbing it. A checkerboard pattern of strings marks off the site; each resulting square has a number. Several excavated artifacts are on display here, including chipped stone tools and pottery.

Two other exhibit areas, reached by paved paths from the Lifeways Building, are the Cemetery Building and the Architecture Building. In the former is a display describing the burial practices of Native Americans of the period. The latter has a display showing the "wattle and daub" method of building using branches woven between posts set in the ground and then covered with clay. (Postholes of the long-gone buildings are still clearly visible on several mounds.) *US-51; closed December through February; 270-335-3681.*

■ REELFOOT NATIONAL WILDLIFE REFUGE *map page 231, A-4*

It seems appropriate that the 100-square-mile Reelfoot Lake is about as remote from any other part of Kentucky as you can get. It was created by the 1811–12 earthquakes: you can expect to feel an occasional light tremor if you spend any length of time here.

The vast cypress swamp, infused with greenish-gold light in summer and fall, seems a primeval place as you drift through it in a shallow-bottomed swamp boat. (These craft are appropriately named "stump jumpers" because they can negotiate the cypress knees that jut out of the water.)

You may catch a glimpse of a black water moccasin snake as it undulates through the water. (These are poisonous, by the way, so no wading.) The sounds of millions of swamp frogs and insects that rattle, croak, and buzz breaks what would otherwise be an utter stillnes, except for the occasional plop of an unseen critter going into the water. Might be an otter; could be a turtle.

Unless you are particularly fond of insect bites, spring is the best time to visit Reelfoot Lake. The waterways are relatively open and it's possible to see varieties of ducks, herons, egrets, geese, and cormorants passing through during migration. The great blue herons start to build their nests of piled sticks in March. And carpets of aquatic plants that flower in purple or white before the overhanging trees have fully leafed out are stunning. They look like floating flower beds. The arrow-shaped leaves of marsh arum look like rank upon rank of sentries growing out of the water near shorelines.

(following pages) Bald cypress trees at sunset in Reelfoot National Wildlife Refuge.

The lake and most of the surrounding wetland is in Tennessee, where it is designated a state park, but the wildlife refuge extends on either side of the border. Fishing for catfish and other bottom-feeding fish is allowed with a proper license. To get to Reelfoot Lake from Wickliffe, take US-51 south 36 miles to State Road 94, which winds its way west through the wetlands and drained farmlands of Fulton County for 22 miles and into the Reelfoot Lake area; *901-253-9652.*

■ NEW MADRID, MISSOURI   *map page 231, A-4*

At the northernmost tip of the bend, across the Mississippi River on the Missouri shore, is the town of New Madrid (pronounced "MAH-drid"). This was the epicenter of the great earthquakes of 1811–13 (estimated at 8.1 on the Richter scale), reportedly so powerful that they caused church bells to ring in Boston and even prompted reports of tremors in Quebec. The New Madrid Fault has been relatively inactive since those early 19th-century quakes. St. Louis and Memphis are major cities within the quake zone that were barely bumps on the map in 1811, and obviously they could be devastated if another big earthquake occurs.

The quakes caused the rerouting of the Mississippi (it even flowed backwards for several hours) and the formation of Reelfoot Lake.

NEW MADRID EARTHQUAKES 1811–1813

This account of one of the New Madrid Earthquakes was recorded by George Heinrich Crist in the north-central Kentucky county of Nelson, near the present location of Louisville. It was submitted by Floyd Creasey—fourth tier great-grandson of the author.

16 December 1811

There was a great shaking of the earth this morning. Tables and chairs turned over and knocked around —all of us knocked out of bed. The roar I thought would leave us deaf if we lived. It was not a storm. When you could hear, all you could hear was screams from people and animals. It was the worst thing that I have ever witnessed. It was still dark and you could not see nothing. I thought the shaking and the loud roaring sound would never stop. You could not hold onto nothing neither man or woman was strong enough—the shaking would knock you loose like knocking hickory nuts out of a tree. I don't know how we lived through it. None of us was killed— we was all banged up and some of us knocked out for awhile and blood was every where. When it got day break you could see the damage done all around. We still had our home it was some damage. Some people that the home was not built too strong did not.

We will have to hunt our animals. Every body is scared to death. We still do not know if anybody was killed. I made my mind to one thing. If this earth quake or what ever it was did not happen in the Territory of Indiana then me and my family is moving to Pigeon Roost as soon as I can get things together.

23 January 1812

What are we gonna do? You cannot fight it cause you do not know how. It is not something that you can see. In a storm you can see the sky and it shows dark clouds and you know that you might get strong winds but this you can not see anything but a house that just lays in a pile on the ground—not scattered around and trees that just falls over with the roots still on it. The earth quake or what ever it is come again today. It was as bad or worse than the one in December. We lost our Amandy Jane in this one—a log fell on her. We will bury her upon the hill under a clump of trees where Besy's Ma and Pa is buried. A lot of people thinks that the devil has come here. Some thinks that this is the beginning of the world coming to a end.

8 Febuary 1812

If we do not get away from here the ground is going to eat us alive. We had another one of them earth quakes yesterday and today the ground still shakes at times. We are all about to go crazy—from pain and fright. We can not do anything until we can find our animals or get some more. We have not found enough to pull the wagons.

20 March 1812

I do not know if our minds have got bad or what. But everybody says it. I swear you can still feel the ground move and shake some. We still have not found enough animals to pull the wagons and you can not find any to buy or trade.

14 April 1813

We lived to make it to Pigeon Roost. We did not lose any lives but we had aplenty troubles. As much as I love my place in Kentucky—I never want to go back. From December to April no man—woman or animal if they could talk would dare to believe what we lived through. From what people say it was not that bad here—They felt the ground move and shake but it did not destroy cabins and trees like it did in Kentucky. I guess that things was as bad here but at least they could see the enemy. On 3 September 1812 the Shawnees that William thought was friendly went crazy and them savages killed twenty four people.

FOOD & LODGING

■ ABOUT LODGING

There are dozens of small inns and bed-and-breakfasts in Kentucky, the majority of which are located in historic properties ranging from 18th-century stone houses and log cabins to ornate Victorian mansions.

Just a generation ago, Kentucky was dotted with 18th- and 19th-century coaching inns and the 20th-century equivalent, the cozy, neo-colonial motor lodge. While some of these remain, the lodging industry today is dominated by chains, ranging from high-end to budget. In the less economically developed regions of the state, these chains are among the most reliable and comfortable places for travelers to stay. Sometimes they are the only places.

On the other hand, Kentucky's state parks (nearly 20) offer fine overnight accommodation. Lodges and cottages are situated in scenic locations and are staffed by people who, in all likelihood, have grown up in the immediate area. So you can ask the desk clerk or lodge dining room server about local attractions and get detailed replies.

■ ABOUT FOOD

Fine Kentucky cooking has Southern roots. Country ham, red-eye gravy, grits, fried chicken, and bread pudding are longstanding favorites that can still be found in independent eateries around the state. Fine dining establishments in Louisville and Lexington like to incorporate these ingredients in updated ways, such as a salad that occasionally graces the menu at Louisville's English Grill. It's composed of Bibb lettuce (bred by a 19th-century Frankfort horticulturist), shaved and fried country ham, and a black-eyed pea vinaigrette. Unfortunately, the state's wet/dry laws have meant that fine dining establishments, whether traditional or contemporary, are rare outside of the major metropolitan areas.

In past decades, fast-food restaurants have run many authentic old Kentucky restaurants out of business, including scores of little blue-plate-special cafes. Your best bet for food in the rural regions of the state is in the local state park lodge.

■ ABOUT DRINK

Nearly one half of the counties in the state in which bourbon whiskey is a multi-million-dollar industry are dry. That is, you can't purchase alcohol of any description in a restaurant or hotel, and there are no liquor stores. After Prohibition was repealed, Kentucky left it up to towns and counties to decide whether alcohol sales would be allowed. The majority of voters in the nonurban areas do not approve of liquor. Wet/dry votes still take place every election season.

After each town name in the list that follows, there's a note in parentheses about drinking status. "Wet" means you can a get a glass of wine, beer, and even bourbon. "Dry" means you are going to have to drink milk. "Moist" (are you still with me?) means that the town allows alcohol sales, but the surrounding county does not. While some restaurants in dry areas look the other way if you bring your own bottle of wine, they are doing so against the law. (I can't tell you which ones they are, or they'd be closed down by the authorities.) By the way, no state park dining rooms or lodges have liquor licenses.

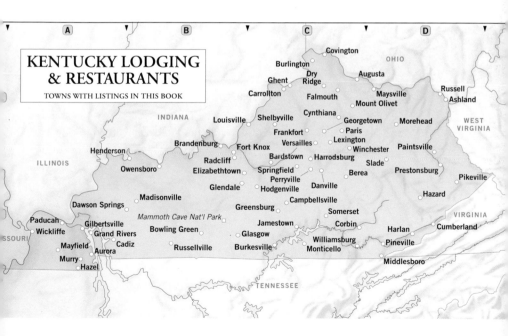

KENTUCKY LODGING & RESTAURANTS
TOWNS WITH LISTINGS IN THIS BOOK

Note: COMPASS AMERICAN GUIDES makes every effort to ensure the accuracy of its information; however, as conditions and prices change frequently, we recommend that readers also contact local sources for the most up-to-date information.

■ HOTEL & RESTAURANT PRICE DESIGNATIONS

Hotel Room Rates
Per person, based on double occupancy:
$ = under $60; $$ = $60–94; $$$ = $95–124; $$$$ = over $125

Restaurant Rates
Per person, excluding drinks and tip:
$ = under $10; $$ = $10–20; $$$ = $20–30; $$$$ = over $30

■ CHAIN LODGINGS

Note: For information, call the national 800 numbers listed below, but for the best rates, make your reservations at the local number; the reservations clerk is frequently authorized to quote discounted rates.

Chain Lodgings

Best Western 800-528-1234	Holiday Inn 800-465-4329
Comfort Inn 800-228-5150	La Quinta 800-NU-ROOMS
Days Inn 800-325-2525	Marriott 800-228-9290
Embassy Suites 800-362-2779	Radisson 800-333-3333
Hampton Inn 800-426-7866	Ramada 800-2-RAMADA
Hilton 800-445-8667	

FOOD & LODGING BY TOWN

Ashland *(WET)*
map page 265, D-1

✕ **Bluegrass Grill**
3505 Winchester Ave.; 606-324-3923 **$**
Casual atmosphere where you can dine inside or out. Blue plate specials dominate the bill of fare, including an open-faced roast beef sandwich and fried shrimp dinner. All the pies are homemade.

✕ **C. J. Maggie's American Grill**
1442 Winchester Ave.; 606-324-7895 **$$**
Old sports equipment hangs from the ceiling, and wooden booths provide a measure of privacy. You can eat in the bar, too, which is in a separate room from the restaurant. Casual American food includes entree-sized salads as well as grilled meats.

✕ **C. R. Thomas Old Place**
1612 Greenup Ave.; 606-325-8500 **$$**
Movie memorabilias dominate the decor, from old posters to black-and-white photographs of screen legends. Hot sandwiches, pasta, steaks, and chicken constitute the offerings in this casual eatery.

✕ **Dragon Palace**
807 Carter Ave.; 606-329-8081 **$$**
A smiling statue of Buddha greets guests as they enter this Chinese restaurant. The menu offers Szechuan, Hunan, and Mandarin dishes, including sizzling entrees and a selection of vegetarian options.

✕ **Texas Roadhouse**
501 Winchester Ave.; 606-325-5188 **$$**
This outpost of a Louisville-based regional restaurant chain offers well-prepared thick, juicy steaks and fine sides such as fluffy baked potatoes (and a bucket of peanuts).

⌂ **Ashland Plaza Hotel**
One Ashland Plaza at Winchester Ave.;
606-329-0055 or 800-346-6133 **$$-$$$**
The 10-story, 157-room hotel dominates the downtown skyline. Ask for a room with a river view. Comfortable rooms have contemporary decor. Health club and business facilities. Bar and restaurant are open in the evenings. Closed Sundays.

⌂ **Carter Caves State Resort Park**
KY-182 N (38 miles west of Ashland);
606-286-4411 **$-$$**
A modern fieldstone-and-timber 28-room lodge with a huge fireplace in the lobby; there are also 10 cottages perched along a mountain ridge.

CARTER CAVES STATE RESORT PARK

⌂ **Fairfield Inn by Marriott**
10945 US-60; 606-928-1222 **$$**
Comfortable, midsized motel a few minutes from I-64 in the rolling countryside outside of Ashland. Three stories, 63 rooms; with suites, business facilities, and indoor pool.

GREENBO LAKE PARK

🏨 **Greenbo Lake State Resort Park**
KY-1 (18 miles north of I-64 Grayson exit), Greenup; 606-473-7324 **$**
The 36-room fieldstone lodge overlooks 225-acre Greenbo Lake. Most rooms have balconies. The unusual feature is a cozy library housing the works of local novelist and poet Jesse Stuart. There are overstuffed chairs where you can while away many reading hours.

🏨 **Levi Hampton House Bed & Breakfast.** 2206 Walnut St. (US-23), Catlettsburg; 606-739-8118 **$$**
A few minutes' drive from Ashland, this redbrick Italianate-style house dates from 1847. Guest rooms have working fireplaces and are furnished with a mix of antiques and reproductions. Three acres of grounds include gardens.

Augusta
(WET) map page 265, C-1

✕ **The Beehive Tavern**
101 W. Riverside Dr.; 606-756-2202 **$$**
Two-story, Federal-style brick building with an upper-story porch, built as an apothecary shop in the 1790s. The restaurant, on the ground floor, has a big corner window, painted woodwork, and antique furnishings. A cozy bar in one corner helps maintain the atmosphere of an 18th-century tavern. Seafood, roast pork, and chicken are specialties.

Aurora
(DRY) map page 265, A-2

✕ **The Brass Lantern**
165993 US-68 E; 270-474-2773 **$-$$**
Rustic hunting-lodge decor, complete with fireplace and an eclectic mix of antiques. Locals like the salad bar. The menu features casual American food—chops, small steaks, chicken. Children's menu available.

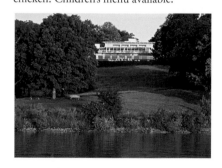

KENLAKE STATE RESORT PARK

🏨 **Kenlake State Resort Park**
542 Kenlake Rd.; 270-474-2211 or 800-325-0143 **$-$$$**
Three-story, 48-room hotel dramatically situated on a low hill on the western shore of Kentucky Lake. A manicured lawn sweeps down to the water's edge. Elegant buffet served on balcony, weather permitting. Woodland and shoreline cottages available, too. Boating, fishing, golf, indoor tennis center, and outdoor pool.

Bardstown
(WET) map page 265, C-2

✕ Dagwood's
204 N. Third St.; 502-348-4029 **$-$$**
Storefront located among the antique shops near the courthouse square specializes in stacked ham and salami Dagwood sandwiches. Hot dishes include turkey Reuben and burgers. Fresh salad bar also features homemade soups.

✕ Kurtz Restaurant
418 E. Stephen Foster Ave.;
502-348-8964 **$$**
Family-run traditional Southern restaurant with exposed stone walls in the back dining room. Furnished with antiques. Dinners include fried chicken, country ham, pork chops. Save room for homemade pie or fresh fruit cobbler.

✕ My Old Kentucky Dinner Train
602 N. Third St.; 502-348-7300 **$**
A pair of 1940 Pullman dining cars, complete with restored wood paneling, white tablecloths, and silver, wind through farmland, woodlands, and even past distilleries on a two- to three-hour-meal journey. Prix fixe dinners have choice of two or three entrees, usually steak, fish, and chicken.

✕ Old Talbott Tavern
107 W. Stephen Foster Ave.;
502-348-3494 **$$$**
Updated Kentucky fare, including pasta, as well as steaks, seafood, and chicken, is served in the dining rooms of this 1779 tavern. When it was redecorated after a fire in 1998, the work exposed historic wall murals in commons areas. Bar has excellent bourbon selection.

A ROSEMARK HAVEN

⛫ Bardstown Parkview Motel
418 E. Stephen Foster Ave.; 502-348-5983 or 800-732-2384 **$**
Owned by the same family as the Kurtz Restaurant next door. The two-story motel overlooks My Old Kentucky Home State Park across the street. Rooms are furnished in Early American reproductions.

⛫ Beautiful Dreamer Bed & Breakfast
440 E. Stephen Foster Ave.; 502-348-4004 or 800-811-8312 **$$$-$$$$**
All four guest rooms in this Federal-style, two-story home have private baths. Three rooms have a double jacuzzi, another, a fireplace. All furnished in antiques and cherry reproductions. View of My Old Kentucky Home State Park.

BEAUTIFUL DREAMER B&B

⊞ **Coffee Tree Cabin Bed & Breakfast**
980 McCubbins Lane; 502-348-1151**$$$**
Log cabin home with wraparound porches overlooking 41 wooded acres. There's a lake, too. Commons room with cathedral ceiling. Four bedrooms are available; three have private baths. Full breakfasts are served, as well as evening dessert.

COFFEE TREE CABIN B&B

⊞ **Jailer's Inn**
111 W. Stephen Foster Ave.; 502-348-5551 or 800-948-5551 **$$-$$$**
This may qualify as the oddest B&B in the country. The stone walls in the 1819 building are 30 inches thick. There are bars on the windows. This was a jail until 20 years ago. Most rooms furnished with antiques. One room is a jail cell, with a water bed bunk, no less, and Elvis posters on the wall.

⊞ **Mansion Bed & Breakfast**
1003 N. Third St.; 502-348-2586 or 877-909-2586 **$$$**
White-brick Greek Revival house located on three acres planted with dogwood. Built in 1851, each of the home's eight guest rooms has a private bath. A meeting room seating 35 is available. Hot gourmet break-

fast served on china with crystal and silver in the formal dining room.

⊞ **Old Bardstown Inn**
510 W. Stephen Foster Ave.;
800-894-1601 **$**
Bargain-priced, two-story motel is located downtown within walking distance of shops and restaurants. Rooms are pleasantly furnished with cherry wood furniture. Complimentary coffee in the lobby; no in-house restaurant.

⊞ **Old Talbott Tavern**
107 W. Stephen Foster Ave.;
502-348-3494 **$$**
Two historic inns under the same management. There are guest rooms above the restaurant and bar in the tavern. Across the street is another building that was originally the town post office. Rooms in both are furnished with antiques.

⊞ **A Rosemark Haven**
714 N. Third St.; 502-348-8218
or 888-420-9703 **$$$**
Antebellum Greek Revival–Italianate mansion located on the row of circa 1830s mansions leading south into the town center. The five rooms and two suites have private baths. Sweep down an oval spiral staircase in the morning to a full gourmet plantation breakfast.

Berea
(WET) map page 265, C-2

✕ **Boone Tavern Dining Room**
100 Main St.; 859-986-9358
or 800-366-9358 **$$**

Students from Berea College staff the restaurant in which famous spoon bread (a soft corn bread) and vegetables are served family style. Entrees include chicken, fish, lamb, turkey, beef. Elegant dining room furniture was also handcrafted by college students.

✕ Dinner Bell Restaurant
One Plaza Dr., Exit 76 off I-75.; 859-986-2777 $
Country cooking includes biscuits and cream gravy at breakfast time and country ham and chicken at lunch and dinner. An attached gift shop sells locally produced preserves, jams, honey, and crafts.

✕ Papaleno's Restaurant
108 Center St.; 859-986-4497 $$
Surrounded by craft shops, this is a good restorative lunch stop. Pasta entrees are traditional and filling. Pizzas are fine for sharing. Jars filled with colored pasta and a display of olive-oil bottles creates festive atmosphere. Grilled entrees at dinner.

⊞ Berea's Shady Lane Bed & Breakfast
123 Mt. Vernon Rd.; 859-986-9851 $-$$
Located just outside the town center on a quiet side street, the house incorporates a smaller home that belonged to a mayor of Berea. The two guest rooms contain artifacts from the owners' world travels, including an African village drum. Garden Room has a collection of hats that guests are encouraged to wear to breakfast.

⊞ Boone Tavern Hotel
100 Main St.; 859-986-9358 $$
Gracious, Colonial-style, 58-room hotel dating from 1909 is staffed by Berea College students. Lobby and guest rooms furnished in handcrafted reproduction antiques. Some four-poster beds are high enough off the floor to require use of a little set of steps.

BOONE TAVERN HOTEL

⊞ Doctor's Inn of Berea
617 Chestnut St.; 859-986-3042 $$$$
Greek Revival redbrick house with stately white columns is furnished with antiques, plush Oriental rugs, and original art. The views from the three guest rooms, each with bath, are of surrounding mountains and the gardens on the grounds. Evening hors d'oeuvres served in addition to full country breakfast.

DOCTOR'S INN OF BEREA

Bowling Green
(WET) map page 265, B-2

✕ Beijing Restaurant
1951 Scottsville Rd.; 270-842-2288 $-$$
Varied Chinese menu (Szechuan and Mandarin) includes lunch specials and Sunday buffet. Orange beef is especially notable. Little pots of hot tea are served. Full bar. Best bet for this cuisine in the region, but the steamboat exterior is kind of an odd fit.

✕ Cambridge Market & Café
830 Fairview Ave; 270-782-9366 $
A favorite local lunch spot, this deli prepares the daily specials, such as marinated chicken pasta or meatloaf, with top-notch ingredients. Freshly made cheesecakes, cakes, and fruit crisps rival the main dishes.

✕ 440 Main
440 E. Main St.; 270-793-0450 $$$
Popular meeting place on the city's Fountain Square has a specialty martini list and the best wine selection in Bowling Green. Menu leans heavily toward seafood and steaks, often prepared with Cajun or Asian seasonings

✕ Mariah's
801 State St.; 270-842-6878 $$
Stately building dating from 1818 has been redecorated with brass and wood. Ceiling goes up two and three stories, creating tall "canvasses" for the colorful murals of 1940s Bowling Green are painted. Casual bistro fare includes excellent trout.

✕ Montana Grille
1740 Scottsville Rd.; 270-746-9746 $$
Hickory-wood smoke permeates the offerings, including rotisserie chicken, fresh salmon, pork chops, steaks, and smoked ribs. Specialty of the house is a tender filet (with a bourbon whiskey sauce). For the less carnivorous, there's a nice selection of entree salads.

⌂ Alpine Lodge Bed & Breakfast
5310 Morgantown Rd.; 270-843-4846 $$
Swiss chalet–style home is set on 12 acres in a quiet residential neighborhood outside of town. Decor is traditional, with handmade quilts as accents. Five guest rooms; two have private baths. Outdoor hot tub and swimming pool; and short nature trail.

⌂ 1869 Homestead Bed & Breakfast
212 Mizpah Rd.; 270-842-0510 $$
Situated on 55 acres of meadows and woods, the 1869 brick house has three guest rooms, all with private baths. Civil War–era antique furnishings fit well with the walnut staircase, working fireplaces, and original poplar floors.

⌂ Holiday Inn University Plaza Hotel
1021 Wilkinson Trace; 270-745-0088 or 800-801-1777 $$$-$$$$
Largest hotel in the city with 218 rooms and suites located around a seven-story atrium. High-speed Internet access from all rooms. Health club, pool, sauna, and game room. Convenient to the campus of Western Kentucky University.

⌂ News Inn of Bowling Green
3160 Scottsville Rd.; 270-781-3460 or 800-443-3701 $-$$
One-story redbrick motel. Red-and-green color scheme extends to the decor of the 52 rooms. Grounds with swimming pool,

playground, grills, and picnic tables. Pets allowed.

SHAKER TAVERN (SOUTH UNION)

☲ **Shaker Tavern**
Hwy-73, South Union; 270-542-6801 or 800-929-8701 **$$**
Located about 20 minutes from Bowling Green in the middle of flat farming country. This Victorian inn, which faces the railroad track, was built by the nearby Shaker community in 1869 for tourists, or as the Shakers called them "the people of the world." Sumptuous country breakfast served. Evening meals by reservation.

☲ **Topper Motel**
427 US 31W Bypass; 270-842-4273 **$-$$**
The 40 rooms in this convenient motel are outfitted with microwaves and refrigerators. The location is its main drawing card, as it's a short drive from Western Kentucky University and the National Corvette Museum.

Burkesville
(DRY) map page 265, C-2

✕ **Mike's Landing Floating Restaurant**
3498 Sulphur Creek Rd.; 270-433-7272 **$-$$**

The casual restaurant looks over the water, and there's a daily buffet. You can get here by road, or, if you're cruising Dale Hollow Lake, you can dock at the boat slips and dine. Fare includes fried fish, as well as steaks and chicken.

☲ **Alpine Resort**
700 Hill St.; 270-864-7100 **$$-$$$**
The red-and-white painted lodge near the top of Big Hill Mountain overlooks the Cumberland River Valley; nearly every room has a balcony with a view. Amenities include a restaurant with working stone fireplaces, and a library of books and movies.

☲ **Dale Hollow Lake State Resort Park**
6371 State Park Rd.; 270-433-7431 **$**
Modern three-story fieldstone lodge is perched on a bluff overlooking the lake. All of the rooms have balconies. The lodge common area has a tall stone fireplace and a restaurant overlooking the water.

☲ **Riverfront Lodge**
305 Keen St.; 270-864-3300 **$$**
Contemporary two-story motel with 40 rooms overlooks the Cumberland River. A launching ramp and floating dock accommodate boaters. Access for handicapped visitors and some nonsmoking rooms (not always available in rural Kentucky).

Burlington
(WET) map page 265, C-1

☲ **Burlington's Willis Graves 1830s B&B**
5825 Jefferson St.; 859-689-5096 or 888-226-5096 **$$$-$$$$**
Cozy suite with fireplace and views of the beautifully tended gardens on the grounds

is one of the options for accommodations. There are two other single rooms. All are furnished in period antiques. Very quiet country retreat within 20 minutes of the Covington/Cincinnati urban center.

BURLINGTON'S WILLIS GRAVES B&B

Cadiz *(DRY) map page 265, A-2*

⌑ Cadiz Super 8

154 Hospitality Lane; 270-522-7007 **$$**
The 48 rooms distributed over two stories are decorated in "modern country" style, which means the gingham-inspired drapes and bedspreads are color-coordinated. Amenities include a pool and business services so you can check your e-mail.

LAKE BARKLEY STATE RESORT PARK

⌑ Lake Barkley State Resort Park

3500 State Park Rd., Canton
(near Cadiz); 270-924-1131 **$-$$$**
The 120-room lodge is circular, and most units have lake views. All have private balconies or patios. Suites are available, too. More intimate is the 10-room Little River Lodge, which has its own restaurant and coffee shop. The park also has several one-, two-, and three-bedroom cottages. All are fully modernized.

⌑ Whispering Winds Inn

43 Channel Court; 270-924-1094 **$$-$$$**
Technically a B&B, since the owners live here, but this large modern house overlooking Lake Barkley is more like a small hotel, with five guest rooms, a suite (fireplace, study, whirlpool, private balcony) and an apartment. Breakfast served in striking octagonal dining room.

WHISPERING WINDS INN

Campbellsville *(WET) map page 265, C-2*

⌑ Lakeview Motel

1291 Old Lebanon Rd.; 270-465-8139
or 800-242-2874 **$**

Comfortable, 16-room motel has a pretty stone exterior and overlooks City Lake. Traditional cherry furniture is used for bedrooms and lobby, where a complimentary continental breakfast is served.

Carrollton
(WET) map page 265, C-1

✕ **Carrollton Inn Restaurant**
218 Main St.; 502-732-6905 $-$$
Beef, seafood, chicken, and barbecued ribs entrees are all served with soup, salad, and sides. The cooking is homestyle. Though not quite "old South," it's very traditional.

⊡ **Carrollton Inn**
218 Main St.; 502-732-6905 $
Small, 11-room inn also has its own restaurant and bar. Rooms decorated with Early American reproductions. Centrally located at Third and Main Streets.

⊡ **General Butler State Resort Park**
1608 KY-227; 502-732-4384 $-$$$
Contemporary stone, glass, and wood lodge has common areas and high windows overlooking the Ohio River Valley that afford panoramic views. Many of the 53 rooms have balconies. There are 23 cottages ranging from one- to three-bedroom. Some are rustic looking and blend with the countryside; others are more modern. The park lodge and dining room are something of a social center for residents of the area.

⊡ **Highland House**
1705 Highland Ave.; 502-732-5559 $$$
This 1920 mansion with its white exterior and sloping green roof looks more like it belongs on Gatsby's Long Island than in Kentucky. It sits on five acres and has lovely views of the Ohio River. Three guest rooms have private baths—one with a hot tub, two with spas.

Corbin
(DRY) map page 265, C-2

✕ **Colonel Harland Sanders Original Restaurant**
Junction of US-25 E and US-25 W; 606-528-2163 $
Part museum and part restaurant. The fare is now strictly KFC, but the restored 1930s–era dining area helps you imagine what eating the original recipe with those "11 secret herbs and spices" might have been like. The Colonel's original cooking utensils are on display.

⊡ **Country Inn and Suites by Carlson**
1888 Cumberland Falls Hwy.; 606-526-1400 $-$$
Chain outlet has a prime mountaintop location. Lobby blends in with the landscape, boasting hardwood floors and a working fireplace. Contemporary rooms are spacious. Suites also available.

⊡ **Cumberland Falls State Resort Park**
7351 Hwy-90; 606-528-4121 $-$$$$
The 52-room Dupont Lodge has a dark stone and wood exterior and beautiful woodwork inside, including massive hemlock beams carved from native trees. The common area has a large stone fireplace and looks out over the peaks and valleys of the Cumberland Mountains. The park also has 26 woodland cottages with stone fireplaces.

CUMBERLAND FALLS STATE RESORT PARK

Covington Area
(WET) map page 265, C-1

✕ Dee Felice Café
529 Main St.; 859-261-2365 **$$-$$$**
Light streams into the dining room through tall stained-glass windows, and live jazz provides the background music in this New Orleans–inspired eatery. Cajun, Creole, and blackened entrées anchor the menu.

✕ Jack Quinn's Irish Ale House & Pub
112 E. Fourth St.; 859-491-6699 **$-$$**
Wood-paneled booths and etched glass are the decor details in this cozy but lively pub offering traditional fare along the lines of fish and chips and hot meat pies. Classic Irish and English draft beers and live music on weekends.

✕ Mike Fink
1 Ben Bernstein Pl.; 859-261-4212 **$-$$**
This small riverboat docked at the foot of Greenup Street features fried seafood, pasta dishes, and sandwiches. Casual, lively atmosphere. The view of the Cincinnati skyline is terrific from the window tables, so try to get one.

✕ Riverview Restaurant
668 W. Fifth St.; 859-491-1200 **$$-$$$**
This revolving restaurant is perched atop the cylindrical Radisson Hotel Riverview. Views of the Cincinnati skyline and the Germanic spires of Covington fan out below. Seafood, pork, and beef dishes predominate. Proper dress required.

✕ Wertheim's Gauthaus Zur Linde
514 W. Sixth St.; 859-261-1233 **$$**
Located in the old Main Strasse section of downtown. The restaurant does a fine job with traditional Bavarian fare and has a good selection of German beers, many on tap. Old-fashioned, it will satisfy that craving for sausages and kraut.

⌂ Amos Shinkle Townhouse
215 Garrard St.; 859-431-2118 **$$-$$$$**
An 1854 two-story brick townhouse in the Licking River district that has seven elegantly appointed bedrooms furnished with antiques. All have baths. Charming pocket handkerchief–sized garden is one of many dotted about the neighborhood. Conveniently located for walking across the Roebling Bridge into Cincinnati.

CHRISTOPHER'S B&B

☷ Christopher's Bed & Breakfast

604 Poplar St., Bellevue; 859-491-9354 or 888-585-7085 $$-$$$$
Bold colors have been used in the decor of what was an 1880s church, now a luxurious B&B a half-mile south of downtown Cincinnati. Hardwood floors remain, and antiques mix with more contemporary pieces. The two bedrooms and one suite have private baths.

☷ Radisson Hotel Riverview

668 W. Fifth St.; 859-491-1200 $$
It looks like a building out of "The Jetsons" but has attained landmark status. The 18-story cylindrical hotel is easily spotted from the I-75 bridge. Well-appointed, contemporary rooms are complemented by amenities including an indoor/outdoor pool and fitness center.

☷ Wallace House Bed & Breakfast

120 Wallace Ave.; 859-261-2717 $$$
The turn-of-the-20th-century Queen Anne Victorian mansion has a wide veranda that guests are invited to use. Each of the three rooms has a private bath and queen-size bed. Breakfast with fresh pastries is served in the formal dining room.

Crestwood
(WET) map page 265, B-1

☷ Fox Hollow Bed & Breakfast

8909 Hwy. 329; 502-241-8234 $$$-$$$$
Guests staying at this 1,300-acre retreat can choose among rooms in the Manor House or three cottages. There's a full-service spa within the complex.

Cumberland
(DRY) map page 265, D-2

☷ Cumberland Motel

2203 E. Main St.; 606-589-2181 $
All 32 rooms in this contemporary motel have full or queen-sized beds. It's not fancy, but then, it's not expensive either. No cafe on premises.

☷ Plaza Motel

18855 US-119 N; 606-589-4911 $-$$
This two-story white-brick motel is far enough off the main highway to be quiet. Half of the 73 rooms were recently remodeled. Furniture is cherry wood, and color scheme runs to hunter green, burgundy, and navy.

Cynthiana
(WET) map page 265, C-1

SELDON RENAKER INN

☷ Seldon Renaker Inn

24 S. Walnut St.; 859-234-3752 $$
Located in the main business district among early 20th-century, three-story storefronts, the late Victorian Seldon Re-

naker Inn, built in 1885, has three guest rooms, each with private bath. A sunny second-floor morning room is the site for continental breakfast.

Danville Area
(DRY) map page 265, C-2

✕ The Tea Leaf
230 W. Broadway; 859-236-7456 **$**
Sandwiches, fresh salads, and fruit dishes, as well as homemade breads and muffins, are the hallmarks of this downtown lunch cafe. It's located in a Gothic-style former Presbyterian church.

⛺ Morning Glory Manor and Cottage
B&B 244 E. Lexington Ave.;
859-236-1888 **$$**
This 1895 Queen Anne Victorian manor house is noted for cherry woodwork, parlor staircase, and fireplaces. Guests stay in private cottage, decorated in exotic Middle-Eastern–style. It is set in a beautiful garden, and is furnished with antiques.

⛺ Old Crow Inn Bed & Breakfast
471 Stanford Rd.; 859-236-1808 **$$**
Built in 1780, this handsome stone mansion is graced with Doric columns. Each of the three antiques-furnished guest suites has a private entrance. The grounds include an organic farm, a pottery studio, and a winery.

TWIN HOLLIES B&B

⛺ Twin Hollies Bed & Breakfast
406 Maple Ave.; 859-236-8954 **$$**
Grand redbrick antebellum house with four massive white columns at the entrance sits on four landscaped acres. Built in 1833, the property is on the National Register of Historic Places. There are three guest rooms, two with private baths. Working fireplaces in common rooms.

Dawson Springs
(DRY) map page 265, A/B-2

⛺ Pennyrile Forest State Resort Park
20781 Pennyrile Lodge Rd.;
270-797-3421 or 800-325-1711 **$-$$$**
The small stone lodge (24 rooms) has the feel of an overgrown cottage. It's surrounded by woods where songbirds sing in the trees, and it is beautifully landscaped with native flowers and shrubs. There are also 13 one- and two-bedroom cottages, some in the woods and a few facing Pennyrile Lake.

PENNYRILE FOREST STATE RESORT PARK

Dry Ridge
(DRY) map page 265, C-1

✕ The Country Grill
21 Taft Hwy.; 859-824-6000 **$-$$**
Decorated with a collection of Kentucky
folk art and antiques, this casual restaurant
serves steaks, burgers, and assorted sandwiches. Friendly servers will want to know
where "y'all are from."

Elizabethtown
(DRY) map page 265, B/C-2

✕ Green Bamboo
902 N. Dixie St.; 270-769-3457 **$-$$**
The menu features Mandarin and Hunan
specialties. Lemon chicken and noodle
dishes are recommended. Fresh, contemporary decor and very efficient service.

✕ Stone Hearth Restaurant
1001 N. Mulberry St.; 270-765-4898 **$$**
For years this has been the special-occasion
restaurant for the residents of E-Town. Old
English decor is complete with horse brass-
es and hunting prints. Subdued lighting

creates an intimate atmosphere. Beef and
seafood are specialties.

⊡ Comfort Inn Atrium Gardens
1043 Executive Dr.; 800-682-5285 **$$**
Most pleasant of the nest of chain outlets at
the crossroads of the interstate and parkways that converge at E-Town. The two-
story inn has 133 rooms. Airy atrium is
focal point. There's an indoor pool, too.

Falls of Rough
(Dry) *map page 265, B-2*

⊡ Rough River Dam State Resort Park
450 Lodge Rd.; 270-257-2311 or 800-
325-1713 **$-$$$**
Park serves as a de facto country club for
many locals, who come here for Sunday
dinner in the lodge dining room and to
play the nine-hole golf course. Most of the
57 rooms in the contemporary wood-and-
stone lodge overlook Rough River Lake.
There are 15 two-bedroom cottages in
woods near the lake.

ROUGH RIVER DAM STATE RESORT PARK

Falmouth
(WET) map page 265, C-1

⌕ Red Brick House Bed & Breakfast
201 Chapel St.; 859-654-4834 **$**

Two-story Victorian Gothic house in the middle of town has four guest rooms, one with private bath. It's furnished with antiques that have been in the owners' families for generations. House also contains a street-level small antique and gift shop.

RED BRICK HOUSE B&B

Fort Knox Area
(MOIST) map page 265, B-1/2

✕ Doe Run Inn Dining Room
500 Doe Run Hotel Rd.,
Brandenburg *(wet)*; 270-422-2982 **$$**

Friday and Saturday buffet features local delicacies such as fried catfish and pan-fried chicken. A la carte menu at other times. Rainbow trout is recommended. One dining area is a screened porch overlooking the stream. Wine and beer are available.

✕ German Cottage Cafe
1285 S. Wilson Rd., Radcliff *(dry)*;
270-352-1966 **$$**

The excellent rouladen and luscious desserts, including Black Forest cake and chocolate torte, may help you forget that you can't get a beer to go with the excellent German food. You're in a dry county.

⌕ Best Western Gold Vault Inn
1225 N. Dixie Blvd., Radcliff *(dry)*;
270-351-1141 or 800-528-1234 **$-$$**

Located just off the military base at Fort Knox, this 94-room, two-story complex has spacious, contemporary rooms. There's also a heated pool.

DOE RUN INN

⌕ Doe Run Inn
500 Doe Run Hotel Rd.,
Brandenburg *(wet)*; 270-422-2982
$-$$

This stone-and-log 19th-century mill has been converted to a cozy inn furnished with antiques. Second-story rooms overlook the rushing stream that powered the mill. Of 11 guest rooms, eight have private baths. A two-story log cabin sleeps up to 10.

Frankfort
(WET) map page 265, C-1

✕ Capital Annex Cafeteria
Capitol Annex Building; 502-564-5126 $
Mingle with legislators and lobbyists in the spacious facility in the basement of the Capital Annex. Hot lunch specials can include fried catfish or barbecued chicken. There are real biscuits and gravy at breakfast. You'll need a photo ID to get past building security.

✕ Gabriel's Chop House
405 Wilkinson Blvd.; 502-227-5100 $$
Popular with hungry state legislators for its enormous buffet offering a choice of soups, salad fixings, and assorted entrees and vegetables. Attractive contemporary interior features lots of glass, stained and clear.

✕ Gibby's
212 W. Broadway; 502-223-4429 $-$$
Corner cafe overlooks the grounds of the old state capitol. Pastas, entree salads and hot sandwiches are features. One of the rare smoke-free restaurants in the state.

✕ Jim's Seafood
950 Wilkinson Blvd.; 502-223-7448 $$
Set back from a busy thoroughfare, the long, rambling restaurant has lots of tables overlooking the Kentucky River. Shrimp, fish, and clam dishes are usually fried; you can also get steak and surf-and-turf. Dine outdoors by the river in fair weather.

✕ Kentucky Coffeetree Cafe
235 W. Broadway; 502-875-3009 $
Made-to-order sandwiches, coffee, and tea drinks constitute the fare in this funky little cafe with book-lined walls. It's the annex to Poor Richard's, a bookstore that sells both new and antiquarian titles.

✕ Serafini
243 W. Broadway; 502-875-5599 $-$$
This wood-trimmed restaurant located in a 150-year-old brick storefront blends Kentucky and continental cooking for lunch and dinner. Duck confit, rainbow trout, and pasta of the day with seasonal vegetables are typical offerings.

⛨ Holiday Inn Capital Plaza
405 Wilkinson Blvd.; 502-227-5100
$$-$$$
This 10-story, 189-room hotel is the capital city's most upscale hostelry and is located across the street from a government office building. Striking decor includes cascading fountains in the expansive lobby. Several luxury suites are available.

⛨ Meek House Bed & Breakfast
119 East Third St.; 502-227-2566; $$-$$
The Gothic Revival house, built in 1869, has striking curlicue-trimmed gables and is within walking distance of the government complex and downtown. Guest rooms have antique furnishings.

Georgetown
(DRY) map page 265, C-1

⛨ Blackridge Hall B&B
4055 Paris Pike; 502-863-2069
or 800-768-9308 $$-$$$$
Contemporary Southern-style mansion has three guest rooms and three suites, all with baths. It's situated on five rolling acres surrounded by horse farms. Four-poster ma-

hogany beds grace the guest quarters. Gourmet breakfast is served on formal china (and by candlelight on dark mornings).

⊞ Bryan House Bed & Breakfast

401 W. Main St.; 502-863-1060 $-$$$
Conveniently set in the center of Georgetown, this 1891 Queen Anne house has three guest rooms. The proprietors offer special rates for visitors attending U of K basketball games or Keeneland horse racing.

⊞ Pineapple Inn

645 S. Broadway; 502-868-5453 $$
Striking yellow Victorian house with white gingerbread trim is located in a 19th-century neighborhood. The four rooms are furnished with antiques and all have private baths. Full Southern breakfast served.

Ghent
(WET) map page 265, C-1

⊞ Ghent House Bed & Breakfast

411 Main St.; 502-347-5807 $$-$$$
This 1833 Federal-style house has views of the Ohio River from its back porch. Three rooms, one suite, and garden cottage, all with private baths. The grounds are landscaped as an English garden, roses and all.

⊞ The Poet's House

501 Hwy-42; 502-347-0161 $$
The name is derived from the building's history as the residence of Kentucky poet James Tandy Ellis. This 1868 Federal redbrick has two guest rooms with baths and an adjoining cottage. Breakfast served in sunroom overlooking the Ohio River. Dinner is available by request.

Gilbertsville/ Grand Rivers Area
(DRY) map page 265, A-2

✕ Iron Kettle

1895 JH O'Bryan Ave., Grand Rivers; 270-362-0409 $
Southern comfort food is the specialty. Think meat loaf, fried chicken, ham—gravy is the sauce of choice. Country-casual atmosphere; staffers in denim overalls clear your plate while you revisit the buffet.

✕ Patti's 1880's Restaurant

1793 JH O'Bryan Ave., Grand Rivers; 270-362-8844 $$
Sit-down table service is the rule at Patti's. Late Victorian decor, though dress is casual. Charbroiled pork chops, flower-pot bread, and lemon meringue pie are recommended. Service is friendly and prompt.

⊞ Cave Spring Farm Bed & Breakfast

567 Rocky Hill Rd., Smith Grove; 270-563-6941 $$-$$$
The white-brick 1850s house sits on 17 acres of woods and fields. The property's trails are ideal for hiking and birding. The main house has more formal rooms; guests can also opt to stay in a contemporary log cabin or wooden house tucked into a wooded hillside.

⊞ Grand Rivers Inn

1949 J. H. O'Bryan Ave., Grand Rivers; 270-362-4487 $-$$
No frills, but this quiet, modest 14-room motel has a bright, crisp decor. No restau-

rant, but rooms have small refrigerators and microwaves. Small outdoor pool.

⊤ **Kentucky Dam Village**
State Resort Park
US-62/641; 270-362-4271
or 800-325-0146 $$-$$$
Contemporary lodge has huge windows looking out over the expanse of Kentucky Lake. Most of the 72 rooms have balconies. There's a striking open-sided brass fireplace in the lobby. Smaller Village Green Lodge has 14 rooms near park's golf course.

KENTUCKY DAM VILLAGE

⊤ **The Moors Resort & Marina**
570 Moors Rd.; 270-362-8361
or 800-626-5472 $$-$$$$
Lodge on Kentucky Lake has 24 rooms, but you can also stay out on the lake by renting a houseboat. Resort also has a marina, restaurant, and cottages.

Glasgow
(DRY) map page 265, B-2

✕ **Bolton's Landing**
2433 Scottsville Rd.; 270-651-8008 $-$$
Pleasant dining room is decorated with original artwork by local painters. Tra-

ditional menu emphasizes chicken, fried seafood, and a selection of pasta dishes.

BARREN RIVER LAKE STATE RESORT PARK

⊤ **Barren River Lake State Resort Park**
1149 State Park Rd.; 270-646-2151
or 800-325-0057 $$
The 51-room lodge has clear views of Barren River Lake. The lobby has a vaulted ceiling, stone fireplace, and slate tile floor. There are 22 modern, pastel-colored cottages set along a winding wooded pathway, and nine wood cabins near the lakefront.

⊤ **Four Seasons Country Inn**
4107 Scottsville Rd.; 270-678-1000
or 877-806-6340 $$-$$$$
Stylishly executed modern inn with Victorian country furnishings. Small motel has 21 guest rooms on three floors. Two have whirlpools. Swimming pool for guests.

⊤ **Hall Place Bed &**
Breakfast
313 Green St.; 270-651-3176 $$
Ivy-covered, 1852 Greek Revival house is located in central Glasgow. Three guest bedrooms all have private baths. Tastefully decorated with period antiques. Full breakfast is served.

Glendale
(DRY) map page 265, B-2

✕ Depot Restaurant
201 Main St.; 270-369-6000 **$-$$**
This 19th-century building with its plank floor was once a train depot. Favorite items include country ham sandwich at lunchtime and a stuffed shrimp entree at dinner.

✕ Whistle Stop Restaurant
216 E. Main St.; 270-369-8586 **$$**
Located next to the railroad track that runs through the center of town—and you know it when the train comes by. Dishes include fried chicken, roast pork, corn pudding, and homemade pies with flaky crusts.

⛱ Petticoat Junction Bed & Breakfast
223 High St.; 270-369-8604 **$-$$**
There are six guest rooms in this 1870s farmhouse surrounded by a white picket fence. Beds are made up with antique linens. Grounds planted with kitchen garden. Full breakfast.

Harlan Area
(DRY) map page 265, D-2

⛱ Holiday Inn Express of Harlan
2608 KY-421; 606-573-3385 **$$**
The two-story motel offers reliable accommodations in a pretty, isolated part of the state. There are 62 rooms, a heated pool, and a sauna. Small pets are allowed.

⛱ Mount Aire Motel
355 Skidmore Dr.; 606-573-4600 **$-$$**
The mountains overlook the rooms rather than the other way around, since the motel is nestled at the base of the surrounding range. Log-faced, one-story facility has 40 rooms, all on the ground floor. Some have kitchenettes.

Harrodsburg
(MOIST) map page 265, C-2

✕ Beaumont Inn Dining Room
638 Beaumont Inn Dr.; 859-734-3381 **$$**
Panfried chicken and excellent filet mignon are featured entrees. Friendly servers will keep pressing extra servings of mashed potatoes and cream gravy on you. Dining room is furnished in antebellum antiques.

✕ Trustees Office Dining Room
Shaker Village
3501 Lexington Rd.; 859-734-5411 or 800-734-5611 **$$**
Shaker specialties are served family style, including roast chicken, a local vegetable called salsify, and a tart Shaker lemon pie. Servers wear Shaker costumes (including bonnets), and the simple but elegant furniture is all handcrafted. No alcohol.

BAUER HAUS B&B

⊤ **Bauer Haus Bed & Breakfast**
362 N. College St.; 859-734-6289
or 877-734-6289 **$$-$$$**
Gabled Victorian three-story house near
Centre College campus has four rooms that
all feature sitting areas. Two have private
baths. Furnished with antiques. New carriage house. Full breakfast served.

⊤ **Baxter House**
1677 Lexington Rd.; 859-734-4877
$$-$$$
Handsome 1911 redbrick house built
around an 1840 log cabin. Four rooms,
three with private baths and fireplaces.
Seven acres of grounds; beautiful gardens.

BEAUMONT INN

⊤ **Beaumont Inn**
638 Beaumont Inn Dr.; 859-734-3381
$$-$$$
A distinguished antebellum mansion furnished with antiques. You can sit in wicker
furniture on the column-flanked front

porch or stroll the manicured grounds. Gift
shop sells Kentucky products and regional
cookbooks.

⊤ **Canaan Land Farm Bed & Breakfast**
700 Canaan Land Rd.; 859-734-3984
or 888-734-3984 **$$-$$$**
The 1785 brick farmhouse is furnished
with primitive antiques and has seven
guest rooms, six with private baths. There's
also a two-story 1815 log cabin on the
189-acre working sheep farm. Full breakfast served.

⊤ **Shaker Village of Pleasant Hill**
3501 Lexington Rd.; 859-734-5411
or 800-734-5611 **$$**
Shaker Village has restored 33 19th-century
buildings, built of a variety of materials:
white limestone, brick, and wood. Fourteen
offer lodging, with Shaker furnishings.
Some overnight accommodations have fire-
places. Beautifully situated on 2,800 acres
of rolling pastureland that stretches down
to the Kentucky River.

SHAKER VILLAGE OF PLEASANT HILL

Hazard
(WET) map page 265, D-2

✕ Cliff Hagan's Ribeye
200 Morton Blvd.; 606-439-3739 **$$**
Former University of Kentucky basketball
great has a mini-chain of eateries around
the state. This is one of Hazard's best din-
ing bets. It's decorated with basketball
memorabilia in Wildcat blue and white.
Sandwiches, salad bar, fried fish, and steak
are on hand. One of the few places in the
region where you can get a drink.

⊡ Buckhorn Lake State Resort Park
4441 KY-1833; 606-398-7510 **$-$$$**
Three-story stone lodge with 39 rooms, all
offering dramatic mountain vistas. One
side faces the lake. Lobby common area has
a handsome, copper-hooded fireplace.
Three modern cottages with decks overlooking the lake are also available.

BUCKHORN LAKE STATE RESORT PARK

Hazel
(DRY) map page 265, A-2

✕ Ann's Country Kitchen
H-641 S; 270-492-8195 **$**

Lively little cafe frequented by both locals
and tourists has a long list of sandwiches for
lunch. Homemade pies and cobblers vary
with the seasons. Casual country decor of
frilled curtains and samplers.

Henderson
(WET) map page 265, A/B-1/2

✕ Bon Ton Mini Mart
2036 Madison St.; 270-826-1207 **$**
Former convenience store has been converted to a small restaurant serving incredible spicy/crispy fried chicken. It's a
hidden gem that's been written up in
Gourmet magazine. Great for traditional
country breakfast, too, with homemade
biscuits.

✕ The Mill Restaurant
526 S. Main; 270-826-8012 **$-$$**
Furnished with antiques, this restaurant is a
downtown landmark and something of a
romantic inspiration. (Servers will tell you
how many marriage proposals have taken
place here.) Steak and prime rib are good
bets, as is the fried seafood.

✕ Wolf's Restaurant & Tavern
31 N. Green St.; 270-826-5221 **$$**
Two-story brick structure dates from 1878
when it was built as a bakery by German
immigrant George Wolf. Homemade
soups, thick pork chops, and dense cheese-
cakes are menu features.

⊡ Henderson Downtown Motel
425 N. Green; 270-827-2577 **$**
Modern two-story motel has 38 rooms with
choice of twin or double beds. Not fancy,

but certainly the price is right and it's centrally located.

John James Audubon State Park
US-41; 270-826-2247 **$$-$$$**
Stay in one of the five comfortably appointed log cabins on a lake, each equipped with a fireplace. Birders and naturalists can hike the trails followed by Audubon and view several of his famous paintings in the park's museum.

L&N Bed & Breakfast
327 N. Main St.; 270-831-1100 **$$**
Two-story redbrick Victorian house has a round front porch and white trim. Design features include stained glass and oak floors. It's furnished with antiques. All four guest rooms have private baths. Located downtown, one block from the river.

L&N BED & BREAKFAST

Monica's 8 Motel
3211 US-41 N; 270-827-9144 **$**
"Small little ol' motel" has 20 rooms, some

of which are furnished with king or queen beds. Clean and quiet, it's the sort of spot where an "upscale" room ($30) has TV with a VCR.

Sugar Creek Inn
2077 US-41 N; 270-827-0127 **$-$$$**
Two-story traditional motel has 65 rooms furnished with cherry-veneer furniture. Six of the rooms have whirlpool baths.

Victorian Quarters B&B Inn
109 Clay St.; 270-831-2778 **$$$**
Century-old four square mansion overlooks the Ohio River. Lovely gardens complete with a wooden gazebo. Period antiques decorate the three suites, all with baths. Choice of full or continental breakfast.

Hodgenville
(DRY) map page 265, C-2

Cruise Inn Motel
2768 Lincoln Farm Rd.; 270-358-9998 **$**
Small, 1950s-style motel with just 10 rooms. They are clean, simple, and cheap. Quiet, convenient place to stay when visiting nearby Lincoln-related sites.

Hopkinsville
(DRY) map page 265, B-2

✕ Woodshed Pit Bar-B-Que
1821 W. Seventh St.; 270-885-8144 **$**
Slow-smoked pork and chicken are the bulwarks of the menu. Fine baked ham is served with homemade corn bread. The decor is country casual and the service is friendly and timely.

Jamestown
(DRY) map page 265, C-2

LAKE CUMBERLAND STATE RESORT PARK

⊞ Lake Cumberland State Resort Park
5465 State Park Rd.; 270-343-3111
or 800-325-1709 **$-$$$**
The Lure Lodge has 48 rooms, a large dining room, and facilities such as an indoor pool and meeting rooms. Lobby with stone fireplace overlooks the lake. The smaller Pumpkin Lodge has 10 guest rooms. There are also 30 cottages on several sites around the park, some of which are chalets.

Kuttawa
(DRY) map page 265, A-2

✗ Cumberland House
5017 US-62 W; 270-388-7722 **$-$$**
While there's an a la carte menu featuring chicken, pork chops, and various steaks, the roadside cafe is known for its seafood buffet. You can pile your plate with frog legs, shrimp, clams, crab legs, and fried fish. Pies are homemade.

Lexington
(WET) map page 265, C-1

✗ a la lucie
159 N. Limestone St.; 859-252-5277 **$$$**
Fringed lampshades and upholstered booths create a Paris Left Bank atmosphere. The cooking combines continental flourishes with Kentucky ingredients. The demi-glace on your duck will have a touch of bourbon.

✗ Alfalfa
141 E. Main St.; 859-253-0014 **$-$$**
Located across from the main entrance to the University of Kentucky campus, this holdover vegetarian cafe and coffeehouse may remind you of your student activism days. Acoustic music and poetry readings are common evening entertainment.

✗ Atomic Cafe
265 S. Limestone St.; 859-254-1969 **$-$$**
Conch fritters in the heart of the Bluegrass? Absolutely, at this Caribbean cafe that also has a great selection of jerk dishes and colorful wall murals that evoke the islands. Good selection of imported beer.

✗ Emmett's Restaurant
1097 Duval St.; 859-245-4444 **$$$**
An award-winning wine list is one reason to visit here. Another is the menu, which features traditional dishes beautifully executed. These include real Southern panfried chicken and pork chops "bourbonnaise" served with creamy polenta rather than grits.

✗ Jalapeño's
285 New Circle Rd. NW; 859-299-8299 **$**
This Mexican place is worth seeking out. Its menu goes beyond tacos to include sev-

eral seafood dishes. Black-and-white photos of pre-1950s Mexico adorn the walls. The sangria is dangerously drinkable.

✕ Marikkas German Restaurant

411 Southland Dr.; 859-275-1925 $-$$
Along with the usual schnitzel, noodles, and kraut, this very good German eatery has 14 tap beers and a 500-bottle selection, mostly from the old country and served up in appropriate glassware—tall weiss beer glasses and steins for lagers.

✕ The Merrick Inn

3380 Tates Creek Rd.; 859-269-5417 $$
Traditional Southern fare, including fried chicken, country ham, and sides such as corn pudding are favorites at this elegant, old-fashioned eatery. The redbrick exterior and white columns complement the period furniture in the dining rooms.

✕ Nadine's

3735 Harrodsburg Rd.; 859-223-0797 $$-$$$
A famous martini list and a leather-covered sofa in the bar mark this as Lexington's little corner of hedonism. The chicken, beef, and seafood selections will be prepared with Southwestern, Asian, or continental seasonings. Great place to make a meal of several appetizers.

✕ Tachibana

785 Newtown Pike; 859-254-1911 $$
The influx of Japanese to the nearby Toyota plant has brought a corresponding proliferation of excellent Japanese restaurants in the area. Elegant rice-paper walls and bonsai create the right atmosphere for very fresh sushi and light-as-as-feather tempura dishes.

⊡ Brand House at Rose Hill

461 N. Limestone St.; 859-226-9464 $$$-$$$$
Four-poster beds with draperies and other period antiques furnish the high-ceilinged guest rooms in this 1812 home. There's an old-fashioned billiards room and a large dining room where breakfast is served. Located in one of the city's historic district.

BRAND HOUSE AT ROSE HILL

⊡ Gratz Park Inn

120 W. Second St.; 859-231-1777 $$$
Charming small hotel dating from the turn-of-the-last-century is furnished with English antiques and reproductions. It's three stories high with 44 guest rooms, and feels much more intimate than a hotel. Entrance courtyard is surrounded by a high brick wall that enhances privacy.

GRATZ PARK INN

Lexington *(cont'd)*

⊞ Hyatt Regency Lexington
401 W. High St.; 859-253-1234 **$$$$**
One of two hotels located right in the middle of the city; convenient for walking to shopping, restaurants, and Rupp Arena. Luxury suites are available in this modern hotel as are indoor pool and business center.

⊞ Marriott's Griffin Gate Resort
1800 Newtown Pike; 859-231-5100
or 800-228-9290 **$$$$**
The center of the sprawling resort on the edge of the city is this Greek Revival mansion dating from 1873. English antiques, crystal chandeliers, and plush Oriental carpeting furnish public areas and some rooms. Other buildings and facilities are more contemporary.

⊞ Radisson Plaza Hotel
369 W. Vine St.; 859-231-9000 **$$$**
This big downtown hotel is a 22-story high-rise. The reason to stay here, besides the chain hotel amenities, is for the view from the upper-floor rooms of the city's his-

toric neighborhoods, which fan out below and the surrounding Bluegrass countryside.

⊞ Scott Station Inn
305 E. Main St., Wilmore;
859-858-0121 **$**
Located in the picturesque little town of Wilmore near Lexington, Scott Station Inn was built in the late 1800s. There are six bedrooms, four with private baths. Popular with guests visiting nearby Asbury College, just three blocks down the street.

SCOTT STATION INN

⊞ Silver Springs Farm
3710 Leestown Rd.; 859-255-1784
$$-$$$$
Located on a 21-acre horse boarding farm, this is a place you can stay if you are traveling with your horse. There are extra turnout facilities. The 1880 white Federal-style house is surrounded by massive oaks and furnished with antiques. There's a guesthouse in addition to the three guest rooms.

⊞ Springs Inn
2020 Harrodsburg Rd.; 859-277-5751
$-$$$
Suburban motor hotel with 223 units spread over two stories is a very comfortable

modern facility. It is close to the attractions on the west and southwest side of the city, such as racetracks and the university. Non-smoking rooms and rooms for the disabled are available.

SWANN'S NEST AT CYGNET FARM

⊤ Swann's Nest at Cygnet Farm
3463 Rosalie Lane; 859-226-0095
$$$-$$$$
Neo-Colonial house is located on 15-acre horse farm just behind Keeneland Race Course. The reproductions of Early American furniture grace the bedrooms. Two suites are available in addition to three non-suite bedrooms. Because it's a horse farm, no children under 16 or pets allowed.

Louisville
(WET) map page 265, B/C-1

✕ Baxter Station Bar and Grill
1201 Payne St.; 502-584-1635 **$-$$**
Upscale pub fare is offered in this former neighborhood bar. Black-bean cakes, burgers, and entrees such as pasta and ginger salmon are typical. A toy train runs on a track near the ceiling, and murals depict passenger train interiors. Two dozen beers on tap. Three-season deck.

✕ Bluegrass Brewing Company
3929 Shelbyville Rd.; 502-899-7070 **$-$$**
Award-winning microbrews are served with entree salads, wood-oven-baked pizzas, and grilled entrees. Comfortable wood-accented interior and a multilevel deck.

✕ Bourbons Bistro
2255 Frankfort Ave.; 502-894-8838; **$$**
First stop for bourbon lovers and neophytes, since tasting flights of American whiskies are customized for both. The bistro has more than 130 bourbons on hand. And the upscale Southern-inspired menu of seafood, chicken, and steaks (often served with a country-ham accent) employs bourbon as an ingredient, too.

✕ Cafe Metro
1700 Bardstown Rd.; 502-458-4830;
$$-$$$
Art deco decor and intimate dining rooms mark this elegant restaurant. Specialties include seafood, duck, quail, and veal, including the signature Jagerschnitzel. Wine list includes a reserve list.

✕ Club Grotto
2116 Bardstown Rd.; 502-459-5275
$$-$$$
Subdued lighting makes the whimsical decor (carvings of flying frogs) somewhat mysterious. Bistro menu includes seafood, pork, lamb, and vegetarian dishes. Award-winning wine list.

Louisville *(cont'd)*

✕ The English Grill
Fourth St. and Broadway; 502-583-1234
$$$-$$$$
Gentlemen's club decor complete with paintings of horse scenes as well as upholstered side chairs in intimate oak-paneled dining room. Located on the second floor of the historic Brown Hotel. Lamb, quail, and seafood are specialties. Dessert souffles are masterpieces.

✕ Jack Fry's
1007 Bardstown Rd.; 502-452-9244
$$-$$$
Live jazz in intimate black-and-white restaurant dominated by a bar give the place a New York cafe atmosphere. Seafood is outstanding, but then so are the lamb and beef dishes. Desserts include homemade sorbets and cookies.

✕ Le Relais
Taylorsville Rd. at Bowman Field;
502-451-9020 **$$**
Located in the terminal of Louisville's original airport (ca. Lindbergh). The French menu is accompanied by an award-winning wine list. Veal, duck, and trout are notable. There's outdoor dining on a deck overlooking a small airfield.

✕ Lilly's
1147 Bardstown Rd.; 502-451-0447
$$-$$$
Green-and-purple decor runs through several small dining rooms, which have distinctive murals. Locally produced, seasonal ingredients. Lamb, chicken, beef, and

seafood served. Nightly veal special incorporates pasta and features sauces.

✕ Lynn's Paradise Cafe
984 Barret Ave.; 502-583-3447 **$-$$**
Formica and Bakelite are the decorator materials, not to mention the toys and mismatched salt and pepper shakers on the tables, and the concrete animals in the parking lot. Big portions at breakfast, lunch, and dinner. Southern specialties in the morning. From meatloaf to lobster in the evening.

✕ Mazzoni's Oyster Cafe
2804 Taylorsville Rd.; 502-451-4436 **$**
Good fried fish, but this modest cafe is known for the invention of the rolled oyster, a Louisville delicacy of plump mollusk rolled in cracker crumbs and deep-fried. Dip the concoction in hot sauce. Good oyster stew, too.

✕ The Oakroom
500 S. Fourth St.; 502-585-3200 **$$-$$$**
Beautiful oak-lined, formal dining room of the Seelbach Hotel. Continental service and menu, but dishes are hybrid Kentucky: spoonfish caviar, bourbon mash bread, farm-raised buffalo, Kentucky lamb, and Appalachian-foraged ginger. Most extensive wine cellar in the state.

✕ Pat's Steak House
2437 Brownsboro Rd.; 502-893-2062 **$$**
Tender filets served with traditional sides such as baked potatoes and lima beans. Good fried chicken and rich fried chicken livers, too. Two-story house near downtown has many cozy dining rooms. Bourbon Manhattans are first rate.

✗ Uptown Cafe
1624 Bardstown Rd.; 502-458-4212 $-$$
Pasta dishes come in whole or half portions, and there are many hot sandwiches as well as grilled entrees. Veal, seafood, beef, and vegetarian dishes. Most wines available by the glass.

✗ Vincenzo's
150 S. Fifth St.; 502-580-1350 $$-$$$
Tuxedo-clad servers prepare many salads, such as traditional Caesar, at tableside. Veal, seafood, and beef are among the Italian specialties. Pastas are elegant. Excellent wine list with many fine Tuscan selections.

🖼 Breckinridge Inn
2800 Breckinridge Lane; 502-469-6130 $$
Handsome suburban motor hotel in white-brick Colonial style. Convenient to major shopping malls and expressway to downtown. Facilities include lighted tennis courts and swimming pool. There are 123 rooms in two stories.

🖼 Brown Hotel
335 W. Broadway; 502-583-1234 $$$$
Grand hotel dating from 1923. Gold-and-marble, second-floor lobby runs the length of the building. Decorated with antique European furniture and artwork. Attentive care of guests; 24-hour room service.

🖼 Central Park Bed & Breakfast
1353 S. Fourth St.; 502-638-1505 $$$-$$$$
Limestone 1884 Italianate house overlooks Old Louisville's Central Park. Ornate plaster and woodwork throughout. The eight spacious guest rooms (some are suites) are furnished with antiques and all have private baths. Full breakfast.

🖼 Columbine Bed & Breakfast
1707 S. Third St.; 502-635-5000 $$-$$$
Massive Ionic columns flank the entrance to this Italianate mansion built for a timber baron in 1896. Interior details include a sweeping hand-carved mahogany and Italian marble double staircase. Five rooms and one suite, all with private bath. Elegant gourmet breakfast.

🖼 Executive Inn
978 Phillips Lane; 502-367-6161 $$-$$$$

🖼 Executive West
830 Phillips Lane; 502-367-2251 $$-$$$$
Belong to a complex of Tudor-style motor inns with a total of over 1,200 rooms. Attentive guest service, even though facility is sprawling. Located by the Louisville International Airport and the State Fairgrounds.

🖼 The Galt House
140 N. Fourth St.; 502-589-5201 $$$-$$$$
Twenty-five-story, 565-room hotel located on the river. Views of the river from guest rooms are unparalleled. Revolving restaurant on top floor.

🖼 Inn at the Park
1332 S. Fourth St.; 502-637-6930 $$-$$$$
Red stone, Richardson Romanesque mansion next to Central Park has five rooms and two suites, all with private baths. Furnished throughout with period antiques and reproductions. Decorated with fine art. Full breakfast served.

Louisville *(cont'd)*

⊞ Inn at Woodhaven

401 S. Hubbards Lane; 502-895-1011 or 888-895-1011 **$$-$$$$**

An 1853 Gothic Revival mansion located in the suburbs has a total of eight rooms and two suites in the main house and matching carriage house. There's a charming Octagon Cottage too, with wraparound porch and upstairs reading nook. Full breakfast served in room if requested.

INN AT WOODHAVEN

⊞ Inn off the Alley

325 Bardstown Rd.; 502-451-0121 **$$**

Tucked away behind the busy storefronts of Bardstown Road, this B&B is perfectly situated for those wanting to check out the nearby boutiques and restaurants. Three suites each include bath and kitchenette.

⊞ Pinecrest Cottage Bed & Breakfast

2806 Newburg Rd.; 502-454-3800 **$$$**

This hundred-year-old, wood-clapboard cottage sits on six acres of woods and gardens certified as a Natural Backyard Wildlife Habitat. Cottage has tastefully decorated living room with working fireplace, king

bedroom, large bath, and food-stocked, eat-in kitchen. Access to host- house swimming pool and tennis court.

⊞ Rocking Horse Manor

1022 S. Third St.; 502-583-0408 or 888-467-7322 **$$$-$$$$**

One of Old Louisville's mansions dating from 1888. Richardson Romanesque house has six guest rooms, all with bath. Has an exercise area.

SEELBACH HILTON

⊞ Seelbach Hilton Hotel

500 S. Fourth St.; 502-585-3200 **$$$$**

City's first grand hotel, opened in 1905. Two-story marble lobby features eight murals depicting Kentucky history. Rooms furnished with four-poster beds. Bathrooms have marble and gold fixtures. You may sense some lingering aura of F. Scott Fitzgerald, who stayed here and used the hotel for a scene in *The Great Gatsby.*

⊞ Tucker House Bed & Breakfast

2406 Tucker Station Rd.; 502-297-8007 **$$$**

Early 19th-century Federal-style house located in the National Rural Historic District, but only 20 minutes from downtown.

Original woodwork throughout house, which is furnished with period antiques. Four bedrooms, each with bath.

Madisonville
(MOIST) map page 265, B-2

✕ **Cody's Steak House**
50 Chelsea Dr.; 270-825-1949 $-$$
Prices, as well as the casual atmosphere, are right for local families. Dining area and bar are decorated with sports memorabilia. Ribs, chops, steak, and fried seafood are the menu mainstays.

✕ **Di Fabio's Casapela**
17 W. Center St.; 270-825-1900 $
Traditional Italian cuisine includes vegetarian pasta dishes. Daily specials include fresh seafood, such as sea scallops. Tiramisu, cannoli, cheesecakes, all made in-house. Reasonably priced wine list.

🛏 **Best Western Pennyrile Inn**
Pennyrile Pkwy., Exit 37; 270-258-5201 $
A two-story, 60-room modern inn with amenities including a 24-hour restaurant, coffee-makers in room, swimming pool, and business services. Pets are accepted; complimentary breakfast buffet.

🛏 **Hammock-Moore House Bed & Breakfast**
129 S. Main St.; 270-821-5812 $$$
The wrap-around porch with red-tile floor attached to this 1892 Victorian house has more floor space than many homes. The five guest rooms are reached via a circular carved-oak staircase. Breakfast options include a Continental "early bird" or a hot breakfast.

Mammoth Cave Park
(DRY) map page 265, B-2

🛏 **Mammoth Cave Hotel**
Park Entrance Rd., 270-758-2225 $$
Two-story, 110-room hotel on the grounds of the park is designed to blend in with the landscape. Wood-trimmed. Several two-bedroom suites. Very quiet and comfortable with private balconies and patios. (Don't feed the cute raccoons that come around begging for scraps. They'll scratch at your door all night!)

Mayfield
(DRY) map page 265, A-2

🛏 **Days Inn**
1101 W. Houseman St.;
270-247-3700 $
Pretty much the only lodging game in town. Two-story motel has 80 rooms, pool, restaurant. Comfortable, if generic.

Maysville
(WET) map page 265, D-1

✕ **Da Sha's Restaurant**
1166 US-68 S; 606-564-9275 $$
Brass- and wood-decorated bistro has a menu that runs to soup and sandwich combinations, entree salads, grilled chops and streaks, and fried or grilled seafood. On "the Hill" overlooking the town. Full bar.

✕ **Laredo's Restaurant**
545 Tucker Dr.; 606-759-8749 $$
Southwestern decor. Menu features steak, ribs, chops, and chicken. Appetizers include

quesadillas and salsas with chips. Cowboy theme extends to peanuts in the shell to munch with drinks.

✕ Union Cafe Restaurant
719 Forest Ave.; 606-564-6049 $
Specialty is "the mini-burger." Selection of sandwiches includes grilled chicken, pork tenderloin. Beer only; no wine or spirits.

⊞ French Quarter Inn
25 E. McDonald Pkwy.; 606-564-8000 or 800-966-9892 $$
Downtown near the Ohio River bridge. Some rooms in the four-story, 64-room hotel have river views. Cherry-veneer furniture in attractive and comfortable rooms. Tippedore's restaurant has New Orleans–inspired menu.

⊞ Kleir Haus Bed & Breakfast
912 US-62; 606-759-7663 $$
Restored 1855 farmhouse with wrap-around porch is located in rolling hill country, next door to a golf course. Three guest rooms, two with private baths, have a mix of antiques and more modern furniture. Full breakfast provided.

⊞ Ramada Inn
484 Moody Dr.; 606-564-6793 $$
Some of the three-story motel's 114 rooms have sitting rooms. Facility includes a swimming pool and restaurant.

Middlesboro
(DRY) map page 265, D-2

⊞ Holiday Inn Express
1252 N. 12th St.; 606-248-6860 $$
Three-story motel with 60 rooms is located almost directly across from the entrance to Cumberland Gap National Historical Park. Rooms are spacious and those not facing the highway look out onto the mountains.

RIDGE RUNNER B&B

⊞ Ridge Runner Bed & Breakfast
208 Arthur Heights; 606-248-4299 $$
Beautiful Victorian mansion with ornate woodwork was built in 1890 for one of the town's founders. Set on hills surrounding Middlesboro. View from antique-furnished rooms and house-length front porch is of mist-shrouded mountains. Four rooms, two with private bath and two shared. Full country breakfast in dining room.

Midway
(WET) map page 265, C-1

⊞ Wallace Station
3854 Old Frankfort Pike; 859-846-5161 $
Former railroad station, now a "Bluegrass deli." Country ham is often paired with locally made artisan cheeses on the thick sandwiches. The house barbecue sauce has a generous lashing of bourbon.

☷ **Rebel's Roost Bed and Breakfast at Dearborn Farm**
1234 Weisenberger Mill Rd.; 846-9799 **$$$**
The four guest rooms of this B&B are in an 1810 farmhouse on an authentic, 30-acre working Thoroughbred-horse farm. The full breakfast includes homemade muffins and locally milled grits.

Monticello
(DRY) map page 265, C 2

☷ **Anchor Motel**
1077 N. Main St.; 606-348-8441 **$**
Two buildings, a one-story and a two-story, in downtown motel have sandstone facades with red roofs. Traditional decor; 55 rooms.

☷ **Beaver Creek Resort**
✕ KY-92 W; 606-348-7280
or 800-844-8862 **$$$$**
Large, modern marina on Lake Cumberland rents houseboats by the weekend or the week. Top-of-line models are luxurious, with king-sized beds. All have galleys and heads (kitchens and baths, to you landlubbers). Dockside restaurant has grilled and fried dishes, mostly seafood.

Morehead
(WET) map page 265, D-1

✕ **Fuzzy Duck Coffee Shop**
240 Morehead Plaza; 606-784-9877 **$**
A "fuzzy duck" is a blend of three varieties of coffee bean. Little cafe has sandwiches, pasta and green salads, and wraps, as well as coffee drinks made from freshly ground

beans. A hangout for faculty from Morehead State University.

☷ **Brownwood B&B Cabins**
1350 KY-801 S, Farmers;
606-784-8799 **$$-$$$**
Modern but rustic wooden home contains a guest suite. There are three separate cabins decorated with country quilts and outfitted with potbellied stoves. Beautiful mountain setting with lake view. Full breakfast includes buttermilk pancakes.

☷ **Carter Caves State Resort Park**
344 Caveland Drive, Olive Hill; 800-325-0059 **$$-$$$**
Guests have a choice of the intimate, 2-room fieldstone lodge or one of the woodland cottages, outfitted with queen-size beds and wood-burning fireplaces. Tours are available of the park's striking caves, featuring a 30-foot waterfall and rare bat species.

☷ **Ramada Inn**
698 Flemingsburg Rd.; 606-784-7591 **$$**
Two stories house 141 rooms, so inn is large enough to support a restaurant and cocktail lounge. Lodging of choice for parents bringing students to the university.

Mount Olivet
(DRY) map page 265, C-1

☷ **Blue Licks Battlefield State Resort Park**
US-68; 859-289-5507 or 800-443-7008 **$-$$**
A new 32-room fieldstone lodge. The view of the Licking River is obscured by trees in

the summer, but the water is within easy walking distance. A 150-seat dining room has an impressive fireplace. Two modern, two-bedroom woodland cottages are also available.

Murray
(WET) map page 265, A-2

✕ Bull Pen Steaks & Spirits
101 S. Fifth St.; 270-759-5030 $

This 1890s building in the heart of downtown has been converted into a spacious bistro specializing in hand-cut Angus steaks. The Bull Pen is also known for its fresh produce and local ingredients, such as locally raised chicken.

✕ 15th & Olive Delicatessen and Grille
216 N. 15th St.; 270-753-1551 $-$$

Located in an art deco building in the middle of town, this establishment functions as a deli by day and as a stylish bistro by night. The deli serves sandwiches piled high with corned beef or curried chicken. Also known for Thai pasta, stuffed breads, and fresh baked goods. Favorite lunch hangout for college faculty. In the evening, the bistro serves seafood, pasta dishes, pork tenderloin, and filet mignon. Smoke free.

✕ Los Portales
Olympia Plaza Shopping Center, #12 ; 270-767-0315 $

Colorful interior and servers who never stand still make for a lively dining experience in this Mexican eatery. Tamales are roasted in corn husks. Burritos are very, very big.

⌑ Amerihost Inn
1210 N. 12th St.; 270-759-5910 $$-$$$

Downtown Murray outlet of chain has con-

temporary design and a striking indoor pool area with an adjacent sauna.

⌑ Murray Plaza Court
502 S. 12th St.; 270-753-2682 $

Two-story family motel has 40 rooms located very near Murray State campus. Decor is simple and attractive. Pets are allowed.

Owensboro
(WET) map page 265, B-2

✕ Briarpatch
2760 Veach Rd.; 270-685-3329 $-$$

Brer Rabbit never had it this good. Large restaurant with pleasantly landscaped grounds is made comfortable with stone fireplace and stained-glass windows. Menu consists largely of beef and seafood, but there's an extensive salad bar, too.

✕ Colby's
202 W. Third St.; 270-685-4239 $$

Located in a restored 1890s storefront in downtown and furnished with antiques, the restaurant gives a taste of what 19th-century Owensboro might have been like. Menu flavors are up to date with grilled Angus steaks, seafood, and pasta offerings.

✕ Colby's Deli
401 Frederica St.; 270-684-2495 $

Favorite local deli for catered box lunches. Stacked sandwiches and fresh salads are very good. Soup selection, from chicken noodle to loaded potato, changes often. Fresh baked goods, too.

✕ El Toribios Mexican Restaurant
3034 E. Fourth St.; 270-683-8361 $

Owned, run, and patronized by Mexicans, so the cuisine is authentic and far superior to that of chains nearby. Fresh guacamole and chile rellenos are notable, as is the flan.

✕ Moonlite Bar-B-Que Inn
2840 W. Parrish Ave.; 270-684-8143 **$-$$**
Sprawling restaurant decorated as a country hunting lodge. Packed at lunch for the all-you-can-eat barbecue buffet. Kentucky burgoo and pulled mutton sandwiches are specialties, as well as smoked pork, beef, and chicken.

✕ Old Hickory Pit Bar-B-Q
338 Washington Ave.; 270-926-9000 **$**
Locals will tell you that the "Q" here is even tastier than that at better-known rival Moonlite. Western Kentucky's specialty, mutton, is represented here pulled and chopped—or, unusually, as ribs. Combo meals available so you can sample widely.

⊞ Executive Inn Rivermont
One Executive Blvd.; 270-926-8000
$-$$$
Main hotel in the city is located on the riverfront and next door to the arts complex. It has a cabaret that hosts traveling entertainers performing music from Broadway to Bluegrass. It has 550 rooms and two swimming pools in its seven stories.

HELTON HOUSE B&B

⊞ Helton House B&B
103 E. 23rd St.; 270-926-7117 **$$**
Arts-and-crafts, mission-style house in one of the city's older neighborhoods dates from 1920. Four traditionally decorated rooms share two baths; living and dining rooms are furnished with antiques. Sunporch is a great place to read; the third-floor suite has private bath. Full Southern breakfast.

⊞ Ramada Inn
3136 W. Second St.; 270-685-3941 **$-$$**
Centrally located, two-story, 145-room motel with restaurant and heated pool. Attractive decor of green and ivory is reflected in the comfortable, well-appointed rooms.

Paducah
(WET) map page 265, A-2

✕ Cynthia's
125 Market House Sq.; 270-443-3319 **$$**
Northern Italian menu with veal, seafood, chicken, and beef dishes. The service is very attentive, and the wine list is well-matched to the cuisine.

✕ Jeremiah's Froghead Brewery
225 Broadway; 270-443-3991 **$$**
You can get frog legs on a plate, but, no worries, there aren't any frogs in the ales, lagers, and porters brewed on site. As for food, the house special is a 20-ounce sirloin, so don't fill up on beer. And you'll want your wits about you if you opt for the cook-your-own dishes.

✕ Max's Brick Oven
112 Market House Sq.; 270-575-3473
$-$$
Max's specializes in big entrée salads and, not surprisingly, brick-oven pizzas. Seafood,

pasta, and veal dishes round out the menu. The Courtyard Bar stays open late.

✕ Parcell's Deli and Grille

2201 Broadway; 270-575-3354 $
This is the place for a quick lunch when you're in the mood for a burger, a freshly made chicken salad, or a classic patty melt. There's outdoor seating in good weather.

✕ Whaler's Catch

123 N. Second St.; 270-444-7701 $$
The Old New England nautical decor includes a hand-carved bar dating from 1863. Among the creative seafood menu's specialties are a seafood, corn, and potato stew and fish stuffed with crabmeat.

⌑ Courtyard by Marriott

3835 Technology Dr.; 270-442-3600 $$-$$$
There are 100 stylish, contemporary rooms in a facility that offers a bar, restaurant, two swimming pools, and business facilities. Monthly rates are available if you are planning an extended stay in the area.

COURTYARD BY MARRIOTT

⌑ Executive Inn Paducah Riverfront

One Executive Blvd.; 270-443-8000 $$-$$$
Four-story, 400-room modern motor hotel is located on the riverfront next to the convention center. If you run out of any supplies on the road, there are a grocery store, gift shop, and shopping arcade within the complex. Comfortable rooms include suites with wet bars and refrigerators. Indoor pool and exercise room, too.

⌑ Fisher Mansion Bed & Breakfast

901 Jefferson St.; 270-443-0716 $$-$$$$
Queen Anne–style mansion has three rooms and one suite, all with Victorian furnishings. A full Southern breakfast is served in the formal dining room or, weather permitting, in a garden courtyard graced with a fountain.

⌑ Rosewood Inn Bed & Breakfast

2740 S. Friendship Rd.;
270-554-6632 $$-$$$
White-clapboard farmhouse with Victorian detailing is located on several acres about 15 minutes from downtown. There are two guest rooms (one with private bath) and two suites. The Garden Room overlooks the landscaped grounds. Breakfast is served in the sunroom.

⌑ Super 8

5001 Hinkleville Rd.; 270-442-3334 $-$$
Two-story motor inn has 91 rooms attractively decorated. There's a heated pool on the nicely landscaped property. Located at the edge of the city just off of I-24 and near the point where the Tennessee River flows into the Ohio.

Paintsville
(DRY) map page 265, D-1/2

✕ Mandarin House

507 S. Mayo Trail; 606-789-5313 $-$$

Not as extensive a menu as you might find in a larger town, but the stir fries, soups, and spring rolls are a nice change of pace in a region where the fare is heavy on chicken-fried steak and pork chops.

X **Wilma's Restaurant**
212 Court St.; 606-789-5911 $
Little cafe with home-cooked specials such as chicken and dumplings with two sides. You'll get change for your fiver. Other fare includes burgers and sandwiches.

⌂ **Days Inn Paintsville**
512 S. Mayo Trail; 606-789-3551 $-$$
All the singles in this 72-room motel have king-sized beds. Contemporary decor is tidy, if unexciting. Pool and exercise equipment, too. Some suites have whirlpools.

⌂ **Ramada Inn**
624 James Trimble Blvd.; 606-789-4242 $$-$$$
Largest lodging facility in the area with 129 rooms. Restaurant, game room, and heated indoor/outdoor swimming pool. Decor is rather incongruously (for the eastern Kentucky mountains) New Orleans–style, but tastefully done.

Paris
(WET) map page 265, C-1

X **B J's Creekview Restaurant**
8 E. Main St.; 859-987-4647 $-$$
Casual eatery backs up to Stoner Creek. Steaks, pasta dishes, seafood combo, and Cornish hen are specialties. Full bar.

⌂ **Colonial Motel**
1493 Main St.; 859-987-3255 $
Small (eight rooms), old-fashioned motel at

town center is no-frills, but in the words of the owner, "That's how we keep our rates down." Good for the budget-minded.

⌂ **Country Charm Bed and Breakfast**
505 Hutchinson Rd.; 859-988-1006 or 866-988-1006 $$-$$$
The 19th-century Gothic revival brick house is in the heart of a working Bluegrass farm. A graceful oak staircase leads to the guest rooms, furnished with four-poster beds and Persian rugs. Suites are available, too.

Pikeville
(WET) map page 265, D-2

X **Windmill Family Restaurant**
90 Weddington Branch Rd.; 606-432-2222 $
Pleasant, casual spot (across the parking lot from the Daniel Boone Motor Inn) where breakfast—including homemade biscuits and gravy—is served anytime Other fare runs to country-fried steak, liver and onions, and fried chicken.

⌂ **Daniel Boone Motor Inn**
US-23 N; 606-432-0365 $
The two-story independently owned motel has 120 traditionally decorated rooms. Despite the name, it is not filled with corny pseudo-pioneer bric-a-brac. Very friendly local staff.

⌂ **Landmark Inn**
190 S. Mayo Trail; 606-432-2545 $-$$
Attractive modern motor inn has 103 rooms in four stories. It's located in a nest of chain motel outlets along the US-23 turnoff to town. It's notable for having a rooftop restaurant and cocktail lounge.

⊞ **Moderne Villa Motel**
1066 S. Mayo Trail; 606-432-2188 **$**
Small, 50-room motel that has added features of a pool and a playground. Good bargain choice for families. Pets allowed.

Pineville
(DRY) map page 265, D-2

⊞ **Pine Mountain State Resort Park**
1050 State Park Rd.; 606-337-3066
or 800-325-1712 **$-$$$**
Comfortable stone-and-wood lodge is set right on the mountainside. Rooms with modern decor have decks overlooking the woods. Covered wooden walkways connect rooms. Grounds are landscaped with native pink and white rhododendrons that put on a spectacular show in the spring. Cottages, from log to modern, are available, too.

PINE MOUNTAIN STATE RESORT PARK

Prestonsburg
(WET) map page 265, D-2

⊞ **Holiday Inn-Prestonsburg**
1887 US-23 N; 606-886-0001 **$$**
The 117 rooms in this three-story motel were recently remodeled, so the furniture

and decor are new and comfortable. There are a restaurant and bar in the motel. Other facilities include a heated pool and exercise equipment.

JENNY WILEY STATE RESORT PARK

⊞ **Jenny Wiley State Resort Park**
75 Theatre Court; 606-886-2711
or 800-325-0142 **$$**
Handsome two-story, 66-room lodge is set right in the dense woods of the park, with a view of Dewey Lake on one side. There's easy access to well-marked hiking trails. This is one of the most "away-from-it-all" parks in the state system. Named for a pioneer woman who was kidnapped by Indians and survived.

Richmond
(MOIST) map page 265, C-2

✕ **Elvira's**
1105 Kim Kent Dr.; 859-625-0319 **$**
This casual Italian eatery offers homemade pasta at fast-food prices. Usually spaghetti with a choice of sauces is the staple (try the freshly made marinara sauce); sausage-rich lasagna and cheese ravioli are also recommended.

⊞ Barnes Mill Bed & Breakfast

1268 Barnes Mill Rd.; 859-623-5509 **$-$$**
There are four rooms (two shared baths) and a honeymoon suite in this 1916 brick house furnished in period antiques. When the weather is fine, you'll want to relax in the wicker furniture on the wraparound porch. Hot, home-baked bread at breakfast.

BENNETT HOUSE B&B

⊞ Bennett House Bed & Breakfast

419 W. Main St.; 859-623-7876 **$$-$$$**
Located in the historic residential section of Richmond, the Queen Anne–Romanesque house is easily spotted because of its four tall chimneys. It was built in the late 1800s and has a massive cherry staircase leading to the guest rooms. Lovely Victorian parlor has cozy wing chairs by the fireplace. Breakfast is served in a spacious dining room.

⊞ Holiday Inn

100 Eastern Bypass; 859-623-9220 **$$**
Two-story, 140-room motor hotel is convenient to Eastern Kentucky University campus, so it fills up fast the weekends parents are bringing students to school or fetching them for summer. Modern decor, pool, and picnic tables on grounds. Has a full-service restaurant.

⊞ La Quinta

1751 Lexington Rd.; 859-623-9121 **$$**
The Southwestern mission design (complete with bell tower) makes the two-story, 95-room motor inn quite noticeable in log-cabin land. There's a heated pool and pets are allowed.

Russell Springs
(DRY) map page 265, C-2

⊞ Cumberland Lodge

US-127 S; 270-866-4208 **$**
Two-story, 53-room modern motel has amenities such as a swimming pool and exercise room. Rose is the color scheme for the bedrooms. There's a complimentary continental breakfast and rooms have coffee-makers.

Shelbyville
(WET) map page 265, C-1

✕ Bistro 535

535 Main St.; 502-633-4147 **$$**
Versatile menu of sautéed chicken and seafood dishes as well as vegetarian and pasta selections. Attractive setting in old storefront with exposed brick walls and eclectic modern artwork. Good wine list. Excellent homemade desserts.

✕ Buffalo Crossing

1140 Bagdad Rd.; 502-647-0377 **$-$$**
The 1,000-acre farm supports 500 head of buffalo, many of which wind up on the menu in the casual family restaurant. Burgers, barbecue, chili, meatloaf, and steaks are all made with the lean meat that sustained the Native Americans and the pioneers.

FOOD & LODGING

✕ Ken-Tex Bar-B-Q

1163 Mt. Eden Rd.; 502-633-2463 **$**
On a hill above the highway is this little log building with the tell-tale iron smokers outside. Inside, the barbecue—ribs, pulled pork, chicken—is served up Texas-style in a savory sauce with equally savory sides.

✕ Science Hill Inn

525 Washington St.; 502-432-2227 **$$**
Elegant Georgian dining room in what was, in the early 19th-century, a school. Furnished with walnut and cherry antiques. Fried chicken and country ham are served with traditional Southern sides including hot-water corn bread. Save room for the bread pudding with bourbon sauce.

⌂ Country Hearth Inn

100 Howard Dr.;
502-633-5771 **$-$$**
Very attractive modern motor lodge that has old-fashioned details like a lobby fireplace, but all up-to-date advantages such as whirlpool baths in seven of its 40 rooms. Two-story, "new country" architecture.

Slade
(DRY) map page 265, D-2

NATURAL BRIDGE STATE RESORT PARK

⌂ Natural Bridge State Resort Park

2135 Natural Bridge Rd.; 606-663-2214 or 800-325-1710 **$$$**
View from the balconies in the 35 rooms of Hemlock Lodge are of ridge after ridge of mist-shrouded mountains, part of the vast Daniel Boone National Forest. One of the best places in Kentucky to enjoy fall colors. Woodland one- and two-bedroom cottages are private.

Somerset
(DRY) map page 265, C-2

⌂ Doolin House Bed and Breakfast

502 North Main St.; 606-678-9494
$$-$$$$
This modern downtown B&B is a reproduction of an 1850s house. Its five guest rooms are named for Kentucky Derby winners. The proprietors are trained chefs, so it's worth waking up in time for breakfast.

⌂ Raintree Inn Bed & Breakfast

3314 Old Hwy-90, Bronston;
606-561-5225 **$$-$$$**
If you saw the movie *Raintree County* with Elizabeth Taylor and Montgomery Clift, you'll know what this antebellum mansion with the huge sycamore out front looks like. It was used as the setting. The elegant main house is furnished with antiques and has three spacious guest rooms with fireplaces, two rooms in the historic barn, and a carriage house with two bedrooms. Traditional Southern breakfast is served in the dining room.

Springfield
(MOIST) map page 265, C-2

⌂ **Glenmar Plantation Bed & Breakfast**
2444 Valley Hill Rd.; 859-284-7791
or 800-828-3330 **$$**
The owners still farm the property surrounding this 1785 Georgian manor house. Barns with log interiors date back to the 1790s. Guest rooms are furnished with period antiques. Full Kentucky breakfast is dished up in the morning.

⌂ **Maple Hill Manor**
2941 Perryville Rd.; 859-336-3075 **$$**
There are seven bedrooms furnished with antiques in this handsome 1851 Greek Revival mansion. Period details include a beautiful hand-carved, cherry spiral staircase and a restored mural in the dining room that was discovered beneath wallpaper during restoration. Set on 14 acres.

Versailles
(WET) map page 265, C-1

✕ **Kessler's 1891 Eatery**
197 S. Main St.; 859-879-3344 **$-$$**
Located a block from the courthouse in a century-old storefront, this old-time eatery has a varied menu ranging from barbecue (smoked on site) to pasta, fried fish, and steak. House specialty is an apple-stuffed pork loin.

✕ **Sweet Potatoes**
520 Versailles Circle; 859-879-1718 **$**
Pleasant, informal cafe in a shopping center just outside of town. Wide variety of sandwiches and burgers with different toppings. Big entree salads include one with blackened chicken, and a chef's salad.

⌂ **1823 Historic Rose Hill Inn**
233 Rose Hill; 859-873-5957
or 800-307-0460 **$$-$$$**
Four rooms, with private bath (including one with a copper tub), a charming brick cottage, and a private apartment are the accommodations in this lovingly restored 1823 Southern Gothic mansion. Interior details include ornate Federal mantelpieces. Landscaped grounds.

1823 HISTORIC ROSE HILL INN

⌂ **Montgomery Inn**
270 Montgomery Ave.; 859-873-4478
or 800-526-9801 **$$-$$$$**
This handsome three-story Victorian inn is filled with Kentucky antiques. Of the 12 rooms all but one are suites with jacuzzi and private bath. Old-fashioned porch has rockers and swings. Full gourmet breakfast is served on an airy sunporch.

Wickliffe
(DRY) map page 265, A-2

✕ **Backwoods Bar-B-Q**
93 Green St.; 270-335-3355 **$**
This is an oasis in a region where there are few restaurants other than fast-food outlets. The ribs, chicken, and pulled pork (tender

shoulder meat) are all hickory-smoked. Sides and sweets are homemade.

☷ Wickliffe Motel
520 N. Fourth St.; 270-335-3121 $
This old-fashioned, privately owned motel is located just a few blocks from the Indian mounds archaeological site. The 19 rooms are clean and quiet.

Williamsburg
(DRY) map page 265, C-2

☷ Cumberland Inn
649 S. 10th St.; 606-539-4100 $$-$$$$
This elegant new inn built in Colonial style belongs to Cumberland College. The 50 rooms are furnished with reproductions of Early American antiques. Dining room serves traditional Southern food. Of interest is a small wildlife museum on the grounds. There are gas-log fireplaces in suites and a very nice outdoor pool.

Winchester
(WET) map page 265, C-1

✕ Engine House Deli
9 W. Lexington Ave.;
859-737-0560 $-$$
Sandwiches and salads are served in this kid-friendly deli in Winchester's first fire station. The desserts alone make a visit worthwhile. A plus: rotating installations from regional artists.

✕ Halls on the River
1225 Athens-Boonesboro Rd.;
859-527-6620 $$

Local favorite gathering place, with a deck out back overlooking the Kentucky River. Catfish, chicken, and steak dinners anchor the menu. The country and western music gets loud, but that's part of the atmosphere.

☷ Guerrant Mountain Mission B&B
21 Valentine Court; 859-745-1284 $$
Unusual setting in what was once an Edwardian hospital and nurses' home. Located in the mountains, and decorated with late-19th-century antiques. Two suites available.

GUERRANT MOUNTAIN MISSION B&B

☷ Windswept Farm Bed & Breakfast
5952 Old Boonesboro Rd.;
859-745-1245 $$-$$$
Three suites with private baths in this 1850s Greek Revival redbrick mansion. Their windows overlook rolling Bluegrass farms. Full Southern breakfast is served at the time you request.

STATEWIDE TRAVEL
INFORMATION

Listings

Note: COMPASS AMERICAN GUIDES makes every effort to ensure the accuracy of its information; however, as conditions and prices change frequently, we recommend that readers also contact local sources for the most up-to-date information.

VISITOR INFORMATION

KY Department of Travel	800-225-8747	Lexington CVB	800-845-3959
KY Road Conditions	800-459-7623	Louisville CVB	800-792-5595
KY State Parks	800-255-7275		
KY Bed & Breakfast Assn.	888-281-8188	Kentucky Tourism website:	
		www.kentuckytourism.com	

METRIC CONVERSIONS

To convert feet (ft) to meters (m), multiply feet by .305. To convert meters to feet, multiply meters by 3.28.

1 ft = .30 m	1 m = 3.3 ft
2 ft = .61 m	2 m = 6.6 ft
3 ft = .91 m	3 m = 9.8 ft
4 ft = 1.2 m	4 m =13.1 ft
5 ft = 1.5 m	5 m =16.4 ft

To convert miles (mi) to kilometers (km), multiply miles by .62. To convert kilometers to miles, multiply kilometers by 1.61.

1 mi = 1.6 km	1 km = .62 mi
2 mi = 3.2 km	2 km = 1.2 mi
3 mi = 4.8 km	3 km = 1.9 mi
4 mi = 6.4 km	4 km = 2.5 mi
5 mi = 8.1 km	5 km = 3.1 mi

To convert pounds (lb) to kilograms (kg), multiply pounds by .46. To convert kilograms to pounds, multiply pounds by 2.2.

1 lb = .45 kg	1 kg = 2.2 lbs
2 lbs = .91 kg	2 kg = 4.4 lbs
3 lbs = 1.4 kg	3 kg = 6.6 lbs
4 lbs = 1.8 kg	4 kg = 8.8 lbs

To convert degrees Fahrenheit (°F) to Celsius (°C), subtract 32 from degrees F and multiply by .56. To convert degrees C to degrees F, multiply degrees C by 1.8 and add 32.

0°F = -17.8°C	60°F = 15.5°C
10°F = -12.2°C	70°F = 21.1°C
32°F = 0°C	80°F = 26.7°C
40°F = +4.4°C	90°F = 32.2°C
50°F = +10.0°C	98.6°F = 37.0°C

■ CLIMATE

Kentucky's climate is temperate. **Summers** are humid and temperatures average in the high 70s and 80s. Temperatures of 100 and above are rare, but do occur. **Winter** temperatures hover in the 30s, but can fall to the teens or below. Yet balmy days of 75 degrees now and then occur in midwinter.

Spring can be rainy and cool, but days in the 60s and 70s start in early April and continue through Derby time. In **fall**, warm days (70s) can linger through October, though the first frost usually happens around the middle of that month. The secret to packing for a trip to Kentucky in fall, winter, or spring is "layering." In the summer, dress to stay cool.

Average **rainfall** 45 inches, half of it occurring in the warm season—April to September. Snowfall varies considerably from year to year. Range is from 10 inches in the southwest to 20 inches in the northeast. **Snow** rarely covers the ground for more than a few days, which places the state within the humid belt. **Ice storms** can make driving far more treacherous than in snow. Ice is most frequent from December to February.

Also see the Travel Basics pages for each geographic chapter: **Eastern Highlands,** page 32; **Inner Bluegrass,** page 86; **Northern Triangle,** page 134; **Louisville,** page 158; **Central Kentucky,** page 182; **Western Kentucky,** page 228.

■ FESTIVALS & EVENTS

FEBRUARY

Louisville: Humana Festival of New American Plays, Actors Theatre.
Runs through the beginning of April.
800-428-5849.

MARCH

Corbin: Kentucky Hills Weekend.
A celebration of Appalachian culture through crafts, music, and storytelling.
Cumberland Falls SRP; *800-325-0063.*
March 3-4.

Louisville: Kentucky Crafted: The Market.
Traditional crafts, Kentucky food,

demonstrations of traditional pursuits such as whittling. Late February or early March. Kentucky Fair and Exposition Center; *888-KYCRAFT.*

Paducah: Civil War History Weekend.
Commemorating the 1864 Battle of Paducah. Raymond Schultz Park.
March 23–25. *800-PADUCAH.*

APRIL

Bledsoe: Wildflower Weekend.
Register in advance for hikes, bird forays, presentations and folk dancing.
Pine Mountain Settlement School;
606-558-5371.

FESTIVALS & EVENTS

Hopkinsville: Dogwood Festival. Third weekend; *800-842-9959.*

Louisville: Kentucky Derby Festival, Thunder over Louisville Great Steamboat Race; third weekend through Derby Day, first Saturday in May; *502-584-6383 or 800-928-FEST; www.kdf.org*

Paducah: AQS Quilt Show & Contest, fourth weekend; *800-PADUCAH.*

Pikeville: Hillbilly Days, third weekend; *800-844-7453.*

MAY

Berea: Kentucky Guild of Artists and Craftsmen Spring Fair, mid-month; *800-598-5263.*

Berea: Kentucky Guild of Artists and Craftsmen Spring Fair. Works by more than 100 regional crafters in the states' craft capital. Indian Fort Theater; *800-598-5263.*

Bledsoe: Black Mountain Weekend. Hikes, bird forays, folk dancing, and more. Register in advance. *606-558-3571.*

Covington: Maifest. Crafts, food, and more. Third weekend; *606-491-0458.*

Hopkinsville: Little River Days Festival, third weekend; *800-909-9016.*

Louisville: Running of the Kentucky Derby. Kentucky's largest single event. *502-636-4400.*

Louisvilllle: Mountain Laurel Festival. Welcomes summer and the blooming of the mountain laurel with crafts, food, and entertainment. Pine Mountain Settlement School; *606-558-3571 or 800-988-1075.*

Owensboro: International Bar-B-Que Festival. Cooking teams compete, judged by the public. Downtown; *800-489-1131.*

JUNE

Ashland: Brass Band Festival. Central Park: *606-325-4250.*

Danville: Great American Brass Band Festival. World-class bands perform during a weekend of free music and entertainment. Second weekend; *606-236-4692.*

Frankfort: Capital Expo. Crafts, food, and fun. First weekend; *502-875-3524.*

Harrodsburg: Historic Fort Harrod Heritage Festival. First weekend; *606-734-3314.*

Henderson: W. C. Handy Blues & Barbecue Festival. The legendary blues musician is honored by his hometown. 800-648-3128; www.handyblues.org

Owensboro: Yellow Dulcimer Festival. Wonderful music, workshops, and crafts. 800-489-1131.

JULY

Ashland: Summermotion. A huge celebration with fireworks, concerts, food, and more. First weekend; 800-416-3222.

Berea: Berea Crafts Festival, mid-month; 800-598-5263

Burlington: Boone Co. Bluegrass Festival. Second week; 606-689-7431.

Harrodsburg: A Shaker Fourth. Celebrate Independence Day the old-time Shaker way. Shaker Billage of Pleasant Hill; *800-734-5611.*

Harrodsburg: Kentucky Shaker Music Weekend. Interpretations of Shaker songs and dance. Shaker Village of Pleasant Hill; *800-734-5611.*

Paducah: Summer Festival. Events happening all over town. Third week; *800-PAD-UCAH.* First weekend; *800-765-7464.*

AUGUST

Goddard White Bridge: Fleming County Kentucky Covered Bridge Festival. Last Saturday. On Rte-32; *606-845-1223.*

Hardin: Hot August Blues & BBQ Festival. Fourth weekend; *502-474-2211.*

Harrodsburg: Pioneer Days. Third weekend; *606-734-2365.*

Henderson: Bluegrass in the Park Music and Folklife Festival; *800-648-3128.*

SEPTEMBER

Bardstown: Kentucky Bourbon Festival. Celebrates Kentucky's finest product; runs Thursday to Saturday mid-month, call for information: *800-638-4877.*

Covington: Oktoberfest. Second weekend; *606-491-0458.*

Dawson Springs: Pennyrile's Septemberfest. Live entertainment, crafts, and food. Pennyile State Resort Park; *800-325-1711.*

Harrodsburg: 19th-Century Country Fair. Shaker Village of Pleasant Hill; call for dates, *800-734-5611.*

Lebanon: Marion Co. Country Ham Days Festival. Fourth weekend; *502-692-9594.*

Middlesboro: Cumberland Mountain Fall Festival. Downtown Middlesboro, last weekend September or first of October; call for information; *800-988-1075.*

Morehead: Poppy Mountain Bluegrass Festival; *606-784-2277.*

Owensboro: Bluegrass Blast. Barbeque and bluegrass on the banks of the Ohio River. English Park; *800-489-2231.*

Prestonburg: Kentucky Highland Folk Festival. Mountain Arts Center; *800-844-4704.*

Springfield: Washington Co. Sorghum & Tobacco Festival. Third weekend; *606-336-3810.*

OCTOBER

Berea: Kentucky Guild of Artists and Craftsmen Fall Festival, mid-month; 800-598-5263.

Cumberland: Kingdom Come Festival. Demonstrations of folk artisanry, crafts, food and fun; *606-589-2145.*

Henderson: Big River Arts & Crafts Festival, first weekend; *502-926-4433.*

Middlesboro: Cumberland Mountain Fall Festival. Celebrates Old English heritage with crafts, food, and entertainment.

The most exciting event is the Official Kentucky State Banjo Playing Championship; *606-248-1075 or 800-988-1075.*

Paintsville: Kentucky Apple Festival. First weekend; 606-789-4355.

Renfro Valley: Appalachian Harvest Festival. First weekend; *800-765-7464.* Also, Fiddler's Festival. Last weekend; *800-765-7464.*

Russellville: Logan Co. Tobacco Festival. First week; *502-726-2206.*

■ KENTUCKY HORSE RACING

Churchill Downs: Louisville. Home of the Kentucky Derby. April–June, Spring Meet; October–November, Fall Meet. Call for dates and post times. *502-636-4400*

Ellis Park: Henderson. Thoroughbred racing at one of the largest tracks in the United States. June– September. Call for dates and post times. *800-333-8110*

Keeneland: Lexington. Kentucky's most beautiful track. April, Spring Meet; October, Fall Meet. Call for dates and post times. *800-456-3412*

Kentucky Downs: Franklin. Thoroughbred racing; September. Call for dates and post times. *502-586-7778*

Tyner: Stringbean Memorial Fall Music Festival; *606-287-0600.*

NOVEMBER–DECEMBER

Ashland: Winter Wonderland of Lights. End of November through December; *606-329-1007.*

Lexington: Southern Lights. End of November through December; *800-845-3959.*

Renfro Valley: Christmas in the Valley. End of November through December; *800-765-7464.*

Players Bluegrass Downs: Paducah. Harness racing; August–September. Call for dates and post times. *800-755-1244*

The Red Mile: Lexington. Harness racing in a beautiful and historic setting; September–October. Call for dates and post times. *606-255-0752*

Thunder Ridge: Prestonsburg. Harness racing in Eastern Kentucky; June–August. Call for dates and post times. *606-886-7223*

Turfway Park: Florence. Thoroughbred racing; January–April, September–October, November–December. Call for dates and post times. *800-733-0200*

I N D E X

ACKNOWLEDGMENTS

All photographs in this book are by Adam Jones unless noted below.

HISTORY & CULTURE:
Page 18, Print Collection, Miriam and Ira D. Wallach Division of Art, Prints and Photographs, The New York Public Library, Astor, Lenox and Tilden Foundations ▪ Page 20, Mildred Lane Kemper Art Museum, Washington University in St. Louis. Gift of Nathaniel Phillips, 1890 ▪ Page 21, The Granger Collection ▪ Page 24 (top and bottom), Library of Congress Prints and Photographs Division ▪ Page 26, Library of Congress Prints and Photographs Division ▪ Page 27, Library of Congress Prints and Photographs Division ▪ Page 28, Library of Congress Prints and Photographs Division

EASTERN HIGHLANDS:
Page 40, Corbis ▪ Page 58, Library of Congress Prints and Photographs Division ▪ Page 67, Private Collection/The Bridgeman Art Library ▪ Page 68, National Archives ▪ Page 69, Appalachian Archive Collections at Southeast Kentucky Community and Technical College, Cumberland, KY ▪ Page 73, Bettmann/CORBIS ▪ Pages 76-77, Michael Ochs Archives, Venice, CA

INNER BLUEGRASS:
Page 93, University of Louisville/Ford Photo Album Collection ▪ Page 95, Library of Congress Prints and Photographs Division ▪ Page 110 (bottom), Churchill Downs, Inc/Kinetic Corporation ▪ Page 111, Churchill Downs, Inc/Kinetic Corporation ▪ Page 112, Barbara Livingston ▪ Page 113 (top and bottom), Churchill Downs, Inc/Kinetic Corporation ▪ Page 115, North Wind Picture Archives ▪ Page 122, Shaker Village of Pleasant Hill, Harrodsburg, Kentucky ▪ Page 128, Buffalo Trace Distillery ▪ Page 133, The Speed Art Museum, Louisville. Gift of Mrs. Hattie Bishop Speed

NORTHERN TRIANGLE: OHIO RIVER TOWNS:
Page 137, Underwood Photo Archives, San Francisco ▪ Page 151, Museum Center, Maysville, KY ▪ Page 154, Library of Congress Prints and Photographs Division ▪ Page 156, Kentucky Historical Society

LOUISVILLE: KENTUCKY DERBY:
Page 162, Library of Congress Prints and Photographs Division ▪ Page 165, The Courier-Journal ▪ Page 171, The Speed Art Museum, Louisville. Gift of Mrs. Lewis C. Humphrey in memory of her grandfather, William Burke Belknap ▪ Page 181, The Speed Art Museum, Louisville. Purchase, Museum Art Fund

CENTRAL KENTUCKY: HISTORY, WHISKY & CAVES:
Page 186, Underwood Photo Archives, San Francisco ▪ Page 206, Library of Congress Prints and Photographs Division ▪ Page 217, The Speed Art Museum, Louisville. Purchase, Museum Fund

WESTERN KENTUCKY:
Page 237, John J. Audubon State Park ▪ Page 241, Ohio County Park, Hartford, Kentucky ▪ Page 243, Library of Congress Prints and Photographs Division ▪ Page 252, Ford Photo Album Collection/University of Louisville ▪ Page 253, Parsons Collection, Science, Industry & Business Library, The New York Public Library, Astor, Lenox and Tilden Foundations ▪ Page 256 (top and Bottom), Museum of American Quilter's Society

  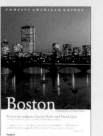 

Alaska (3rd edition)
$21.00 ($32.00 Can)
0-679-00838-1

Arizona (5th edition)
$19.95 ($29.95 Can)
0-679-00432-7

Boston (2nd edition)
$19.95 ($27.95 Can)
0-679-00284-7

Chicago (2nd edition)
$18.95 ($26.50 Can)
1-878-86780-6

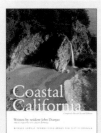   

Coastal CA (2nd ed)
$21.00 ($32.00 Can)
0-679-00439-4

Colorado (5th edition)
$19.95 ($29.95 Can)
0-679-00435-1

Florida (1st edition)
$19.95 ($27.95 Can)
0-679-03392-0

Hawaii (5th edition)
$21.00 ($32.00 Can)
0-679-00839-X

Idaho (2nd edition)
$21.00 ($32.00 Can)
0-679-00231-6

Las Vegas (6th edition)
$19.95 ($29.95 Can)
0-679-00370-3

Maine (3rd edition)
$19.95 ($29.95 Can)
0-679-00436-X

Manhattan (3rd ed)
$19.95 ($29.95 Can)
0-679-00228-6

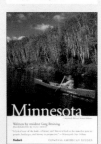 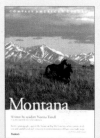 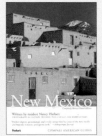 

Minnesota (2nd ed)
$19.95 ($29.95 Can)
0-679-00437-8

Montana (4th edition)
$19.95 ($29.95 Can)
0-679-00281-2

New Mexico (4th ed)
$21.00 ($32.00 Can)
0-679-00438-6

New Orleans (4th ed)
$21.00 ($32.00 Can)
0-679-00647-8

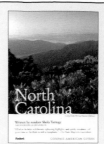

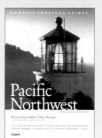

North Carolina (2nd ed)
$19.95 ($29.95 Can)
0-679-00508-0

Oregon (3rd edition)
$19.95 ($27.95 Can)
0-679-00033-X

Pacific NW (2nd ed)
$19.95 ($27.95 Can)
0-679-00283-9

San Francisco (5th ed)
$19.95 ($29.95 Can)
0-679-00229-4

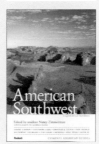

Santa Fe (3rd edition)
$19.95 ($29.95 Can)
0-679-00286-3

South Carolina (3rd ed)
$19.95 ($29.95 Can)
0-679-00509-9

South Dakota (2nd ed)
$18.95 ($26.50 Can)
1-878-86747-4

Southwest (3rd ed)
$21.00 ($32.00 Can)
0-679-00646-X

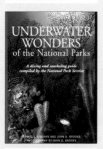

Texas (2nd edition)
$18.95 ($26.50 Can)
1-878-86798-9

**Underwater Wonders of
the Nat'l Parks** $19.95
0-679-03386-6

Utah (5th edition)
$21.00 ($32.00 Can)
0-679-00645-1

Virginia (3rd edition)
$19.95 ($29.95 Can)
0-679-00282-0

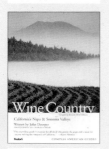

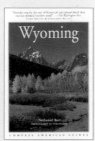

Washington (2nd ed)
$19.95 ($27.95 Can)
1-878-86799-7

Wine Country (3rd ed)
$21.00 ($32.00 Can)
0-679-00434-3

Wisconsin (2nd ed)
$18.95 ($26.50 Can)
1-878-86749-0

Wyoming (3rd edition)
$19.95 ($27.95 Can)
0-679-00034-8

CINDY STUCKY

■ ABOUT THE AUTHOR

Susan Reigler was born in Louisville the year Swaps won the Kentucky Derby. Except for a two-year sojourn at Britain's Oxford University, where she earned a masters degree in zoology, she's lived all her life in the Bluegrass State. Since 1992, Reigler has been the restaurant critic and Kentuckiana Style travel writer for the Louisville *Courier-Journal.* She has also written about Kentucky for Fodor's travel publications and about Kentucky bourbon for *Malt Advocate, Wine Enthusiast* and *drinks.com.* Reigler lives in a 200-year-old stone cottage on a historic farm and nature preserve outside Louisville. Her back door is a mere 100 yards or so from the site of the first licensed whiskey still in Jefferson County.

■ ABOUT THE PHOTOGRAPHER

Adam Jones is a nationally known photographer whose work has appeared in numerous publications including *National Geographic, Natural History,* and *Montana* magazines. He also has won the prestigious BBC Wildlife Photographer of the Year contest. Jones makes his home in Lexington, Kentucky.